Digital India

Digital India

How Technology is Reshaping a Billion Lives

By

Ananya Mehta

Vij Books
New Delhi (India)

Published by

Vij Books
(Publishers, Distributors & Importers)
4836/24, 3rd Floor, Ansari Road
Delhi – 110 002
Phone: 91-11-43596460
Mobile: 98110 94883
e-mail: contact@vijpublishing.com
www.vijbooks.in

ISBN: 978-93-48738-97-4 (PB)

Contents

Introduction

Not Just a Revolution—A Rewriting of the Indian Story

There is no earthquake of culture in a civilization that lets us know what is going on. Furthermore, there is no sound that announces a culture's transformation and the people's hidden composition. Nonetheless, very quietly and almost invisible, this process is taking place all around us. India, a civilization as old as empires, as wide as no borders, is not in the digital age, but it is also the source of the changes that this age could not have anticipated.

It is not a book attending to the themes of applications; it is not even a celebration of the technological novelties, nor is it a discussion of the startup valuations. What it is, however, is a revelation—a reflection of a billion humans in the process of inventing something new. Something that is neither Silicon Valley nor Vedic, and additionally not describable as 'developing' or 'emerging'. Digital India: How Technology is Reshaping a Billion Lives is not an excavation of code, but a discovery of consciousness. By analysing the philosophy and culture, we can recognise the subtle yet essential changes that Indian society is undergoing.

We have heard immemorably the story of the orphan who used to live in the middle of nowhere and who became a king by just climbing the ladder. However, what if the ladder is placed on shifting sand? Suppose that and, above all, technology is not a form of access but a creator of identity. Suppose further that, perhaps, it is not the warmth of a billion mobile screens that is the story, maybe there is a sub-plot going on—one in which the outlines of opportunity, power, family, language, morality, and memory are being altered.

This book has been written in hopes of doing justice to those questions.

More Than Connectivity

Let's first acknowledge a simple yet often overlooked truth: having technology is not equivalent to having the ability to work that technology. For many Indians, the smartphone is more than just a gadget; it serves as a reflection of their lives, a means of storing information, a place to write their thoughts, a stage for their play, and, most importantly, a bank- and now, a teacher. However, the process of acquisition, transformation, and use of these tools is heavily influenced by indigenous cultures, caste, religious patterns, and linguistic environmental regulating factors.

Most of the things said about Digital India are written from situations that are outside and looking inward. The perspectives they come from are Western analytical frameworks, tech-centred policy agendas, and market-generated success metrics. On the contrary, this book's point of entry is the lives of the people themselves. It does this by listening to the rhythm of the pulse of Tier 2 cities and tribal districts. It narrates how a grandmother is not only a practitioner of live streaming puja, but also teaches her younger relatives how to navigate modern technology. It explains how a young girl in Jharkhand decides to be noticed, not by seeking migration, but by using technology. It follows the progression of platforms from regular online places to modern temples and emojis, from a characteristic emoji to a dialect, and, lastly, how memes can be transformed into mere mantras.

India's quest for a digital world can be summarized as a technological jump combined with a social shift; the latter is often overlooked. What is at stake here is not only that of market but the collective mind and world-view.

A Second Independence?

To have a clear vision of where we are, it's wise to know where we came from. The first act of change was India's independence from Britain in 1947, which is directly linked to India's underdevelopment during the period that followed. That period was characterised by institution-building, planned development, and a tremendous struggle to unite a vast and plural nation into a coherent democratic whole. In the near future, it will be India's second great act of becoming.

What we see today is the unfolding of a second act—this time it is not about the declaration that comes from the Red Fort, but rather about the people in their living rooms, street sales, WhatsApp groups, and rural data centres. This act is not a political one, it is about the infrastructure that

India possesses. What really takes place here is the birth of digital India. This has freed them from the harsh restrictions imposed by the knowledge, financial media, and opportunity gatekeepers up until now.

Nevertheless, it is not total freedom without compromise. As history witnesses how colonizers transform the meaning of and erase the inequality, the emergence of digital systems is no different. Algorithm will store biases, platforms will introduce the value system, and the design solutions in Palo Alto will definitely stimulate Pune's behaviour. The tools we willingly use do not come empty—they have specific ideologies, language defaults, and governance assumptions.

If the first independence was about freeing the land from the colonial rule, the second must be about ensuring dignity in the realm, which is borderless, invisible, and ever-changing.

This book does not try to narrow down the digital field to just technical aspects. Of course, we will talk about interfaces and platforms, but always stressing the context of the way they change human experience. The screen is more than just a way of communication - it can certainly be a mirror and a maker. A teacher and a temptress. A tool and a trap.

What meanings do we imply when AI-powered astrology advises a young man in Varanasi who to marry? When a woman in Karnataka streams her protest live to prevent her arrest? When a child in Tamil Nadu learns Sanskrit, who is not native to the country, from a gamified app developed in Estonia. The examples are much more than just the digital spread, as it is also about discussing authority, aspirations, and authenticity.

And perhaps, more importantly, who becomes the main creator of the kind of change in question? Who works on the code, who processes the data, who goes over the comments, who has the rights to the infrastructure, who is the real beneficiary of this contagious activity? In each bit, a contest is omnipresent.

Emphasizing the People's Perspective

This book is based on people, not products. The chapters in the book are not a technology show, but rather are a mode of thinking through anthropology. It discusses women taking charge of their lives through selfies, nomadic tribes that record their oral histories with laptops, farmers who fly drones over ancestral lands, and transgender individuals living their own lives on Instagram.

Each of these stories, like a prism, gives an account of the intricate mesh between the digital, the social, the historical, and the spiritual. The aim of this project is not to admire the inventions of technology only. Our mission here is to explore how technology is consumed, given our Indian origin, which is a space where mythology, modernity, and memory are in constant negotiation in everyday life.

This book, by reintroducing real-life experiences at the forefront, asks the reader what the true meaning of living a digital life as an Indian might be—does it entail not only doing business, searching, or consuming, but also feeling, questioning, dreaming, and dissenting through digital means?

Philosophy in the Feed

This work is in line with the idea that Indian data on GDP and the number of internet users taken on their own will not be sufficient to get to know the country. To understand the shifts happening in digital India, one must engage in conversations that reflect the philosophical thoughts of the age.

India used to be a hotbed of metaphysical speculation—its classical traditions were more concerned with the live perceiver than the things perceived. These same questions are now broadcast on screens. The attention economy is now vying with ancient forms of inner peace. The notion of karma questions the anonymity of the digitally executed actions. Public shaming is a reflection of ancient ideas of social sanction while algorithmic virality is like a new divine justice.

With traditional values and build communication built on argument and justice, is it possible that India will be a digital ethics creator without being influenced by foreign ideas? Can this country's cultural heritage be used to shape the future of technology rather than be consumed by it? While the book suggests that the answer could be positive, it's not an easy one, and the first step is to be honest about the situation we are in and to talk about it using words that do justice to the richness of our being and our creative potential.

The time is now

This is not a book that predicts the future; it is a book that opens people's eyes and their minds to the world around them. Although the digital world gives humanity the promise of better life, beyond this hope lies a new horizon with threats like the abuse of the privacy of individuals that a company can induce through the provision of a service, the role of schools being reduced to the level of content distributors, the spread of confrontation due to the presence of echo chambers and the spiral of attention drawn by commercial stimuli, among many others.

The disease also carries its cure: the possibility of the vernacular experience blooming amidst crises, of silenced voices that now sound, of the homegrown idea of technology that makes the impossible possible, of the inheritance that preserves and allows for growth.

India does not sit back and let the world provide it with technology. It actively throws the bait for it to take a new form. The manner in which we conduct ourselves while using the digital tool will not only determine whether we end up being the leaders in the market but will also be indicative of our moral direction.

Our coding is not just about the creation of applications. Nor is it just about building platforms, but also about establishing patterns.

Features of This Book

Each of the subsequent chapters delves deeper into a particular feature of this significant change that has taken place from revamping Indian identity in this age of the screen to reimagining faith, family, and femininity. We will be the first to venture into the most peculiar network of dualistic tendencies due to the fact that personal offline authority can lead to online accounts being hidden; the popularity of the digital media may result in the person being both rescued and devastated in their life.

We will be taking up the uninteresting questions: about privacy in a culture of proximity, about ethics in a terrain full of automation, about language in an area still dominated by English. On top of that, we are going to illuminate the people who are not just technology users, but creators of a new narrative.

This book isn't a manual on how-to. Rather, it's more of a book that speaks to the present moment. It's only for those who feel that a very fundamental thing is taking place though they would want to talk of the issue in more profound terms. For students and scholars, of course—but not only for them, but also for the people who are citizens, creators, teachers, parents, policymakers, people interested in the future of India as more than just a market.

An Invitation

That which comes next is an emollient for you to ask you to be patient and look lazily. To enable the consumers to be inquisitive, not just about what

India is reaching, but who we are attaining during the process. We opt for the understated and unboisterous change instead of the burgeoning and broadcasted change to be our new form as a society.

You might feel that the stories in the forthcoming section are yours as you browse down. You might identify with familiar contrasts, dilutions, conflicts. This is our plan. For this is not just a book about digital India.

It's a book about us. All of us. Coding, swiping, uploading, resisting, transforming—one signal at a time.

Chapter 1

The Second Birth of India

India has eternally been a land of multitude of things. The social structure that was in the past a place where both science and the mystical domain coexisted, where the ancient and the aspirational dwelled together, and where the spoken word and the computer algorithm had a place. The dawn of the 21st century in India marks the birth of a new age; it is happening as a silent process without any apparent changes, yet it is actually a strong force that is refashioning every aspect of life in India. If the year 1947 marked the political start of modern India, then the present moment announces the onset of the country's second birth, driven by innovation through code, connectivity, and data collection, as it attempts to engage with the invisible world of data. India's first birth was associated with national identity while the second is all about digital ontology: being, acting, relating, and remembering in a world that is increasingly controlled by the interface.

According to the general narrative, the painting of digital India portrays it as an availability issue showing smartphones in the hands of the people from the rural areas, real-time payments in tea stalls of roadsides, e-governance, and ed-tech. These are valid points but are very limited to show the whole picture. They ignore how the screen has evolved from being a passive mediator with the world into an active shaper of behaviour, memory, ambition, and belief. Nor do they talk about whether the social and cultural hierarchies of India, that have existed for centuries and were decided at birth, have been altered or reinforced through digital technologies. All that is happening is not a mirror image of old India but the creation of something that is much more complicated, that is, a hybrid culture that has tradition as well as a touchscreen, and where operations are controlled by silent algorithms that dictate the choices, beliefs and sometimes the moral principles of each one of us.

Imagine the WhatsApp power in India where a staggering amount of people over five hundred million are using it for all kinds of needs, not just for talking. Also, consider how the new age of the economy is ritualized. Services like PayTM and PhonePe are part of the daily routine, so it is no longer a matter of choice but rather becoming an instrument of that society, like the temples used to be for the trading because they provided a schedule to the bazaar. This analogy is not at all far-fetched, and its level is not exaggerated. Just as temples in previous eras used to collect and graciously hold people's trust, today's platforms are the very places where the artifacts of the new world are housed and display the people's faithfulness to systems that symbolize safety, communication, and the possibility of working out the way that the smartphone is. Simply put, the smartphone is as much of a place as any.

In this chapter we will dissect how this representation has changed beginning with the question whether the data taking place of our dharma is the idea of exploring further. I mean that seriously. If we think back in the past, the dharma ideal as an allusion to an ethical compass for the people in India is one that is well sustained-it is not a mere regulation or plan of actions but a lifestyle that is really culturally sensitive and agrees with the role, duty, and association of the society. In addition to the digital system, another key point comes into existence that claims to be globally applicable as well and that, through its advanced technology, says it knows better who we are and what we want. The digital machine, which is running on data and functions, and is not straightforward, reveals and controls our likes, our purchases, our trusted people, and our convictions gradually. With the advancement in technology, we see that the moral codes of the new world have moved from the scripts to the recommendation engines and content filters keeping along their consequences, not likely as cosmic reincarnation, but in plain sight, in the spread of ideas, and in social and economic advancements.

Many people may prefer to think of data as neutral and that the algorithms are totally fair. They may also be of the opinion that the platforms are nothing more than conduits of information. Yet, investigation has shown that none of these assumptions is valid. In reality, algorithms are created by human beings, trained with existing prejudices and not optimized for justice or wisdom but for user engagement, retention, and monetization. Consequently, it is obviously an incontrovertible fact that moral choices are increasingly left to machines—not to a priest or guru, but to those behavioral models which not least we have become to optimize for clicks. The objects of the attention, those that aren't, and those that are punished online are part of a hidden logic, a logic by which we usually don't even question, and at the same time one that constructs our ethical construction. Who is to say what is a hate speech? What counts as misinformation? What bodies are to be followed as examples? What is the language that is to earn money, and what is the one that is to lose it? The answers are mainly more computational than cultural, based not on the decision-making at a local level, for example, in New Delhi, but on the influence of a global network of data centers distributed throughout the world.

The consequences are huge for Indian society. Over the years, in a country that has been known for accepting and debating moral ambiguity—through narratives, proverbs, principles, and the like—the inexorable rise of the binary nature of content moderation is a negation of the notion of progress. It is the virtual world that encourages the extreme, the categorical, and the uncomplicated. In India, however, real life is not so easily reduced. It continues being complicated, multilayered, and blessed with temporal truths. Therefore, when a society that is built on complexity grapples with a technology built on dichotomy, the two will certainly come into conflict.

This significant change of direction from the moral to the cognitive aspect can be best described as a psychological reboot—a parallel transformation unfolding on a different level. Digital life is no longer an option to the younger generation in India but the only reality they have. Their attention, memory, and even self-esteem are increasingly dependent on the apps and the interfaces that silently reprogram their neural pathways. The change doesn't stop at the level of the individual's behavior but is clearly reflected in his/her neurological functioning. It has come to light through many different studies that a high level of digital presence among the youngest members of the society is necessarily connected with shorter attention spans, increased anxiety, and a decrease in the quality of the work undertaken. At the same time, in India, the implications of these are both cultural and traditional. What once were the three mainstays of the Indian teaching method were memorization, recital, and the practice of extended concentration—all of which are now endangered in the face of a swipe-first, notification-saturated environment.

This is not to indicate a moral panic but to admit a change. The classroom, the temple, the living room—all spaces where only simple and direct interaction is possible—have now become places of another kind with a fragmented, accelerated, and reactive rhythm. Even the goal itself is being redefined. For many young people in India, the image of a successful person is not a bureaucrat, an engineer, or even an entrepreneur, but an influencer. This is not just a superficial change; it indicates a broader refocusing of desire: from the quantity of things to be known, and the degree of one's competence to being prominent and the ability to be seen.

The problem, on the other hand, is that the being seen factor is in fact altered—this is regulated by platforms following nothing but a set of obscure metrics. The very contrast lies here: while so many Indians never before had an opportunity to show up, today, the concept' visibility' has never been so determined, so manipulat-able by some algorithm. One day you are viral, the next, you are invisible. In such an atmosphere, the demarcation between acknowledgment and being unnoticed is no longer in human hands, but the algorithms of the respective platforms decide

And this is where the metaphor of the chapter becomes crucial: the platform of a thousand gods. Indian gods, throughout history, have been numerous thousands and have each had specific domains, devotees, rituals, and avatars. They were not just in the realm of spirituality, but were also active in the material one—ruler of harvests, cause of births, provider of justice, and source of kings. In the present day, a new pantheon has started rising—decidedly non-deity|holy]], but nonetheless digital. Their Luther are not Krishna or Kali, but Instagram, YouTube, Flipkart, and Tinder. Each of them has their own set of rituals: scrolling, swiping, liking, streaming. And it's their unique way of promising people happiness: love, celebrity, well-being, and knowledge.

The temples were once the heart and soul of the collective where people not only prayed but also learned social standards, justice, and knew who they are. But today it is the platforms that take on this function. People's identities are formed and torn apart there. Platforms are the uniformed centres for disseminating information, for creating new local moral communities, and for isolation.

Just like in the past, the temples determined which social class and who their patrons were, the present-day platforms regulate them as well, e.g. by follower count, blue tick, and algorithmic favour. Even though democratization is promised, the platforms are characterized by the reproduction of the old inequalities in a new, virtual shape.

Realizing this parallel does not have the romanticization of the past or the demonization of the present as its goal. It is to see that India] has a talent to take external influences through deeply rooted frameworks and make good use of them that other nations do not have. Therefore, the issue is not finding out whether the platform will substitute the temple, but determining if it will indeed take on the social responsibility of the temple. Here the platform can mimic the temple's authority but not its ethics.

Henceforth, the chapter serves as a reminder that the Hindi would-be knowledgeable people who are now experiencing the digital-heavy era feel at ease in it. And specifically, it urges them to have a deep knowledge of what switch from the conventional concept of governance to subscribing to a digitalised environment means. It also acquaints them with the idea that in the age of big data, dharma could find new creative application, attention could change discipline, the platform could supersede the institution. All this points to the observation that India's digitalization is not only a process of turning to the internet—it is a complete transformation from one thing to another. This observation, if conducted with the utmost honesty and rigour, will most likely reveal an India that has been reborn. This India will neither be a continuation of the old nor a mere embrace of the new, but a full-scale redesigning of the Indian way of life—bit by bit, page by page, soul by soul.

From Postcolonial to Post-Screen

At midnight on 15 August 1947, India got freedom—although not without a lot of confusion. The British had departed, but the ground was far from settled as they had wielded the scalpel of empire politics: the borders were bleeding, the institutions barely borrowed and still running on stingy means, and the people were still not sure about the grammar of citizenship. Independence was the fork in time and the offering of hope—a reset of history's scale that was searching for an identity in an extremely diverse diversity. The period that ensued saw a concentrated effort, which, though it was sometimes inconsistent, was directed towards modernizing India: via the construction of the Parliament building and steel plants, the coinage of a single political language, and a number of Five-Year Plans, all of which looked upon planning as the new spirit of progress. Still, there was also the flip side in the bureaucratic, centralized, and slow-moving project. The doors of luck were kept by language, place, caste, gender, and the fact that the state, struggling to regulate the scale and not having enough entrance, had limitations in terms of technology of an analog nature.

Today, India's change is auspicious a different realm of freedom, not one characterized by the abolition of foreign rule, but from the clutches of the opaque system. It is not the leaders with the flags and revolutions, but the code, communication, and access that are leading the way. It is not only about having paperless offices—digitization is, rather, the act of breaking free from the black & white world and saying NO to waiting in long queues, filling out forms, getting stamps, and being unheard. Earlier, the nation had to be raised brick by brick, just like the postcolonial dawn of India. The postcinema India is a land in the process of being rethought.

To understand the extent of this transformation, it is necessary to go back to the earlier times. The Indian postcolonial identity was based on the notions of scarcity and self-preservation. The early years of independence portrayed a story of forced reserve: frugality, being self sufficient, the planned economy. The definition of the nation was not only political but also educational. It was through the medium of the textbooks of civics, All India Radio, and the cautious approach to the massification of education that this idea was purveyed.

Access remained central and linear, and information was scarce. The media was almost totally centrally controlled, and it was privileged to have access to a telephone, and only the cities had the privilege of bank work done. All this coupled with the way the bureaucracy operated was so unfathomable that one could not penetrate it even if he wished. The top of the pyramid was helmed by English, European language, and had the consequence of becoming a barrier to entry to the corridors of the contemporary towers of those of high status.

The foreign coin in this bore was the shared dream of making a giant leap together which was the conviction that modernity could be achieved through collective sacrifices. That conviction was of a moral nature. It was the reason why people stood in the queue of rations, wrote letters to MPs, or filled endless forms with carbon copies. To participate in the state's machinery was to signal faith in the system, however inefficient it might have been.

Digitalisation has redefined the social contract between the state and its citizens. The screen is acting as a layer parallel to the physical world in Indian society—it is reshaping things from the ground up. Previously, the country's residents interacted with the government through its officials. Now it is the citizens who are the direct users of the services, facilitated by various apps. Aadhaar, India's biometric identity system, is the epitome of digitalization: formerly, a billion people were divided among various documents and states. Now, everyone is digitally connected to a single entity of identity. This has not only made it possible to pass on benefits with minimum bureaucracy but it has also reshaped the trust infrastructure. The main advantage is not having to get in touch with somebody, you have to be now aware of only a number.

But this switch is not just about admin work. There is a lot more to it, it cuts deeper. Digital technology turns the entire spectrum of citizenship qualities the other way round. The India of the post-independence era taught its people to deal with shortages patiently. The India shaped around the screen teaches its citizens to demand everything immediately. The ration shop is now a mobile application; complaint has turned into a tweet; protest is now a hashtag. Time which in the past was demarcated by office hours and government schedules has now been reinvented and is accessible at the user's convenience. So it is fair to say that today's citizen is a user—who has become empowered, yet gradually losing the ability to make decisions, as he is placed within interfaces, whose design is aimed at efficiency rather than conscious evaluation of issues.

This shift has far-reaching consequences. Initially in the postcolonial period, you were required to be fluent in the rituals of the state to be able to access it—always in English and administration. The transition from analogue to digital has removed many barriers, which have now been replaced with new ones: digital literacy, smartphone access, algorithmic visibility. It is not the same people who issue the approvals, but the gates have not disappeared. They have simply been re-programmed—no longer through the clerks behind the counter, but the backend systems, filter bubbles, and design biases have preserved them. Though you can open the system, do you have any control over it?

What characterizes the post-screen transition in India as distinct is the fact that it is one that is happening at the same time. India is not one-mindedly migrating from analog to digital; the fact is that it is living in both the worlds at the same time. A rural Odisha farmer can still use his thumb impression to avail the subsidies, but at the same time, he can also benefit from watching the crop tutorials on YouTube. A housewife in a Tier 3 town could carry out virtual transactions through voice assistants and at the same time, she could be in a situation where she may need to ask her son to interpret English error messages. A young Dalit originator can have a lot of followers on the social media app Instagram and yet he/she can be experiencing the caste system.

This complex reality does away with the traditional approach that followed a single line of the way of life of people, which is progressive. Culture is now looking for another way of being, speaking to clashing features of the country, where discontinuities and substitutions are part of the description of the digital path of India.

Moreover, the transition brings with it an evaluation of national identity. The postcolonial identity was based on the idea of coherence and it was quite a united and diverse picture as the phrase of Nehru. The storytelling from only one source was secondary and the state itself was the narrator of the national tale of being. In direct opposition to that kind of world, the post-screen imagination team is owing allegiance to the shattering away of the centers, the multitude, the task-force. The matter of discussion is not the integration of the nation but the dissemination of the narrative. A cell phone, which each person has, has also become the center for making his voice and worldwide underscores. Every person, who was formerly discriminated in terms of the region, religion, or the class, identity, can now be built from the public through followers, content, and screen-time.

However, this profusion was at a great price. The demise of shared spaces (national newspapers, the Doordarshan broadcast, or the school civics class) gave birth to the fragmented realities. In the digital space of India, there would be several groups living in different informational worlds, possibly formed by different feeds, vernacular media, and ideologically segregated echo chambers. How is the unity in such a context realized? Is it that the identity of a nation is maintained together with the citizens being overseen by various algorithms and commercial segments?

Such issues are not distant. They not only determine policy and public issues but also have a big influence on politics. The best evidence is digital mobilisation that is used largely in the election process, for example, the formation of election publicity groups in WhatsApp to micro-target ads. Another case is the way misinformation quickly travels on existing fractures, thus making an identity a weapon and erasing trust in government. At the same time, there are those who were previously silenced, who, through new media, are now visible, though they are met with trolling, harassment, and digital policing. The displacement of the middlemen has not meant the removal of the powerful.

It would be a mistake, however, to solely concentrate on the threats, and not see the prospects that underlie further down. Despite its contradictions, the post-screen moment is indeed a fundamental departure from the limits of the old analog order. The information which was before hardly accessible has become abundant and readily available with just a tap of a finger. Women previously silenced from open discussions have instead become the economic force of the silent culture through the use of social platforms. Through social media platforms, the young people in the outskirts of the towns are the change-makers, educators, and entrepreneurs, who are not bounded by their localities, castes, or money. The moral imagination of the Indian is reaching new heights. A Ladakhi child can learn coding from a Bengaluru teacher from Telegram. Similarly, a transgender activist in Chennai can do legal education through Instagram reels. They are not just individual examples but rather signs that a new infrastructure of respect is being formed.

To characterize this as a second freedom does not mean that it is being likened to the struggle against colonialism. Rather, it means identifying that a different type of freedom is emerging—freedom from the systemic inefficiency, information asymmetry, and institutional exclusion. This is the freedom to transact, express, learn, and aspire without intermediation. However, it also brings about a novel form of vulnerability. While the colonial subject was subjugated to the Empire, the digital citizen is subjugated to the algorithm. The latter manipulated labor and land, while the latter manipulates attention and data.

It is simply stated post-screen India is not a simple notion. The tools are both powerful, inform and control. The platforms are both paradigms and watchdogs. The systems are both inclusivity enablers and an instrument to sift, classify, and punish. Thus, the redefinition of national identity is no longer only through history and law, but by design choices made by private corporations and then incorporated into the public realm. Now the identity of individuals, those who are seen, who is not seen, and who is served are the decisions that are coded and mostly without democratic oversight.

The requirement, therefore, is to move away from missing the simpler past and to forge ahead with clear vision about the future being built. A digital India is not debatable, and it is coming soon. However, a digital India where everyone is justly treated is no such. That is, as the government is no longer in the hearts of the people but in the platforms, and as the citizen is turning into a dataset, we must be in a position to ask ourselves the right questions: What kind of participation should we promote? What kinds of exclusions should we say no to?

How can we make sure that the birthday of the new India reflects the promises of the first one is, therefore, a question that requires an answer besides the recall of the nostalgic past? A digital India is a matter of course. A fair digital India is the real issue here. As the government (state level, in particular) withdraws into platforms, and the individual is transformed into a dataset, our duty is to question: What forms of participation do we want to promote? What kinds of exclusions are we ready to tolerate?

The aforementioned issues do not relate to technology; rather they are philosophical, ethical, and extremely political. They require the audience to alter the prevailing discourse of identity: from being something only inherited to realizing that it is something that is co-created by them in a world where history interweaves with the interface and a country is not a single voice but rather a composite signal. The screen is not the only frontier. It is the screen that India goes forward to with the inclusion of being increasingly—itself.

Is Data the New Dharma?

The concept of dharma in the view of the ancient Indian sages was not that of a set of unalterable principles, but a changing concept leading to the changes in society and hence being a moral compass of the time, context, and duty. It did not only bind the individuals with moral principles, but it also set the direction for the social order. The king's dharma was different from the teacher's; the householder's was different from the monk's. However, they were all committed not to the one who gave them the orders but to their own sense of what is right within them. In modern-day India, another set of rules is being developed, no longer by carving on palm leaves or stone but by using algorithms, storing them in cloud servers, and protecting them through platform policies. If dharma was a concept of a person's ethical behavior in conformity with the cosmic and the social world order, then today's digital systems proffer the same concept of compliance to the norms generated by the data. The question here is, is data going to be the new dharma and what are the consequences accompanying the restructuring fact? Not to say in some fancy way, but really and not only in words. To have a better understanding, let us examine the ethical implications of the emergence of digital and see what possible impacts it might have on the Indian ethical plane?

On the first look, drawing a comparison between the two may not look valid. The way of dharma was metaphysical, whereas the current treatment of data is purely empirical. Dharma contained the sense of duty, while data is a method of reward based on optimization mechanics. Nevertheless, they have something in common—they both regulate behavior. They both define what is normal or tolerated and what is not. They both, as people say it, play a role in shaping the seeming stable factors of decision making, action, and the behavior of a person/client. Forming the basis of these unseen similarities, evidence of the similarities are replicated in two ends; the continental and the analytic sides of LEDs (the philosophical symmetry) and the digital, thexx moral vacuum in India's digital reach, hindering its progress.

Let credit scoring take, for example, the case of how a change of the operating model from manual to analog has happened. In the old payday loan industry, people get to know your credit score by your printer at the company, bank history, employment records, tax filings. Credit scoring now almost utterly relies on digital data in a cashless society. This is illustrated by the fact that a person's relationship to the mobile phone, social contacts, or posts/time and location on social media, are used to evaluate that person's creditworthiness. The assumption here is that the data new facts about the candidate's behavior which the candidate would not disclose. Although the methodology is not clear to the public and no one can fight it. In this system, there is no representative of the sabha, and the moral side of one's problem has no room to be mentioned. The migrant's irregular digital footprint is condemned without the possibility of clarification, which is far more than just technological efficiency—it is a new form of moral adjudication, where data rather than testimony decides the case and code plays the part of the judge.

In a society, in which mental attitude was comprehended of the same importance as the actual outcome—the Gita gives a direct distinction between actions and feelings—the cutting down of actions from human behavior into digital ones was a very big new view. The ancient ethical standards of India were based on ideas that there are areas of gray wherein duty went into opposition with the law or in which personal sacrifice defied social conventions. However, against that standardization, the data processing systems function. They look for likeness, remarks in the same class, and the possibility of being it's the case of one's situation. They do not pay attention to the details. The criteria are that a thing is not profitable unless it has specifics. But still, it is those specifics that are the basis for ethical conduct in society. The algorithm is silent about the cause of default of someone that could be due to health problems, loss of work, or digital illiteracy. It is the reason for classifying it as a risky one.

This new order is ironic because the state does not force this order, instead, it is the people's choice for its convenience. Datafication is not opposed by Indians, they are actively datafying their lives. Data is the norm now. From using biometric authentication for social benefits to the utilization of facial recognition in public transport to accessing AI astrology apps. Additionally, data has been a normal means of making the decisions. The foundations of data seem to be seducing the logic, better services, tailor made experiences, and immediate feedback. Somewhere in this euphoria, the ethical frameworks stand still, always trailing the technical developments. Right, in the old times, dharma went through the processes of philosophical debates and public discourses, but today's technology-driven data systems differ in their evolution, by being more of engineering sprints instead of human-factor-driven and being more of the interests of business shareholders than concerned people. The outcome is the presence of not only the technical but also the epistemological gap: data systems provide the inferred but not reasoned decisions.

This epistemic gap is most conspicuous in governmental affairs. For example, predictive policing tools predict the future situation of crime, and based on predictably known historical data, outsource the task of allocating resources of law and order to the lower-risk (in the opinion of the system) areas, even if this means that police will not respond fast to critical situations. Although this seems like good resource succeeding, it ends up being harmful and intensifying stereotypes such as policing communities that are already discriminated., at times it also refers to the extension of surveillance without the owner's consent as well as going against the due process. The very idea of justice is changed in the way that it does not require the well-argued reason of the people but the mere factor of prediction. It is not guilt that is proved but guilt is anticipated and then the suspect is taken to be guilty. This shows a sharp break with India's traditional legal system where nyaya (justice) was based on public reasoning and the presumption of innocence. Instead, in the data-hung state, speculation becomes a systematical thing and justice is a far cry.

The private sector at the same time with the same or similar drives is a different entity with its understandable profit objectives. For example, content moderation is increasingly regulating the borders of permissible speech. What is removed or shadow-banned or amplified is the job of automatic systems following the policy of a social media platform. As a matter of fact, those policies are rarely clear, not uniform, and many times a cut-and-paste of foreign jurisdictions. Ordinary Indian netizens constantly come across content that is removed and yet they are provided no explanation, while in some other cases harmful content is made more visible due to the present engagement metrics. The algorithm is not neutral—it embodies values. Which values make the decision is the question? What constitutes harm, hate, or harassment is deeply contextual in India's polyglot, multi-religious, and caste-stratified society. A joke in one language could be interpreted as an insult in another. A symbol in one region may be considered inappropriate in another. Without cultural sensitivity, algorithmic governance runs the risk of both excluding and intervening too much.

On the contrary, data systems that demand a certain kind of behavioral change also provide the tools through which resistance can be seen. Civil society organizations have started reacting to concealed data practices through litigation, as well as public relations activities and they have also cultivated alternative technologies. One of the steps at the government level was the introduction of the Personal Data Protection Bill, a bill representing a distorted shadow of the original and hugely delayed, but still a trial to try to gain a much-needed moral oversight of the digital systems. Digital literacy campaigns run by communities have put chips in the hands of users to take their data's path under their control. A step towards this direction is made by religious leaders, educators, and community organizers who initiate debates on ethics in regard to screen-time, algorithmic addiction, and digital disinformation—such debates are no longer seen as only technical problems but instead, they are raised as moral concerns.

Significantly, a small but growing number of Indian philosophers are shaking the foundations of the debate by offering new perspectives in their native languages. Digital ethicists are wondering if dharma can be the source of an Indian way of ruling or organizing data that will respect the rights of every individual as well as the well-being of the collective, which will be both transparent and trustworthy, innovative but accountable. It is not intended to be only religious but also ethical in nature hence the term plurality is changed from the religious to the ethical. Here, just as an Indian activist of the environment was able to bring out the idea of the sustainability of the earth through the use of prakriti that goes beyond merely the carbon index, so as well, the ancient Indian notion of dharma can be put into the service of the critique of the ethical impoverishment of datafication. For example, what if we were to develop algorithms that promote the anubandha concept—being interconnected—or algorithms that have the human factor in the decision-making process as they respect the samvada—dialogue—principle?

These objectives face a variety of strong challenges, nonetheless. Surveillance capitalism defines the global technology stack, and the prevalence of such architectures makes it a challenge for the mentioned ideas to be materialized. Indian platforms are not built keeping Indian users in mind and such platforms also do not follow a business model centered around behavioral manipulation thus making it difficult to follow moral reasoning. In any case, the issue has already been resolved and the extent to which the country datafies is not in question—India has already taken this step. The question is, therefore, if it is still possible to make India be unique ethically by datafication. May it form digital systems that indicate not only efficiency but also the sense of the dignity?

This tension between tradition and algorithm is not only the case in India, but the depths of the country's rich culture are what make the tensions apparent. When we consider that the Indian culture has always addressed the ethical aspects of speech (vak), memory (smriti), and action (karma), and that this has always been a topic of debate, it therefore becomes necessary to reflect on the reduction of human behaviour to data. The major objective is not to dismiss the data but to make it more fitting for the people. This is to allow the algorithms at work; hence, they are in control so as not to lose the adikara, they observe the niyama and must still be truthful.

India need not be a passive consumer of digital morality. Instead, it can be a contributor. What India needs to do is to regain the moral authorship, but not through nostalgia; rather, through critical, plural, and context-sensitive thinking. Data should be embraced not only as a resource, but importantly as a relationship – a fabric of consent, responsibility, and mutual recognition.

Perhaps this is where the analogy of dharma has the most to offer. Dharma was never a set of fixed rules. It was situational, problematic, and open to the complexity of life. Therefore, our own data ethics should be the same. Meaning, that they are not only practiced with the help of laws and technological solutions, but are learned through education, public debates, and the reform of institutions. The digital society of India will not only be created by the actions that we take, but it will also be shaped by the values that we hold dear. Should data be our new dharma, we must decide who will be given the task of writing its scripture and to whom it should be responsible.

The Psychological Reboot

What is most truly going on in India's social structure now is not something the infrastructure or economy can change, it is the thinkers' mindset that tells the real story. The change in the society is not in the speed of the Internet or in the number of people using electronic finance tools, but in a quiet process of changing attention, ambition, and memory, particularly among those who make up the country's youngest generation. The average Indian person under twenty-five, which is a number of more than 600 million individuals, is growing up in a totally different psychological environment than any of the previous generations. For this group, the mobile phone is not just a tool but a co-processor. It is not only their mediator in reality, but it also determines the architecture of young people's lives. To claim to have understood the contemporary India without looking at this psychological reboot would be like avoiding the most important element of success.

Most Digital India stories are really about giving power: information access, market inclusion, digital literacy. These are results that are easy to measure, see, and politically market. However, what is rarely debated is the inner price of being always connected—the tacit yet influential changes in the mentality of the people, their wants, and the way they see themselves. The question here is not whether the digital contact of the people's brain will have a different result; science has already given an answer to this. But the essential point is how these effects will be depicted in the new social and cultural context of India and what that implies to a society that is in the process of modernization in the era of the infinite scroll.

The giving of attention is the first thing that gets lost in such transformations. In schools and universities, teachers report an alarming decrease in the level of concentration of their students. Anecdotal evidence is getting corroborated. A study, conducted in 2022 by the Indian Institute of Technology Bombay, found that students' retention of information during traditional classroom instruction was negatively affected when they were continuously engaged in digital multitasking. Nonetheless, the cause is not just diversion; it is also a designed-in development. As when cognitive inputs are broken up, and pleasure mechanisms are immediately gratifying—e.g., likes, shares, and views—our brains are retrained to give preference to quickness rather than to potentiality. In a culture which previously fostered memory and deep thinking, the transition to the quick scanning and low-friction gratification represents a radical shift.

They are still the generation that gets referred to as Gen Z and Gen Alpha, and they are the ones that are updating the concept of ambition. The traditional paths to the American dream of medicine, the civil service, and engineering are still being followed by many, but these coexist, in parallel, with the new digital dreams such as: content creator, game streamer, start-up founder, and crypto investor. What is important is not to criticize these lifestyle changes, but it is imperative to admit the increase in the tempo and the raised visibility at the same time. The generations in the past aspired through deferred pleasure, whereas the young folks nowadays look for confirmation not in the future but in real-time. This is not narcissism—

it is construction. When the structures one lives in are built to measure the engagement of an individual in currency metrics, then the construction of one's identity moves in the direction of numeration naturally.

One of the outcomes of this is the formation of a new performative self: curated, algorithm-aware, audience-sensitive. Teenagers on Instagram use cliches not because they do not have any originality, but because it is what the algorithm appreciates. A 17-year-old girl from Coimbatore, who creates reels about beauty tips, is not only copying Western influencers due to imitation – she is translating the language of visibility. The thing that is happening is the not death of realness but the birth of a new kind of strategic selfhood, which is not run by social morals but by the logic of the platform. Even the morality is seen through this glass. If honesty once demanded internalized codes of behavior, it is now largely an issue of brand management: being esteemed as 'good' by a fractured, often unseen public. The identity is no more created by thinking—through feedback, it is pieced together.

This gives rise to deeper psychological issues. What does it mean to grow up in a world where your identity is constantly measured? Anxiety, envy, and impostor syndrome have ceased to be the problems of adults only; they are fast becoming typical teenage states. A 2021 survey by the Centre for Internet and Society revealed that Indian teenagers had disproportionately higher levels of stress due to online comparison, and FOMO (fear of missing out) as compared to their global counterparts. But what makes this particularly difficult in India is the conflict between collectivist family structures and hyper-individualised digital environments. A young person might still live in a joint family, attend religious festivals, and be subject to conservative norms, yet have an online presence where rebellion, sexuality, and self-expression are money-making. The outcome is not necessarily always conflict – it can also be cognitive dissonance, compartmentalization, or double lives.

One of the lesser-known parts of this rebirth is the shift in memory. Word of mouth narratives that were traditionally used in Indian education for a long time to pass knowledge and culture have been now largely replaced by outsourced memory. The question we need to ask ourselves is, why would you want to remember a verse if you could google it? Why learn a phone number, or a time schedule, or even a mantra, when all the information is just a notification away? Digital memory functions as a prosthesis, but like any other prosthesis, it leaves a lasting impact on what the body is not actually compelled to do. Indian education, which in the past was built on memorization, today, is faced with a generation that has the "not remembering" concept embedded in their DNA. This is not necessarily a negative point, but it does request a bit of pedagogical reorientation—more specifically, the focus should be on acquiring synthesis, critical thinking, and context-making skills, since all of these are skills that hardly come naturally in the generation of media satiation.

The psychological reboot is not just a matter of individual preparation. The same audience's preferences for shorts over essays, and hashtags over arguments, not only influence their ability to actively participate in public life but also condition this ability. Political awareness, for many, comes not from the spoken word or the written text, but from funny videos and the exposure to memes. The vocabulary, therefore, includes the hashtag "Justice for," visual protests on the Internet, and symbolic avatars. This can be a sign of the country being fueled, but it is also a sign of the country being very instable. People easily get through anger; they do not have the time or the desire to go through the layers of things. The reason is not that these people are indifferent to the complications that the issue they are discussing carries, but because it is not the habitude to multitaskers to be trending. This medium both offers and restricts the content.

Nevertheless, in this regard, some paradigm shifts have entered the scene. New personalities rise constantly all over the globe. Applications such as "Stop, Breathe & Think" have leapfrogged social media. Some of the highly educated families in the show business have given their students, in this critical period for the implementation of digital tools, the mandatory ruling. Thus, some of these programs at the crossroads of media and wellness that are being run by teenagers often, although deemed as out of place, are seen as a support group for the repressed people in the society. The most important change probably is that all this is a mix of current technology with the resources of the Indian tradition. The move is not a move from one to two-dimensional but one in which different levels of the same reality run at the same time. So, while deep attention is a loss, the same loss, in the end, provides more accessibility. It is a situation of a gain in online comparison while the number of online communities that provide emotional support increases. The website is not just a decline; it is a development.

The real challenge is in creating deliberate shifts in the mindsets of people rather than just making the changes through manipulation. In Indian society, buoyancy and change go hand in hand, but the absence of any introspection regarding adaptability can lead to a disintegrating self. What the young generation needs is not the absence of technology, but rather the presence of deliberate effort. Schools must change the "screen time" guidelines and implement digital cognition on their students as part of the curricula—how algorithms are shaping our thoughts, how platforms are manipulating time, and how to identify content that is informative from content that is addictive. Besides parents, those who are improving their literacy with the skills of blocking the apps need to understand their children's psychological settings. Of course, the most important thing is to make the platforms responsible for what is not only allowed but also designed for the sake of exploiting it.

The mental reorientation of the younger generation of India is not just a short-term change but a permanent one. This will give birth to the next generations of new citizens of India who will be different from their predecessors in behavior, beliefs, and decision-making. In case, it is regressive, transactional, and attention has become a commodity it will be felt in various ways within the institutions—starting with the political, the educational, the interpersonal relations, and up to the religious. However, in the event that this is that kind of upgrade, which is glowingly self-examined ethically with a decisive stand and is aware of its own design, then, yes, this could be a second rare psychological upgrade scenario inside India only.

Not only psychologists or educators are responsible for this issue but also policymakers, designers, and ordinary citizens play a crucial role. A reboot of minds is in motion. The pertinent question is, will we leave it to chance, or will we endeavor to direct the course of the next frame with precision, context, and transparency?

The Platform of a Thousand Gods

In ancient India, a temple was where people gathered for more than just worship; it was also an economic enclave, a museum of cultural heritage, and a political symbol. It not only regulated daily life but also projected the social desires of a population. In the precincts of the Temple, records of donations were maintained, land sales were attested, musical debates and compositions were carried out, and justice was sometimes delivered. The factions of the society also used temples for fulfilling their spiritual needs as well as fundamentals of trust, identity, and social order. In India today that is digital, a new type of infrastructure has arisen that shapes values of a similar nature, behavior, belonging, and power relationships. However, in contrast to the rise of stone, this is a growth from the code. The usage of it is neither the rule of the priests nor the ritual of the developers and product managers but something totally different. These entities are the platforms, such as WhatsApp, PayTM, Instagram, YouTube, etc. They are not merely tools but are the digital temples, and they are sovereigns of belief, conduct, and congregation.

No, this is not an ornamental metaphor. As the temples were never just for the gods but the organization of human life around shared rituals and meanings, the platforms of today are not just apps for their functions. They not only fulfill the function of community-building but also dictate our way of life, success, devotion, truth, and identity. A temple was the middle of a village; a platform is what links you to your networked life. The issue is not whether they are replacing the old institutions. The central question is rather the role they are taking on, which presumably does not comply with the moral duty the traditional fabric used to force them into.

The strength of confidence was established first in the act of building the temple. The place of worship prompted unwavering belief through its being easily understood, linked to the local way of doing things, and guided by the memories of the people. Conversely, the platform has a trust that is based on casual use, big scale, and the impression of neutrality which are not very intelligible. The common Indian consumer, for example, may trust and use WhatsApp for personal communication, UPI for financial transactions, or simply gain social capital from Instagram, but without any consciousness of the algorithms, data flows, and governance structures involved. It is not faith; it is a case of addiction disguised as convenience. Nevertheless, just as the devout of the past who never questioned the temple's officials or its treasuries today's users also, not rarely, question the implied codes that influence the shaping of what they see, whom they interact with, and how their attention can be turned into money.

An example of the platform-temple comparison that stands out is the comparison of the rituals that happen in both places. In the temple, devotees offered food and chanted sacred mantras as they worshipped. But on the platform, the primary ritual is user engagement: the day-to-day activity of logging in to the site, swiping through content, liking, commenting, and forwarding it. The latter behaviors are far from neutral as they are shaped by material incentives, guidance, and quite often, cunning. For example, before the ban on its Indian operations, TikTok had designed a user interface that was irresistible to young people of different languages. Consequently, this act was a kind of both performance and petition: the user's prayer was no longer for the divine's favor, but for the algorithms to recognize it. Thus, instead of divine revelation, virality becomes the new norm. Despite this, the all-powerful algorithm remains invisible just like the deity hidden behind the curtains but controlling the whole show.

Payment platforms like PayTM or PhonePe have already transformed into close equivalent intermediaries for the financial transactions that were previously carried out by deities or their attendants—not in the religious sense of the term, but in their ability to decree value. Similarly, as temples of the past controlled economy through the way of land grants and donations, modern day financial apps make the financial trust system under the control of the mobile with proper KYC verification services, QR code identification, and digital records. Probably the fifth generation of a fruit seller in Surat puts an adorned QR code rather than a calendar of Lakshmi. On the other hand, in today's context, a pilgrim in Tirupati may use the mobile phone to give a donation, a destitute person in Delhi could be seen holding a phone with GPay stickers. The situations have changed, it is not that money is no longer the sacred property of sanctuaries but it has now become the property of smartphones.

The community part is also experiencing a change in the way it is organized. Platforms create affinity communities, which do not depend on geographic confines, but are linked through the similarity in their users' interests. For example, a housewife in Kanpur might be in several devotional WhatsApp groups, a mutual aid Telegram channel as well as a community of like-minded parenting influencers on Instagram. Each group member acts as a trustee and develops trust, conversation and stool pigeon traditions in the designated community. Still, the difference with traditional temple-based communities is that the platform-based communities are more transactional and fleeting. They can be set up and destroyed overnight, they are not eventually shaped by social consensus but by the content that is currently trending and the instantaneous mood.

The change in the structure of belief is perhaps the most palpable one. At a temple, truth was diverse—mythic, symbolic, scriptural, personal. On platforms, truth is not only made overly simplified but also made into a game. Credibility is visually represented; repetition makes the truth. Untruthfulness does not thrive on the platform, it is there with the help of its deliberately structured incentive system. WhatsApp forwards are the modern form of oral transmission—albeit one that is bereft of any contextualization or sense of culpability found in traditional storytelling. A video showing the love for a deity, a rumor about a politician, a conspiracy theory—all ride the same vehicle, use the same tools, and often evoke the same feelings. The holy and the false are now co-users of the same server.

The two things mixed up have a great effect on the ways the citizens of India perceive the public domain. While temples in the past were the ones to set the example of what virtue, obedience, sin was, the platforms do it today in shaping the public sentiment. Rage has been ritualized. The hashtag campaigns are no different from holly processions, just in this case, people gather, chose their camp and, most interestingly, expect loyalty. It should be noted how the whole country rebelled on the issues such as #JusticeForHathras or the Shaheen Bagh movement which received so much publicity from social media. This is where the situation is similar: digital congregations, like temples, can not only rouse the community but also serve as the center of a narrative, and foster a moral momentum. Still, lack of a traditional structural memory or an obligation to the movement may lead to the mobilisation being one of transient nature, thus, easily manipulated or dismissed.

However, the notion falls short in defining the roles of the two institutions. Temples were, no doubt, ruled by local social class structures, i.e., the powers of the time, the priests, and councils. Oppositely, digital platforms are managed by big corporate leaders, often times living thousands of miles away, with little to no awareness of the Indian subcontinent. A Tamil Nadu community banned on Facebook for using "hate speech" might be part of a culture that accepts the same words as a form of satire. A Bengali influencer getting on Instagram's nerves might just be employing some local idiomatic expressions only his fellow Bengali origin users of the social network would understand. Social norms are no longer explained by headmen and then exercised by community members, they are obeyed according to the content moderation code taken from Silicon Valley. The outcomes of these changes are not limited to only the virtual space but are transferred to the cultural and knowledge domains.

Even so, the platforms have not managed to achieve something that no traditional institution in India was able to get to a point of: empower the citizens with a voice that is truly democratic. A Dalit poet in Bihar publishes his viral spoken word video on YouTube. A sex worker from Kolkata uses Instagram to give a human face to her life. A teenager of the Chhattisgarh countryside can voice his own disagreement of the state propaganda via a WhatsApp voice message. Such advances are no less than a mere redistribution of the right of expression. It needs no emphasis that the platforms on which new voices become loud are more like fragile crutches. It is not difficult for them to be affected by the change of the policy, monetization alteration, and content policing since the decisions are made without consulting the interested parties locally.

What it implies is actually a paradox. Temples have been substituted by platforms in the function, but not in the legitimacy. The latter support the identity and actions of people, although the rituals of trust, once accounted in temples, are missing. They do manage the public sphere, however, they escape the regulation of the public power. These also give authority, while responsibility is refused. India is now in a situation with such institutions that some of them centralize the behavior of people in no civil foundation.

The solution is not just a sense of longing for the past. Temples were certainly exclusionist and hierarchical, and often were accomplices to social injustices. But they were also imbedded, localized and, very often, they were under negotiated codes of conduct. The word one has to think of the governance of a platform, is not so much as a technological or policy exercise but as a profound cultural one. If indeed, the platforms are our new religion, then they have to be driven ethically to represent the diversity of Indian life—many, non-aligned, and familiar with unsystematic changes.

India has a history of creating institutions in accordance with its diversity. The sabha and sangha, the gurukul and the panchayat, were all flexible structures. The digital public square has every right to be treated with care like that. Although the developers are not priests, they act as behavioral architects. Product design is not scripture, but it is doctrine. Furthermore, engagement metrics are not higher beings—but they are obeyed more than a lot.

If one were to regard platforms as they are temples without the knowledge that institutions receive the respect and inquiry that comes in their direction is tantamount to giving up one's rights of governance. The act of worship has now been initiated. The real question is whether India will also set out the rules of holiness.

Chapter 2

The Digital Divide Isn't What You Think

The term "digital divide" has an image that is widely accepted. The idea is that the digital divide standings in Asia. The digital divide is not only about those who are affected, who are online; it is also about the existing ones who are online, but are there due to difficulties, and it is the persons who cause the trouble. The terms "digital divide" and "splinternet" are used to describe the current state of the internet. Frustrated internet users lament the "good old days" when the net was open, safe, and global.

The chapter explicates code without context, a frequently ignored concept in the digital age. Most of the digital systems that make 21st-century India what it is —social media platforms, mobile apps, search engines, fintech, online education, and so on —are not produced in India. This is the kind of logic that comes from the culture of the First World. The assumptions are made from cultural and socioeconomic factors and the designers believe them to be universally acceptable: instrumentalism, nuclear family structure, direct cause-effect, high digital literacy, unchanged courts, and privacy rights equal for all, public interest as a core notion. When such assumptions are not a match to India's very dense, complexal, and diverse nature which includes multilingualism, caste, another kind of labor, joint families, shared devices, and low textual literacy for that matter - this conflict results in the worst-case scenario being excluded.

This chapter would like to make the concept of code without context relevant. A part of the digital foundation on which the life of present Indian citizens rests -- social media, mobile apps, search engines, fintech, online education, and such -- is made exteriorly. This architecture is grounded on cultural assumptions from the Northern Hemisphere that include high digital literacy, linear time thinking, a nuclear family world, the individual at its center, clear and standardized legal frameworks, and unlimited privacy conventions. These general assumptions present in the designing of digital technology, when hitting the multilingual, multicultural, and traditional in India, the latter bear the brunt of the former's exclusiveness.

For instance, let me take user interface design. A banking app which takes for granted that the user has a personal device, a private login, and basic literacy either in English or Hindi is the perfect alienating example for those who share mobile phones, use visual cues for literacy, or are confined to the regional dialect. Also check out algorithmic content moderation on social platforms, for instance - Western-trained AI models that do not understand and often misclassify the local culture with satire, vernacular idioms, or religious symbolism, thus, wrongly silence legal speech or cannot identify hate. These are not exceptional cases either. This demonstrates a particular shortcoming of digital system architecture in terms of Indian society, the root of which is the false assumption that being on the internet is equivalent to being part of a community. However, inclusivity without cultural literacy is not genuine inclusivity.

The paradox of offline power and online poverty illustrates the situation even more. India's complex inequalities—caste, gender, kinship, local influence—give birth to communities with offline command over the situation. Panchayat chiefs, local political intermediaries, religious leaders, local artists, and teachers of an informal nature are the ones who are the direct drivers for everyone. And yet, many of these actors are disenfranchised in the digital environment— not because they do not have access, but because they come across platforms and systems that do not acknowledge their power or existing authority. A Panchayat head might have no presence on Twitter. A local healer might have never monetised a YouTube video. A grandmother whose oral histories are central to her community may find no interface designed to archive or disseminate her knowledge.

This is just not a simple mistake. It means the value systems are not in line with each other. In the real world, knowledge, status, and power are disseminated through relationships, reputation, and continuity. Online, value is measured in a different way, it is recalculated by metrics such as views, shares, likes, subscriptions. The people who understand the platform, mostly the youth who are urban and English literate, tend to be visible and impactful even when they don't have any real capital. On the other hand, those who were rich in traditional authority may become invisible in the digital world. This inversion not only creates economic tension but also questions of epistemology are raised. What is credible, what is loud, and what is saved are all influenced by algorithms that have been trained by standards and norms quite irrelevant to the communities whom they claim to serve.

Despite all these, a force most dynamic, transformative, and yet unexamined in the by lanes of this same terrain is Digital Middle India. These are neither the celebrated "early adopters" of India's digital economy nor are they the so-called digitally illiterate. It is the new breed of world who are the main players: the people that live in second and third-tier cities and who are using technology in a way, not predicted by the developers or the business analysts. They are the people of Solapur who are teaching math on YouTube in Marathi, the women of Gorakhpur who are doing the bookkeeping of the household with the help of PhonePe, the farmers of Punjab who share their tips on pesticides in the local Facebook groups, and the teenagers of Jabalpur who make their Bhojpuri rap videos. These people are not only consumers, but they are interactive co-creators, who transform the platform to get the best of it fitting their world best.

Uniqueness of this demographic derives not only from the local aspects or the possibility to use spoken language, but also from the facility to speak or write seemingly on the spur of the moment. The representers of these clusters may not correspond to the standard definitions of digital literacy, yet still, they gain proficiency in dealing with chaotic digital systems—by using multiple languages, extracting the meaning of icons, and taking screenshots as a reference. The community of learners evolves by means of WhatsApp, gaining visibility in return for the help of others, and benefitting from influence at various levels such as offline businesses and an online presence. They cannot be classified as regular user personas, but definitely, they are the group that is setting the stage for the new technological wave in the Indian subcontinent.

These points the question is from where come the notions used to measure progress. If digital transformation would be based upon the users' uptake and product downloads first and foremost, there is the probability to mistake usage for empowerment. A farmer using a weather app may not be economically secure. A teenager uploading dance videos is not necessarily safe from online harassment. A household with two smartphones may still have only one person with functional digital autonomy. In conclusion, we have to inquire as follows: Who can not just consume but also shape technology and content? Who are viewed as authorities in a particular area, who are the content creators? And who are the target markets for, but not the data of the algorithm?

New kinds of order that appear in the digital sphere also have to be taken into account. Analogous to the way in which the Indian physical map was redesigned with the introduction of colonial railways, privileging of some regions and omitting the others, digital platforms are creating a new map of the online world, which includes trends like over-represented English content, the visibility mainly from the north, and the urban users' ruling of the interactions. This new geography is entirely non-impartial. It generates loud and silent voices at the same time. And unless we start to seriously investigate it, human efforts will only be focused on creating a digital structure based on old inequalities but in new, less obvious forms.

Just to reiterate, I want to specify that this is not a discussion related to digital infrastructure or the equal opportunities provided by the platforms. This is a plea to completely change the reference and become more person-centered, i.e. design, policy, innovation should learn the high level of lived experience needed for their emergence. Sociologists, together with engineers, should form the product teams. Not only should the work of regulation be focused on data privacy and antitrust, but also on the native culture of a country. In light of the above digital literacy should involve not only the practical use of computers but also certain complex ideas such as platform behavior, algorithmic manipulation, and narrative framing.

The reader witnesses this chapter not as a criticism of digital India, but as an illumination of its undiscovered areas. It acts as a guide for readers who are supposed to think about what the digital divide means in a country where matters of education, language, caste, and the labor market are already entwined with each other in a complex manner opposing the usual sectorial theories. This also takes us to see the struggles beyond the distinction between those connected and those unconnected and puts forward differences in such parameters as who is heard, who is seen, who is catered to and who is excluded, not out of ignorance but due to the structural misrecognition.

Our Indian users will be our companion in the journey which through their experiences, we will go rural people, tap the finance sector, and the swaths of socially vital people who despite not having access to technology, they will be coming up with their own smart alternative life. Indian society will grow not only as an adopter but also as a transformer, and that will be a great day for the country. Additionally, it is by figuring out the limitations of the existing digital architecture, e.g., its basic assumptions, exclusions, and undersights, that we become aware of the true extent of the gap that needs to be bridged. This evidence will not only teach us but it will allow us to understand more about the social dynamics and ways to redesign our systems or use them in a future of our own shaping. In this sense, it would not be about scaling up digital technologies but about giving people the right to participate in decision-making in a dignified way and at the same time not to be written off as passive consumers of global technologies. That is why the actual dividing line is not so much the lack of necessary goods that would give one access but rather it represents a lack of sovereignty in terms of being the builder of the system.

Beyond Urban vs. Rural

The most frequently debated dimension of the digital divide in India is the spatial one: the city-rural one. This is the representation that can be found in almost all of the media, policy papers, and general discussions. Urban India is being depicted as the one with the most high-tech solutions, moving fast, and full of digital natives, while rural India is being portrayed as the place where technology is not being taken up, has the poor infrastructure and needs help. Furthermore, this dichotomy, which seemed to be very practical in the past, is now no longer relevant and is to be regarded as intellectually lazy. It is causing more problems than it is being accurate about. Access to the Internet facilities had gained a rapid improvement; now almost all people in villages are able to gain a mobile connection just as much as most people in the cities can. Nonetheless, another deeper and more intense divide emerges out of this situation. This divide is no longer in the physical space but in skills, the will to use it, and the design."

This is the division, and the spatial aspect holds no relevance anymore. Spatial issues have driven the Internet and its development; spatial emphases have been the focal point of the debate. This is the new digital divide that is neither about shoulder to shoulder neighborhoods or wired ones and squared ones nor about fronts nor about rear spaces.

This is a digital divide that is very subtle, very persistent, part of the noise of the city, invisible and at the same time, present. It is the chasm between those endowed with abilities and those who are only linked.

In education, you start with literacy. But you have to understand it broadly. Literacy as being able to read and write not only means this. It is being able to swim through the sea of information and create knowledge out of my making the right and critical selections. A farmer in Madhya Pradesh, the Indian state, has a mobile phone and he often visits the weather updates but he still may not be quite sure that he can differentiate trustworthy and sponsored content. For example, a woman who is about to use the internet for the first time might live in a rural area of Bihar and might be comfortable to receive messages from her son on WhatsApp, but she isn't brave enough to switch on her privacy settings and to take the case to the police in case of harassment. The functional literacy, in general, found among city dwellers, does not apply to digital competence. The platform's interface such as symbols, which are used in combination with gestures or written words, has a meaning, and this is seen as a language; for that reason not all individuals are able to interact with it as it is not the mother tongue of the user community.

This difference becomes noticeable when we talk about the matter of intention. The presence of a device is not an indication of agency. Intent is the result of confidence, options, and cultural allowance. A lot of Indians, particularly women and older people, are not much into the mobile phone as an exploration tool, rather it is a necessity. They use it to receive, not to search; to comply, not to create. From the product metrics side, the Read more... to profile of a girl who met an online Runyoro native appears as mostly the result of one's deep ingrained social conditioning. Can the idea of speaking be That of Who is actually permitted to talk? Which groups claim they are the rightful participants of the internet? These can't be taken as questions in a technical manner; they are sociological ones

Deficiencies in design are likely the most widespread. Most of the top applications used in India are not at all intended for India. They are structured with the expectations of privacy, individual device ownership, a high degree of text literacy, and the Western-style design metaphors. In this regard, just take a simple password: the concept that sets the tone of an individual's privacy contradicts the values creating in the family by the sharing of devices, the uneven level of resource management and the family norms of openness. It doesn't take a regional content recommendation engine that is solely based on the intention of maximizing visitor numbers leaving cultural differences behind and getting the risk of. Such recommendation engines may have the effect of information distortion, political polarization, or unintentional insensitiveness to various cultures. This insensitivity, being unintentional, is not only the weak point of the platforms as they are the

From digital finance and healthcare to education, the combination of literacy, purpose, and design is the force behind advances in these three areas and beyond. Even though the woman in a Tier 3 town may very well have her bank account linked to Aadhaar, access to a mobile app, as well as a government welfare scheme designated, she might still not be able to take that money all by herself. It is also possible that a student who is in an online class for free may be lost not only in terms of how to communicate his/her idea, but also how to switch between tabs, or even non-text submission of assignments. A patient in need of vaccination scheduling may not be in want of good internet service but rather be confused about the complicated interface and the time-sensitive situation. These are not individual exceptions; they are actually the lack of a systematical sortof inclusion or in other words fake individual limitations.

However, these exceptions often fall outside the scope of the current policy metrics. Governments keep on reporting the number of "connected" citizens or devices per capita and use these statistics to indicate digital inclusion. Tech companies often do not even attempt to explain how this daily engagement is beneficial to their real empowerment. The problem goes beyond the narrow concept of measurement, it involves also the whole conceptual apparatus. It is not true that if there is access there is also agency. To use a tool is not the same as to shape its outcome. Inclusion, in the real sense, is not merely the presence on a platform but it is the cognitive and influential abilities of a person to take away something of value.

This misinterpretation of the understanding issue has extremely important and dire consequences; there is no more space for abstracting about it. It is a problem that goes way from the public authorities and passes through the layers of platform design straight into the choices of capitalists. The result is the lack of channels except the final decision, or the limiting expansion of one side. Policymakers, in case they presume that rural areas already have enough virtual access, they cease to invest in community-led digital literacy or innerself-brought of funds. In case a designer highly believes in the mental model bid of his/her user base, he/she is less likely to be taking into account such things as symbolic overload, local hues' symbolism, or uttering the particular emblematic gesture of the place. Investors, if they run the machine towards the scale monthly without putting into a more deeper analysis of the situation, immediately turn into executing taskmasters, who, in the end, understate retentiveness both in user acquisition and user dignity. The results that result are systems that are optimized at the surface level for growth but are shrouded from within to the intricacies of power and access.

We can overcome this deadlock by changing our lens of diagnosis. To make sure that all of India carries the message of digital inclusion, it should be seen as a gradient, not as a sharp division. It must take into account the different levels of competence, the various levels of self-assurance, and participation in various degrees. It must be seen as not only the rate of users but also the qualitative side of access: who can look for something, who can do a transaction, who can produce, and who can argue. Also, it should not be without the presence of questions that almost never come up like Is the user capable of denying? Does the user grasp the terms of the contract? Can the user, when necessary, quit the system? If inclusion does not give an opportunity to the user to say 'no', it is not inclusion, it is dependency.

A number of initiatives conducted by the community for digital literacy, and generally, if not exclusively done by NGOs and self-help groups, are the ones that have been producing great results. An example of an initiative that works is the one in Kerala where the public libraries are transformed to become digital skill centers for seniors. In these centers, the elderly learn something more valuable than just how to use a smartphone. Quite to the contrary, they learn also how to spot fake news and critically evaluate their sources of information. On another note, over in Rajasthan, we find people of the YouTube community who without the direction of a professional teacher have taken it upon themselves to teach their local community in their local dialect, thereby bridging the local and the global through innovation by those who live below the economic scale. These success stories are therefore not just stories but they underscore the fact that by localization, something can work better in a local environment.

Conversely, there are some teams of designers that have advanced in their thinking and have started confronting the assumptions embedded in the digital infrastructure. Spoken, regional language AI interfaces, apps designed for rural areas, visual representations of Indian culture, and intuitive use of features to cater for low literacy contexts are some of the things that we can see in as a new outlook. However, these initiatives are not visible to all. They have to become part of the mainstream, and not only as corporate social responsibility, but as standard good design practice and sound public policy.

As an end result, the urban-rural binary continues to exist due to its convenience. It brings out the simplicity in complexity, allows for easy storytelling, and justifies gradual progress. However, it no longer represents the world as it currently is. The future of India's digital landscape will not depend on the construction of towering buildings in cities or the placement of Wi-Fi hotspots in villages. What is important is whether we can create systems that value the diversity of human intelligence, respect cultural plurality, and be context-sensitive. We need to establish spaces in which the ability to get connected to someone leads not just to participating in something but to authorship.

The divide that matters most today is not that between cities and villages, but the one that separates the rest from those who determine the technological future. Disparities exist between those who are able to steer the digital narratives in a particular direction and those who continue to be invisible. To bridge this divide, we need more than just gadgets and data plans. We need design that listens, policy that learns, and literacy that liberates. Anything else is mere digital development without any substance.

Code Without Context

Even if logic is the foundation of technology, it is usually placed in an environment of assumptions. Behind each digital tool, there is not just a string of code but also a worldview: a series of assumptions about human behaviour, values, and system operation. As a result of these assumptions being taken as is into contexts that are the complete opposite of the originating social fabric, friction will necessarily result. In a country like India, characterised by its diversity in languages, infrastructure, behaviour, and cultural codes, this friction is not a little thing. This is a massive exclusion. The mistake that is being made is so simple; the code that is written for one context does not usually work in another. Still, it is an error that the digital ecosystem continues to make, often with global scalability.

India is the land of infinite digital possibilities, and yet a major part the software that changes its face every day such as social media, fintech apps, online education, and advertising content producers—delegates it as its source, mostly design studios and engineering teams, from the other end of the world but are not far from Indian users. Many of the teams work based on the European and American point of view; they use monolingual interfaces, a digitalized world where people have individual possession of devices, high per capita online literacy, fixed address systems, and commitment to privacy and declarations of consent as the standard. In a situation when such ideas are in interaction with Indian realities—multilingualism, shared living, community-owned devices, the informal economy, irregular supply of electricity, and deep social hierarchies—the system doesn't collapse, but the sense gets lost. The software continues to operate technically, but it is a failure regarding cultural attributes.

Think of the case of WhatsApp groups. Acting as a straightforward messaging application, WhatsApp was best for usage between two people or a small group of individuals. However, in India, it has been only used apart from its original purpose as a tool for mass mobilization, informal education, religious coordination, micro-entrepreneurship, and community governance. The application became a success primarily due to the fact that it could easily adapt to different circumstances. Nonetheless, it was the inability of its moderation systems to change that prevented its growth. There was no doubt that WhatsApp in India did not have enough of a solid local content control mechanism, so it became the largest source of misinformation, hate speech, and incitement during election cycles and the rise of communal tensions. The platform waited to respond until the problems got so big that it introduced message forwarding limits, labels that show if a message has been forwarded many times and lastly, the platform started some awareness campaigns. These attempts, however, did not mean that the code has been designed anew for a society where information channels run through the tradition of families, connections of clans, and linguistic communities as well as the self-sufficient entities though.

What is at stake here is not just user interfaces but also the question of how systems carry and reproduce power. If we consider the case of Google Maps, it becomes evident that in the Western cities with the systematic address and well-functioning transport systems, one can rely on the maps with no fear of misleading. In the Indian locales and rural areas, where addresses are typically given as 'near the old banyan tree,' 'behind the mandir,' and where some roads are not officially registered, the precision of the digital navigation system is lost. Besides, the algorithm wrongly takes speed and efficiency factors as constant. The reality in India is very different from the perspective of most covered by the first two measures, why because the quickest way might not be the safest or the most locks of way, which is particularly true for the women or the marginalized group in the place. In so many words, what is optimal for the system is a complete mismatch with the local culture. Therefore, the insufficient cultural adjustment by the system while optimising leads only to negative connotations.

To demonstrate the above argument even more vividly, let us examine the case of AI assistants such as Siri, Alexa, and Google Assistant. The operation of these smart devices is based on language technologies that cannot cope with the diversity of Indian accents, the switching over of languages, or the prevalence of regional dialects. Here, for example, a Tamil-speaking farmer may repeatedly ask for a weather report in his own way of speaking and still not be understood--not that the question is difficult, but that the system is not built to recognize that particular linguistic model. This is not because of a technical defect but a weak point of the product idea to the disadvantage of not only some representations of the culturally diverse data but also all those consumers of the product who are not recognized as a part of the dialogue. In contrast to the reality that when the machine fails to understand one the cause is not the person but the institution, the machine's failure to understand one's speech is usually assigned the stigma of one's manner of speaking.

The cultural mismatch and resultant consequences in fintech are even more severe. These apps presuppose users who are already acquainted with financial terminology and numerals, who are capable of speaking English or Hindi, and banking procedures. However, the economy in India is primarily cash-based, borrowed informally, seasonal in nature and entails gender-specific financial behavior. For the females of Vidarbha or a weaver in Kanchipuram, the software design of an investment app—drop-downs, graphs, OTPs, credit scores, etc., could be a way of sending a message that either they are out of the zone or they are provided with an opportunity.

The problem is not engendered by the people's aspiration but the solution was to bridge the gap. Still, quite many tools made without a knowledge-based perspective may end up bearing the seed of unequal rights even when it is the kindest to use.

In the education sphere, some developments suit as case illustrations. During the pandemic, ed-tech platforms were enthusiastic enough to make provisions for digital classrooms, video lectures, and online assessments. However, most of the systems were created for students having their private devices, quiet and right places for study, and stable and good internet. However, the reality was that many students—especially in semi-urban and rural India—only had one smartphone per family, studied in limited homes, and tackled low and unstable network signals. Most video platforms were found not only to be irrelevant but also too much of a burden. This was related to the delivery of content in formal Hindi or textbook English, which mostly did not help the learners conversant only in regional dialects. What was supposed to make education open to all turned out to reinforce the exact opposite in practice. Unadapted access is not inclusion but abstraction.

One might wonder why there are no tools designed specifically for Indian users. One part of the answer to that is the way international tech companies are incentivized. Localization is very costly, and a very time-consuming process that takes place at the backend of core business objectives. Moreover, India seems to be nothing more than a testing ground for other countries' tech companies. This makes it an ideal market for rapid scaling, data collection, and experimentation. The mindset of the tech companies, a majority of which are global is, unfortunately, focused on extraction - where the users are treated as data points and their say becomes irrelevant. The outcome of this method is inclusion phylogenetically, from where, quite naturally, users are not part of the scene. Actions like decisions relating to UI, privacy, moderation, and monetization are all done by the people living thousands of miles away, and the users have absolutely no say. What is more appalling is the absence of structural humility, not absence of feedback loops.

But there are Indian developers and platforms who naturally have a preference for moving in the opposite direction of this design. Start-ups exemplified by the likes of Koo, ShareChat, and BharatAgri which execute local context-based design—i.e. voice-first interfaces, local language interfaces, community-based content. However, such companies are rare. The general environment still remains a one-size-fits-all approach with the ideas of the universality of design that comes before specificity, and sensitivity before scale.

This should not be taken to mean a statement that advocates threatening or protecting one's own sector only. Neither is it an assertion against the concept of global platforms. What the writer wants is simply referred to as design justice—a concept that those most affected by the technology have the right to influence its foundational principles. In India's context, this calls for the understanding that reaching the underserved communities through digital connectivity is not enough to ensure their self-reliance. The interplay of codes between people and technology is the determining factor of the latter's being instrumental in the self-reliance or estrangement of individual users of the former technology.

Now, getting this right is a game of high stakes. In countries like India, which are increasingly governed by digital tools across sectors like education, health, finance, governance, and identity, a bad design is not just to be sneezed at. It can be seen as a form of exclusion. When you are not heard, read, or guided by a system, you become invisible to that system, and invisibility in the digital age is not neutral. It is a form of exclusion that is deeply rooted in the structures.

But what is the way forward? One of the strategies is to give a second thought to the person in the driving seat driving design: i.e. teams should be diversified with ethnographers and not just engineers. AI trainers should teach the language to locals, not just competency in NLP (Natural Language Processing). Policy guidelines are made to stress the importance of doing usability studies in lieu of just ticking compliance checkboxes.

The second thing is to stop and think what constitutes the criteria of success. Many times it's about simple information rather than empowerment. The number of downloads does not measure the depth of what has been held. And the level of retention does not equate to the level of comprehension. The most important thing is to bear in mind that it is the empathetic aspects of design that are crucial, which means that effective design is not just about the efficiency of the design, it depends on a good amount of empathy - of course when efficiency is rated high in a digital health service non-formal convention, that is a signal of empathy.

As the closest term to one's understanding, India neither lacks nor, for instance, would adapt better to simple Western platforms. A country like this needs more in-depth and in-out-of-the-box thinking. The kind of systems which are compatible with the conditions to make sure the result that the relays work with these not only the major thing to keep but also the very existence of the of the moral knowledge passed. That take away not unity, but the existence of different things in place of one, systems.

This is a problem not of technical descent but of raising philosophical questions. Creating software with a given context is to admit that human beings are not mere puzzles to be solved, but universes to be grasped.

Offline Power, Online Poverty

Power has never been singular in India. It has been in many hands holding different entities: land ownership, kinship networks, caste status, religious authority, and regional influence. Definitely, well before the time when India got updated digitally due to broadband and data packs.

In those days, there were still people and groups with positions of authority and some communities who were treated with respect. Those individuals and groups did not expect their status to change even though they were not in line with the digital technologies used those days. They were an integral part of the local fabric and held all the power and knowledge. Still, with the rapid digitalification, their position as top power has not been sustainable. The paradox is striking as the more offline leaders dominate, the more likely it is that the online world will make them powerless. The great many who are still lords offline are quite often treated as least of all under the online regime. Their wisdom, accumulated over years or generations is not judged as valuable by any technology. They might not necessarily be leaders in their physical locations but in the online world, they are unacknowledged. The problem mostly lies in monied interests who control search and advertising who will not let their knowledge get currency, their networks be crossover and remain selling their identities that are not tracked by any metrics. In short, they are rich in social capital, but poor in digital agency.

This is not a question of pure technical illiteracy; it goes much deeper than that. There is an intrinsic mismatch between the way offline power is constructed and the structure of the digital platform. In India, the system of offline power is different because it is primarily related to human beings, it has the context on its side, and it is developed through various relationships. It is not like in other places where power would be dependent on digital discovery alone.

Offline power in India tends to be localized and embodied and also very interpersonal in nature. These people are models in their village because of their proximity to the people they serve but they are influential enough to make decisions. They make a decision to distribute resources, they are a focal point in resolving conflicts, and they are respected for their cultural knowledge.

Take the scenario of leaders from caste-based communities who, at times, are pinnacles of influence that can gather all their followers within their locality. They are the key people whose opinion possesses an alluring magic and can convince the masses for political rallies, marriages, social rituals, local governance and so on. However, if we take the same leader and place them in a digital setting, their influence evaporates unless they know how to communicate through the codes of the internet. The authority of these people was spoken, but the platform necessitates a visual performance. They used to speak in a manner that was multi-layered and rich in context, whereas the platform values shortness and infectiousness. The very qualities that were beneficial, namely, slowness of thinking, personal credibility, and relational nuance, are, unfortunately, seen as disqualifications for success in the digital epoch.

An outstanding case in point is that in contrast to the immense space online cultural performance exists in, indigenous folk artists are marginalized and silenced. Even when the situation appears that the artists are the ones who carry the torch of the oral traditions, their content containing Bhojpuri ballads, Baul songs, and Lavani dance, has little to do with formal digital distribution channels and is rather lost in those circuits. Their material is generally not approved for posting, yet if it happens, it is subjugated by parasitic middlemen who times the re-release for maximum financial and algorithmic benefits. The artists lack the knowledge and technology to record themselves, edit the songs, give them metadata titles, or promote them. As a result, they are pushed out of the loop of the value they have created where they should have gotten a major share of it. Their situation is in no way different from that of a viral influencer because they also create even if they do their creative work without fulfilling the epistemology of the platforms. Their knowledge is not simply recorded but is a life practice; their influence is more of an intergenerational nature rather than easy financial exploitation.

Political actors experience similar disturbances. This means that a sarpanch who has built a reputation for effective local governance could very well be rendered ineffective online through manipulation by a rival who is less experienced but knows more about the media. WhatsApp groups and Facebook pages are usually run by political consultants or tech-literate youth and often become the center of online influence. It is necessary to understand that digital messaging, coordinated campaigns, and algorithmic targeting are now the keystone of political success. Through these means, symbolic performance always outpaces actual leadership. The people who have credibility have thus shifted from the voices in the bazaar to the videos that are trending.

Religion in the digital world has introduced us to a new face of power. It is no longer necessary to be a leader figure in the real world to be a prominent personality in the online world. Most of the time, the ones who head the local church, mosque, and an elder of the community being the keeper of religious and ritual knowledge are not visible in the digital world. Unlike this, spiritually influenced and mostly younger 'life coaches', gurus, self-styled influencers are online favorites who are renowned for converting the most profound spiritual pieces into short-form content which may include inspirational quotes, lifestyles changing ideas, and simplified teachings. The language of spiritual domination, at present, is the aesthetic and algorithmic part of the social media network; the divine literally becomes searchable, and the others who remained unteachable or inaccessible got nudged out. Their off-line associations in the existing world, as a matter of fact, are not completely eliminated from them

Digital disruption is not being denied here. However, the goal of democratising access to a voice, a place and capital is praiseworthy. Disruption, in the absence of reflecting on ethical aspects, has a setback of making the ground unbalanced. The transformation from the physical to the digital space cannot be viewed as neutral in terms of values.

Even though, what is also noticeable here is the bias towards men prevailing. Women who are seen as informal leaders in self-help groups, family networks, or neighborhood associations have excluded themselves digitally. Even if these women possess community capital, their digital capital occupies a very low status since the digital world is still not very inclusive. Their digital systems do not include caregiving, mediation, or informal education as forms of labor or leadership. Furthermore, the platforms that are built around transactional logic only, e.g., selling, subscribing, and commenting, lack the element of relational forms of power. This mismatch is a vivid example of what experts have termed as a "feminization of digital invisibility" where women's informal activities aimed at social cohesion are usually unacknowledged in data-centric systems.

However, in the middle of all this there are still some people who are doing their best to cope with this situation. There are cases of communities whose members found the way to leave the darkness of the digital gap behind and become a part of the digital inclusion—they are the ones showing us the examples of how communities with interactive relationships can work: the young people helping the elders to upload content, the non-governmental organizations adding digital elements to the folk traditions with the help of the local people, and the panchayats having their leafy-belt pulling the digital trigger, as these are the things that the tech-savvy intermediaries are supposed to handle in the digital channel- of which among other things are; collecting and running social media pages, and even assisting in the interpretation of official pronouncements of the government. As the author points out, such remedies are patchy but they do have the potential to demonstrate a new kind of co-autho.

The overall lesson is quite evident. The offline power is still in use and of great importance to social cohesion, cultural continuity, and political mediation. However, its legitimacy is persistently questioned by systems that do not recognize it—systems that simplify matters, reward for extroverted character more than for the depth of knowledge, and institutions of governance that consider access as universal. The necessity is not about whether traditional power structures should evolve with the time, but whether digital systems can be designed in a way capable to recognize.

To make this change, it is necessary to change the way we perceive inclusion. This is no longer just about getting the unconnected online, but about transforming their knowledge and authority into formats that are readable and respected. It includes the idea of setting the conditions for the platforms to provide as much reward for trust, as for users' engagement. This way, grounds of authority within the community would have value not only from the popularly supported but also through the algorithm. It is the way of weighing perception, understanding as well as the literal, and not just the rapid, the scalable, and the monetizable.

Epistemic justice is the next level of digital inclusion, which is far beyond rural outreach or the regional language support perspective. It means making a way for the different ways of knowing, leading, and influencing to be given credit. Until the time that digital India becomes inclusive of various groups of society, it will remain incomplete, not for the lack of internet accessibility, but rather for the lack of recognition. The gap is not simply a technological one, it is a human one, as well. People with power in the real world must not be excluded from the virtual one. They should be made visible. What is next is to make a human legible and, therefore, be taken as an author rather than just a user.

The Rise of Digital Middle India

Until the 2010s, the digital story of India was mostly represented by two archetypes: the modern, global early adopter in the metros—technologically literate, English-speaking, and aspirational—and the rural, offline, and disconnected Indian who was normally depicted as the victim provided for by inclusion programs. This dichotomy shaped policy decisions, formed companies' strategies, and also set the tone of global investor opinions. The real narrative, however, didn't resemble the dichotomy above, instead, it was more of a complex, ever-changing, and revolutionary nature that was acting up in between the two. Digital Middle India, which is made up of the cities of Tier 2 and Tier 3, and the towns that are currently emerging, is not in a contest in the digital revolution; it is the driving force behind it.

Their distinguishing trait is not the pursuit of the newest or exclusive but their ability to change, to fill in the gaps, and to expand. The consumers are not seeking the technology just because it is a gadget, but they are interested - how can it be used: for income, identity, expression, reputation, and community. They do not personify the users of Silicon Valley, but undoubtedly, they become the most important ones. They would use their skills in an unusual way, break the limitations as well as collect a lot of user data that would help in reshaping local platforms in India. Better still, they are not only users in the proper sense of the word; however, they are also creators, distributors, and innovators—while the grammar of their digital modernity is a replica of theirs and not someone else's.

For example, meet Shubham Raj. The guy is from Gaya, Bihar. He runs a popular YouTube channel which is based on the topic of competitive exams in Hindi and with a Bhojpuri accent. The number of followers from Uttar Pradesh, Bihar, and Chhattisgarh has tasted north of 300 thousand now. Having no studio or crew, he makes use of a second-hand ring light to shoot straight from his own room. His style of teaching is quite unpretentious, and the main ingredient is the personal experiences he puts in. His conversations are fully packed with folklore and sayings from the local culture which the urban elites may be at a loss with. But, the content is highly more trusted by the community than that of most professional platforms. Shubham has not only made sure that they have all the necessary means to reach his audience but he has also solved the problem of being likeable.

On the other hand, there is the case of Sangeeta Yadav who is 28 years old and comes from Rewa, Madhya Pradesh, and is giving us her example. She entered the world of social media showing, in the first place, recipes and household treatments from Bundeli Hindi. Her follower base quickly reached the figure that exceeded 150,000 within a year. At that time, she was not doing mainstream digital marketing but her referral traffic majorly came from WhatsApp forwards and regional Facebook groups. Money mainly flows from affiliate links and brand promotions- particularly regional FMCG brands which are her source of local credibility. She isn't just an influencer, that isn't exactly the term to describe her. She can be categorized as a micro-entrepreneur of regional culture, very spontaneous while living within a system that values tradition over modernity, and that positively impacts her growth.

Timbergrove, Antigua, Liverpool, Rethymno, Georgetown, and finally Cairns are other cities that are experiencing a similar phenomenon. The informally employed sector of digital creators in these cities is growing and includes many different professionals such as content creators, astronauts, private teachers, and gurus, who earn a living directly from people of the same class, even though they are not covered by media houses and other traditional channels. Fast development of technology, augmented by careless deforestation and climate change, has significantly altered the nature and characteristics of soils, leading to issues with erosion and decreased fertility. The rapid expansion of cities, especially the big refugee camps like Kutupalong, has been a source of daily disturbances to the natural terrain, and therefore, it has also been a significant threat to the stability of the soil. As a result of the frequent changes of the soil, there can be adverse effects like the destabilization of the food security, infrastructure as well as the increase of the disaster risk, hence the region's future will be impacted in a great way.

The ecosystem we are speaking of is not digital-like a digital-only enterprise it also needs to have cultural fluidity. There is no one face of Digital Middle India. It encompasses sectors like caste, class, language, and gender in ways that cannot be simply segmented. Though not sharing the same spot, a Dalit woman from Aurangabad leading a local governance oriented WhatsApp group and a Muslim tailor from Bhopal who expands his business by making short Reels are examples of people who, although in very different situations, are basically the same people: people who form a new public and are nowhere on the radar of elite media and urban analytics.

However, they are significant. Literacy in digital still has its highs and lows, the policies around the platforms used are unclear, and the algorithms they use are biased towards the urban areas. Many content creators from lower-tier cities in India may have difficulty in finding consistent means of monetisation, given that often they will not be the target of ad networks, or there will not be systems of monetisation that consider the specific conditions of a semi-formal economy. In addition to this, there is a noticeable gender gap, which consists in women continuously increasing their role in content creation. This, however, is not without challenges such as the structure restrictions around mobility, privacy, and fam...

There is a situation of continuous balancing where one is responsible for their own aspirations and at the same time remain authentic. Many creators feel obliged to use metro-centric language, aesthetics, or values in their content to make it more appealing to the audience. However, in doing so, what happens often is they lose the very uniqueness that was the cause of their success. The platforms themselves usually prefer that their users think the same way and in the same direction and not go off in different cultural directions. This, in essence, means that along with being 'local', creators are also 'global' and yet, they cannot abandon 'local' in favour of the 'global' trend. Learning to live in this contradictory environment is a huge burden on one's emotions as well as a strategic task.

It is true that the policy and platform design have not been able to keep pace with this developing scenario. Training programs still speculate that 'digital illiterates' are the personas to be reached; hence, they are designed to support these persons through the basics of using platform analytics, IP rights, or multi-channel monetization through the existing users in question. Regulation mainly covers privacy and competition, but the subtopics like regional language infrastructure, content equity, or vernacular data representation are not taken into account at all. The user model that has been followed traditionally is the urban, English-speaking, and upper-middle-class which is too restrictive. This should be changed—no longer just for the sake of appeasement, but rather something new and more powerful is happening beyond the top.

The future of Indian internet is actually not being designed in tech parks or in the pandemic-afflicted cities, but in the open balconies, studios, and bus stops of Digital Mid-India. This is a world that is capturing events using second-hand phones, doing editing using free mobile apps, sharing content by peer networks, and reaching a wider audience through trust rather than strategies. It is a future that not only operates in the local language but also becomes a source of vernacular data, markets the proximity between individuals, and generates resourceful ideas, but has still just been born to its understanding of power.

The interaction that should be done with this kind of India requires one to understand that the digital divide is not the matter of who gets access and who does not but who is the organizing force behind visibility and value. The digital divide turns even more multifaceted as it asks if the internet could host the polyphonic, plural, and the provincial-not only as user categories, but as system architects themselves. It is clear that the Digital Middle India is different from the traditional mainstream. It is creating a new stream - wilder, more localized, though, transformative as well. The major question now revolves around whether platforms, policymakers, and institutions are willing to not only absorb lessons from DMIs but also make them their target.

Chapter 3

Language, Identity, and the Politics of Code

In India, language has always been used as a tool of communication. However, it was not just merely communication- it has also been a bearer of history, caste, aspiration, geography, and rebellion. It is through language that power has been exerted and resiste. Also, it is through language that culture has been sustained and rethought, and it is through language that identity has been made and unmade. Nevertheless, today, with India rapidly becoming a subject to digital platforms and algorithmic architectures, language is not only being used but being deliberately designed. The way Indians talk, write, search, share jokes, and express their emotions online is being subtly but very decisively shaped by the rules and habits of code. A core concept of this chapter is the discussion of the ongoing process of restructuring the linguistic identity which, being necessarily multiple and sensitive, is in process affected by the aspirations and goals of the current digital medium that both bear and put the value of a certain set of alternatives into the practice of people living in the same society

This issue is not trivial. India has around 22 officially recognized languages, and hundreds of active dialects. Still, the digital infrastructure of that supports life in India—from smartphones and computers to content moderation algorithms to search engines—has at that time and space appeared to overwhelmingly adopt the one-language model. Even those platforms, which were allegedly created to "support" regional languages, often do so in a superficial way: they use translation widgets, script switches, or content groups that turn the reality of multilingualism into binary options. In such an environment, the language in which one types is no longer just a matter of practical consideration but a political, and cultural decision. Choosing to use Devanagari script or to write captions in Malayalam-English mixed language, or even to replace words in a text with emojis, becomes a form of expression of oneself or of one's identity. This can be said to be an opposition to being suppressed and marginalized by forces in society. The choices that a person makes reflect their will to be recognized but still remain faithful to themselves, although the systemic demands are not in their favor.

Keyboard as identity is a point of origin. In the age of non-digital communication, language management is mainly oral, or written. The spread of digital communication, especially via mobile devices, has made the device the main weapon in language wars. The choice between the use of the local language script or the Latin transcriptions (e.g. "namaste" in contrast to "नमस्ते") is a decisive factor for the survival, mutation, or legibility of the language in the public. A Tamil speaker who writes in the Roman script may get to readers from other languages but will also be, most probably, one who has the cultural traits of the expression decreased. In contrast, the use of the native script can involve fewer people, due to the lack of platform support, device compatibility, or asymmetries of literacy, but it is the way to be followed that can lead to any kind of participation in a specific range of actions that are mostly conducted through language.

When we observe the growth and spread of digital dialogues like Hinglish, Tanglish, and Benglish, it is crucial to note that these are phenomena that go much beyond just language. More than being a form of communication, these languages reflect the social ferment that is taking place in India today. These new forms of communication not only allow the users to display transnational identity while still being tied to the region, but they also encourage some level of linguistic mixing and this process is most eager in the digital space. In a great number of small and medium-sized cities, Hinglish is not considered an exaggeration, but is rather a must-have thing. It eases the young users to switch the code between online consumption and offline community, between global memes and local idioms. However, these hybrid dialects are often disregarded by both formal linguistic systems and data mining based on "pure" language. Anything not officially recognized by an algorithm runs the risk of being misinterpreted, diminished, or eliminated.

This matter takes us to the underlying issue of whose algorithm it really is. The algorithms responsible for determining what's trending, the ones that suggest content to users, those that filter comments, and also those that recommend friends, are not neutral tools but in a way, they are power structures which are influenced by the data they were exposed to, the goals they were aimed at accomplishing, and the assumptions that determined their code. In situations where these systems are not built with respect to the linguistic complexity of India, they become the primary sources of cultural colonial representations, i.e., they become the forces that generate cultural uniformity. Hindi and English have the most visible platforms, not because they are the most spoken languages, but because the backend systems push forward content that can be easily and accurately figured out, moderated, and monetised. The content of a Bhojpuri video is not the main reason for its trendless life; no one is less interested in it. However, it happens because it falls outside the comfort zone, which is obscure to the algorithm.

As a result, the consequence is the suppression of linguistic diversity in the favour of content that brings higher user engagement. The platform economies, as they currently exist, do not encourage diversity; on the contrary, everything becomes increasingly similar, and thus, it also becomes a reward. The more the country's digital presence, the more the problem with under representation and the danger of linguistic colonisation by algorithm. In other words, there is a slow but systematic process of marginalising the languages that do not fit easily into the existing system of tagging, moderation, and analysis. The role of the algorithm in that sense is similar to the behavior of a colonial administrator in so far as it awards those who abide by the system and punishes those who do not. The case is not just about the languages spoken, but also about those that are made available for research purposes.

Nevertheless, the resistance to this homogeny is noted in several places, as in the transitions of some phenomena from oral to viral. Especially the shift from oral to viral is a space where cultural diversities are being preserved and communicated, but more interestingly, the phenomena listed above have not been part of the mainstream of the textual literary world, they have always been out of the literary canon, and out of the policy discussions too. Hence, digital platforms, particularly the short-form video subspace, have unintentionally become new media zones of expression, albeit the force remains organic and viral. The possibility of a folksinger, for example, from Chhattisgarh making a video going viral on YouTube is a sign that not only such people are performing but they are also contributing to the survival and recollection of the very same knowledge that was not only forgotten but also marginalized by literary and policy canons.

The phrase that the article uses, "the digitisation of language alone", is not the only thing we see in today's digital culture. In this era the form-- the 30-second video, the short thought, the voice note--gives the frame of the talk, shapes the expression of the message and defines the audience of that message. Storytelling, which was once in a specific place, bounded by the time of year and done together with others, is now without a place and time, and instead, its frame is changed by virality metrics. This creates a dichotomy where on one side, the digital platforms permit the oral cultures to have a much larger reach than they ever had before, while on the other side, the platform's structure often is the reason for the reshaping, abbreviation, or aestheticization of the content to make it perform better. The platform's need to label may make a local case with a global algorithm come up because a story still needs to make sense algorithmically, but local color is not an algorithmic preserve.

The change from oral to viral communication channels also defines which members of society will take on the role of language watchdogs. In societies tightly constructed around tradition, the language was not lost but conserved in the community's older generation, which preserved it for themselves and for future generations. In the new age, an influencer who combines software for editing and knowledge about platforms gets the kind of access that a person who carried the past through oral speeches did. This transfer of power through digital makes language open to all, but the old ways of doing things are tampered with. What used to be a local success story in the past has today been turned into a global clamor, with sometimes little to no attention being paid to the local context and understanding of the dialect due to the desire for fame.

The larger question that then needs to be answered is: How do we ensure that the expansion of India's digital infrastructure does not come at the expense of its language diversity? Additionally, how can we develop algorithms that consider and do not overlook regional idioms, rather than simply eliminating them? Language is not just a problem in information technology, but something that affects both technological and democratic levels, requiring public policies for its restoration.

The question of how code and culture, platform logic and linguistic plurality, algorithmic power and identity assertion coexist in the digital space is the basis of this chapter. The chapter explains how everyday acts, such as texting in Tamil, captioning in Hinglish, or posting a Gondwana lullaby, are not trivial; they are acts of cultural engineering. The chapter goes on to illustrate how design choices determine what kind of linguistic behaviour the users eventually end up. The reflection touches on the algorithm's invisible influence on those who speak on the online platform and who stays quiet, and asks the question of whether technology is becoming a new layer of the already existent linguistic gatekeeper in the country.

The main point here isn't whether the language will become digital. This has been happening for quite some time now. The main question is: will the digital world leave the chaos, texture, and brilliant diversity of Indian languages untouched or will it reduce them to be seen as data anomalies? The language, we all know, is more than just a tool of communication—it is a system of memory, a way of doing politics, and a way to show that you have space. The act of typing, speech, posting, or uploading in our own languages is the user's way of insisting that the platform meets them where they are and not the other way around. Particularly in India, insistence is not only a matter of ease of use but also a matter of justice.

The Reign of English

In India, the English language has not only become a medium of communication but it also represents a particular status, a class, and even a key to access doors of opportunities. In societies that are divided by a plethora of factors, fluency in English has proven to be very helpful in acquiring more education, higher salary, and better social standing. However, the new era of computers has seen the phenomena of the English language not only persist but also gain more ground in software, platforms, and algorithms, each of which is set to the preferences of the English-speaking users. The passage of time has seen millions of Indians acquiring inf..."

The English language is used in designing apps, operating systems, and users' onboard experiences in the great majority of the current digital world. Although some platforms include multiple languages, users often experience inconsistent, poorly localized and visually disorienting designs. Let us take, for the example, an everyday person in Khargone district, Madhya Pradesh, a first-time user of a state mobile app. In this situation, the fact of the matter may be that the app has only a Hindi option, yet the quality of translation is still bad, the fonts that are used are of the lowest standard, and due to the heavy use of English, the communication through the interface is totally meaningless. Every now and then, such words as "Submit" or "Proceed" placed over the buttons become a real obstacle fostering confusion; surprisingly, along with that, they also betray no sense of belonging to the person addressed.

These are hardly insignificant mental frictions. They carry and pick up more seams of frustration. Thus, a person who encounters difficulties in making a payment, misses the privacy alert, or gets no response when he/she tries to get a new password owing to the fact that the help is available in English only, may feel that he/she is not digitally efficient to a greater or lesser extent. This fact is not caused by a lack of intelligence or potential, it is, rather, a failure of the realization of the human being behind the design. The platform here requires the user to adapt himself accordingly, thus falling short of adapting itself to the user's real language context. This, in its turn, evokes and is very similar to the former policy of the colonial times which imparted the philosophy about the English language not being a subject only, as it was considered, but a definite demonstration of civility, a culture that has found its place in modern times through the avenues of technology though it is less visible but very real.

Additionally, the predominance of English on content hierarchies is a forceful tool. The video results for a query in Hindi, "how to fix a fan," on YouTube are disproportionate in terms of the number of quality and high-viewed videos when compared to a similar search in English. The same trend is observed on Google, where English users receive more complete and specific suggestions through autocompleting their requests. And, the search frequency of the text on e-commerce platforms shifts the English version of product descriptions and user reviews in the first-line position. Even in popular media, it is most likely that content that is in English and/or "urbanised" is displayed in the spotlight, while the local content of high quality stays neglected behind the first layer of category filters. These systems are not explicitly barring access to non-English speakers. They are still leaving them a bit aside, making them choose their way through the internet by means of linguistic improvisations, which, in their turn, cost extra effort, patience and mental energy.

Nonetheless, the linguistic scenario of India does not readily comply with the process of centralization. More than 121 languages are spoken in the country, each by over 10,000 people and 22 scheduled languages are given the Constitution's recognition. In urban metros, people are often changing their language within a sentence in their talk, which is code-switching. In rural and semi-urban India, language is linked to a community's memory, their identity, and their cultural legitimacy. For a country of this nature, the presence of English occupies digital platforms not just as a functionality matter but fundamentally it is an epistemological issue. The kind of knowledge that appears, is stored and whose voice shapes the digital space is therefore dictated solely by English.

A counter movement, however, has been seen gaining strength and seems to be becoming a major wave: the surge of local language platforms and digital ecosystems that put the vernacular first. They are not simply translations from English-first but ground-up creations that have been ideated on, and have been given form by the people who have the best understanding of what the local people are aspiring for, of their culture and their behavior patterns. Let's consider the Indian Social Media app- ShareChat a major example which provides a social media platform exclusively for non-English users. Among the 15 languages supported, ShareChat was not only a copy of Facebook or Twitter but was also a platform where Bhojpuri jokes, Tamil devotional content, and Assamese memes were at the center of digital life, not on the edges only. The content design, the moderation of the community, and the interface all were able to convey the local speech rhythms and perfectly reflect cultural expectations.

Koo, the Indian version of Twitter, also a microblogging platform, has thus taken a position of being a vernacular-first product. The platform does not only offer multilinguality but also it is convenient for users to express themselves in their mother tongues by the use of easily accessible toggles and the feature of dual-language posting. This situation is not just about accommodating linguistic differences but also about the celebration of diversity as the central value of these platforms. Such platforms are not only expanding access but also creating new power centres in the digital landscape. Content creators who were never seen on these English-dominated platforms now have their own audiences, regional brand representatives, and community say. They are not just part of the digital economy, but they are also those who are creating its future landscape.

Let me give you one more example from Moj, Roposo, and Josh, which shows plainly the change that happened that is the success of vernacular video apps, especially after TikTok was banned. These innovative platforms have not only taken short videos to the next level but have put regional music, idioms, and other local content in the millions of possible theme and content combinations. This further means that dance trends in Haryana or a satirical act in Bengal can now enjoy millions of views without needing to go international to English-speaking countries. By this action, the platforms empower a great number of users to express themselves and also a parallel effect is that English isn't holding the place of visibility gatekeeper any more. Such content as it was thought once to be only for a very small percentage of users has grown so big that it has become a cultural common Umbrella for so many individuals.

However, vernacular creators do have to face a number of obstacles. For instance, it is very difficult for these creators' income to earn them profit, with the reason lying in the payment model that depends on ad-tech systems, and with brand agencies that still regard English-speaking audiences as elite witnesses. AI moderation tools cannot cover

new slang of regions, neither can they handle humour and sarcasm correctly which is why reports of misclassification of content are numerous. Speech recognition for languages such as Maithili and Konkani is also not an easy task while predictive text keyboards, are not capable of language combined scripts entering the calculus of language, of exponential growth. In an ecosystem of language diversity, linguistics is not just a formal program that makes content close to words. Conversational transactions emerge, with speech making and codes sending the data to be used in the video game concerning language that needs to be presented with an edge case.

The problem has reached beyond tech, to phones, ideology and to the heart of the people and has also had a deep impact on English as English is the aforementioned language. Through the choice of language, the history of mobility, which is connected to the dominance of English here. For decades, English has been the symbol of social elevation. Parents who live in households where English is not spoken, see it as a language that creates success. Not because the language is superior, but because the system has been programmed to reject its users disproportionately. This belief also goes on in the digital domain: most users consume and create the content in their mother tongue, but they are forced to use English. The fear of the language is at stake, which in turn results in a dual state where a person may think wisely, whereas he/she is not able to express himself/herself well, not because of any incapacity but rather because of the illegitimacy figured out by his/her mind.

Policy, platform design, and pedagogy are the three things that need to be transformed. If we look at translation, it actually uses the diversity of the language as a means of inconvenience. At the same time, the crowd that wants to know how English-first platforms can be "localised," should start asking a different thing: if the platform were initially vitally for Kannada speakers, what would it look like? This is a technical as well as a cultural and ethical issue. This reconfiguration literally means understanding the language and acknowledging that it is a neutral medium, but one deeply embedded with the ideals, hegemonies, and histories of its culture.

English will not and should not vanish. In the era of a globalized economy, it will consistently take a central position as the communication vehicle across the world. But in this new scenario, its existence must be reconsidered. The future of digital India either grows with the change from an empire to English to a linguistic pluralism ecosystem or perishes, if the mother tongue of each user, regardless of the nation where he/she was born, will reach the level of feeling not only welcome but empowering. This is not only a challenge in appearance, but one that is structural. The user interface, the algorithms, the content curation, and the monetisation strategies ought to be rethought and done so bearing in mind the value of diversity, not the level of lip service.

To tear down the empire of English is not to enter into a war with a language. It is the action of acknowledging and addressing a hierarchy. It is only the mutual intelligibility of multiple voices, each with their own syntax, slang, cadence, and code that can guarantee the birth of a truly inclusive digital India. It is only then that the sense of justice communities can be built from the ground up can be based on a realization that language is a fundamental part of justice and not just the end of access. Language should start to flow as the source of justice, not the final step toward it.

Keyboard as Identity

In the olden days, the keyboard used to be a mere dull tool for the office, for the typing machine or for European languages. But, today, just the opposite has happened in the Indian context, where the keyboard has become a very intimate location for cultural bargaining. The way Indians type in the digital world just looks like the way they breathe, work, get things done, etc. As one writes here in Indian digital spaces, one sees the phenomenon of the language, the culture, the aspiration, etc. being mixed and bonded together live, traits which cover a wide array of types.

The QWERTY layout used for English is still the default in most of the devices, even in India, where its daily use does not embody the meaning of the standard anymore. On a regular basis, users reconfigure, alter, and reinvent the QWERTY layout in multiple ways such as writing Tamil using Latin script, introducing Hinglish as a lingua franca, and blending emoji sequences to communicate caste subversion or romantic feelings. As a result, the keyboard has undergone a complete metamorphosis; beyond serving as a plain mechanical instrument, it now literally has taken on human behavior traits in that it reflects our present and future changes.

From the social media to the comment sections and to the WhatsApp shares, the mingling of languages has taken such a firm root that it looks rather normal nowadays in India. For instance, if we see the phrase "*Kal ghar pe aaja bro, biryani ready hai*" in Roman script, although the language used seems to be a mix of Hindi, English, and regional styles, it would still leave an impression of a grammatically incorrect sentence. But, for those who are present at the dialog, it is not a misspoken language but a language that continually develops and is more flexible in expressing meaning. The keyboard serves as the platform for introducing this change, and typing thus becomes the means of implementing this importation.

The extent to which the Hinglish language is on a steep rise is more visible nowhere else than the digital space. From a language spoken only by the poor in the streets of the northern cities of India, to be heard now on every digital platform across the country is quite an achievement. Enterprises seek it. Celebrities will not shy away from using it. Comedians derive inspiration from it. This rhythm is India's multiculturalism in a note: a celebration of diksha as well as cosmopolitan ambition, of people who have more than one tradition and more than one mode of expression. Unlike pure English or pure Hindi, Hinglish is the voice of generation that does not want to be limited to just one place or class, but flows across regions, scripts, social classes, and even ideologies. And to the greatest extent, it is a user-driven language. There are no stringent rules, no grammatical slate of what Hinglish must be like.

Also regional languages have found a place in the digital world and in most cases, by using the Latin alphabet as a surrogate script. For example, Tamil speakers write English characters phonetically, and Bengali users publish complete fan-fiction threads in Romanised Bangla. The choice hardly ever happens because of linguistic laziness. This is an expression of pragmatism, inclusion, and comfort. Very often, Indians have not been trained in typing in the script of their own language, that is, English as the medium of language of instruction. But it did not prevent them from giving the digital world Indian flavors. Writing to type and use is like a bone showing itself. By writing "*nalla irukkinga da*" on a Facebook post, a person is not merely conveying information, but they are also transmitting a multilayered identity propelled by language, spirit, and sitcoms.

So what if the expression is already beyond the letters? The emoji, so prevalent, unpunctuated, and sometimes not taken seriously, has been recognized as a separate semiotic language. Emojis are the new form of communication for the majority of Indians, who are either new in the digital world or whose literacy level is compromised. This visual language is a quick way for people to express themselves, making them find more time to engage with others and connect deeper. A prayer emoji 🙏 conveys its cultural context of devotion, supplication. The fire emoji 🔥 is most often an expression of friendship, victory, or appetite. A string of figures that is,

💃 🎉 🍾 sent in a family WhatsApp group tells the others about one's party mood without any words used. It doesn't mean that emojis are just useful and fun in expressing oneself but they actually help those that are less fluent in current dominant scripts to participate in the digital world. They are actually more effectively communicative than one could have ever thought back then.

Yet, these linguistic expressions are not neutral at the same time. They are processed by algorithms, grouped, and sometimes filtered by the algorithms. Autocomplete, search, content moderation, and trending topics algorithms mostly support the standard English that is a bias of visibility. For example, a post in Hindi or even Romanised Bhojpuri may have less outreach, be subjected to more frequent flags, or not be properly indexed. The much-vaunted democratization of the keyboard is in fact takeaway of infrastructural asymmetries. The teachings are more inclined to only those literacies, and the back-end data systems are highly biased towards sanitized commercial content as opposed to the grassroots kind of content.

The gendered angle is also an essential part of this matter. Young women who live in various parts of India - but mainly in Tier 2 and Tier 3 cities - are the group that typically faces a much more critical approach to their digital activities. Speaking in English can be considered as a confident and inspiring act, especially as spoken in the country itself. However, speaking one's mother tongue might be considered as "too local." Evidently, being reliant on emojis could lead to the judgment of immatureness or being unserious. This puts those who are typing in a position to be in a dilemma. Nevertheless, some handle it by just choosing the right digital accents - using standard English in their posts, while being free to comment using their language. Or they employ various identities through pseudonyms or multiple accounts to express different aspects of themselves. What is more, the end result of this practice is neither simple code-switching nor mere identity-building - it is art, as it suggests a person's identity is shaped by, and constructed for, the perceived audience, the platform's existing norms, and their safety.

Even political discourse is not immune to the power of technology, as that, too, has become intertwined with computer keyboards. Hashtags intended for political demonstrations in Indian languages such as Hindi and Tamil do not become as popular as if these hashtags were in English. Also, those slogans which are typed in local scripts are equally difficult to promote. Even in a movement as significant as #MeToo or #FarmersProtest, it was the English posts that got the lion's share of the media coverage. In the digital space, language is used as a criterion for the authenticity of ideas and their reinforcement. It is not the case that grassroots-wise the voices of vernaculars are inaudible -- but rather they have to swim against the current. The keyboard, far from being a neutral medium, acts more like a gate that goes slightly in one direction with regards to the signs posted near it.

All the same people have found different ways of defying this. The rappers from Uttar Pradesh, for example, apply Hinglish bars and transliterated Hindi to pinpoint the caste injustice. Khara Lahariya, that is a media outlet among others, carries out its work by translating, inter alia, all the village news into Bundeli and Awadhi languages supported by the hybrid scripts. And Influencers in Coimbatore find fame by inputting witty reels in Tanglish and building in the process big followings. All these possibilities are more about taking back the domain of the keyboard from being mere instruments to being territories. Digital life may thrive without causing self-culture no harm. And the act of writing in one's own language, even if the system makes it hard for you, is a silent kind of rebellion.

The consequences of this are felt not only in culture but also in trade. Fintech's lightning in a bottle in small-town India exemplifies how important it is to allow consumers to use their language on digital platforms rather than the platforms dictating only English or any other language. Payments apps have had to adapt by now offering more onboarding in Hindi, Marathi, Telugu, etc. Voice recognition solutions are getting ahead, but the majority of them are not still equipped to process the queries involving different languages and that, too, in the same sentence, for example as "mera balance check karo bhai." The chatbots in local dialects of India are not yet fully operational either. The root cause of the quoted problems is a basic oversight - language is the fundamental medium of communication and hence of trust. Without the freedom of writing and talking in one's mother tongue, no AI or the most advanced tech stack are able to ensure communication, felt in a human way.

Are we already aware that the keyboard bypasses the user's way to go to the internet?

Does the keyboard, indeed, only serve as the interface through which users access the Internet? Of course not! By being so much more, it is the place from which the individual can establish the power and voice as well as the one who defines the legitimacy of their position. The keyboard is a way for the users to express themselves, both their comfort with self-expression, and their negotiation with the standardized scripts, and their ability to shape their digital environment. The use of cyberspace-related metaphors in the text reflects the user's comfort and self-expression. The keyboard has become a theatre of power, voice, and legitimacy as a result. The users are negotiating the standardized scripts and, hence, portraying the skills of their user interface. Our work in the digital world reveals that much more is at stake, such as an individual's sense of self, especially in the communication of themes of culture, social demands, and rites such as the use of technology without assistance or ...

It can even be called a power exchange stage, the place where the user files a claim of... to the rest. The fact that even a wrongly spelled word, a Devanagari WhatsApp status, or an emoji thread are not considered as errors goes to show that they have become inscriptions of a plural India that refuses to be reduced to the colonial grammar on tech platforms.

India is going through a digital phase where linguistic diversity is not a problem to be solved but-is the way the country operates. The multiplicity of languages is accompanied by the design of the keyboard that doesn't only mean a connection to a desktop but rather with the whole social-economic milieu in which the language is used. It is where people are featured in all their elements of diversity, toying, comforting, protesting, and celebrating the same in their self-made languages. To ignore such would not only represent a wrong understanding of the way t... India, but also show a lack of knowing who the people are.

Whose Algorithm Is It Anyway?

Stories told in a society are the ones that build it. There are the algorithms in the digital age, which are also major contributors to the decision-making process about what gets told. They decide on the content of your feed, what videos are viral, which tags are ranked, and which languages are "relevant." Besides, they are said to be neutral; this is actually not the case. Every suggested video, music promoting song, or meme becoming a trend is representative of an invisible structure consisting of values, personal preferences, and design choices that the social space is primarily influenced by. In India, a country which is multilingual, multi-religious, and characterized by uneven economic distribution, this situation poses a very relevant question: whose algorithm is it anyway?

First and foremost, an algorithm is a set of strict instructions. Nevertheless, in the case when these engineers are situated in California, who write those strict instructions and when the data on the basis of which the algorithms are trained are mostly of Western users, and more importantly, the algorithms are set to increase engagement rather than diversity, the influence on the Indian culture could not be downplayed. Suppose the recommendation engine of YouTube is taken as an example. In its early stages, the engine resulted in unfair advantages towards the content in English and Hindi, even if the cases had no conscious bias and were purely the result of a poorly drawn feedback loop: more users watching such content meant more visibility, which led to more views, which in turn led to further reinforcement of its dominance. Meanwhile, it was the creators bringing up the topic of Marathi, Santali, or Khasi who had difficulty in breaking through, although in some cases, their work was of significant artistic or social value.

This is not just a question of representation; it raises the question of epistemic access as well—the power of individuals to see themselves represented in the wider knowledge eco... (12 characters are hidden) ...space, and be reflected back. If the content that is dominant across all platforms is not a reflection of your language, humor, rituals, or lived experiences, then subconsciously you have changed to be a parody of what the algorithm rewards you to be rather than who you actually are. It's a shift that is not without effects; it truly shapes the future of your aspirations, relations, and even political opinions.

There's no better example of this than the rise of pan-India influencers. Their language is usually polished, modern Hindi, or English, which they even speak when they are from non-Hindi-speaking areas. The way the algorithm functions is transparent: the farther the reach, the more views, brand deals, and platform support. Cultural impact, on the other hand, is not felt so directly. A tribe from the Northeast or a young creator from the tribal areas of Odisha without switching the language is the last that are hardly ever heard. The algorithm doesn't target them maliciously—it merely works out decisions that choose whatever gets things done fast. Things are defined now, which subordinates the complexities and nuances quite a bit.

Furthermore, it is not a one-sided situation. We can see a counter-trend happening and a group of creators, developers, and platforms are stirring up the whole idea of things. One example is the Indian social media app called ShareChat, which comes with a feature of posting in more than a dozen regional languages. While most of the global platforms consider Indian users as a single entity, ShareChat's interface is clearly divided by language, region, and interest. Through this decision, users are granted the power of mannerly content spin and consumption in their own language without the obligatory Hindi-English filter.

Local YouTube channels specializing in comedy from Bhojpuri, cooking from Telugu, or folklore from Manipuri are also striking a chord with the audience. Typically, these channels have their popularity on home turf but today the idea of community-led virality has taken off and this audience has quickly spread to new areas. These channels are not successful in spite of their exclusivity but rather because of it. They bring something that is beyond the capacity of the mainstream algorithm: cultural intimacy. This intimacy is the one that many get when they see their grandmother's dialect on the screen or understand a joke that only Tamil Nadu Doordarshan viewers can relate to.

However, these success stories are viewed as rare even now. The preset options typical of major international platforms are still supporting the concept of one cultural identity. It is not only the nature of the content that is visible—it is also about how the content is commercialised and controlled. Videos that are marked as "low engagement" in minority languages may go down the priority list for a variety of reasons, and this would be the case even if the videos carry cultural importance. Automation moderation systems, rooted in Western norms, may wrongly disallow the use of the local language, political slogans, and religious expressions, while considering them as hate speech or fake news. The outcome is that in the digital world, culture and algorithms become one.

Furthermore, the algorithm influence over public discourse as such is another aspect. In the case of Twitter (now X) and similar platforms, trends are usually employed for gauging the pulse of society by media outlets, political representatives, and social activists. However, what the algorithms identify as a "trend" is a result of an automated process that is based on speed, quantity and exposure. English language and mainstream Hindi tags are already privileged. A local land rights protest in Chhattisgarh might not see the trend line, but an incident of a break-up involving a celebrity in Mumbai changes the situation much faster. Soon the algorithm which initially was to control the culture ends working as well in political agenda setting.

It is not enough to offer representation for counteracting this system clarification is mandatory, and this includes the public recording statistical accountability—understanding how software changes or affects people's understanding and viewpoint, and what can be changed through the same technology. To this end, the authors of the Data Protection Bill are, it is clear, prompting the implementation of provisions that will require the platforms to make public the logic behind the decision of visibility and access to resources affected by their algorithms. Structured visibility is, however, just the starting point of the challenge; the construction of new models is the ultimate goal, which should be carried out with the proper sensitivity and innovative spirit of the software developers and managers of the products, who would give to the term 'diversity' a place among the general rules and not at the hem of society

This kind of perceptiveness can convert the discovery engines into "Bhojpuri"and a location-based tool which prioritizes regional creators without punishing them for the lower initial audience. The tool should also allow the users to list their language preferences, and a constant reward-maximization feature does not necessarily lead them to abandon those preferences while also enabling them to output the artists they want. It can expand the way that databases categorise music so that the lyrics of Bhojpuri folk songs and oral histories of Santhali are classified as meaningful content instead of being eliminated and dumped in the generic "Other." Though the goal is not to antagonize code, it becomes instead humane to code it in such a way that it becomes fully aligned with the pluralism it seeks.

Data is no less important than sensitivity when preparing these systems for use. If the data-sets containing Indian references are voted by the hidden programmes to be sent to the Indian market, and these data-sets don't represent entirely the local cultures, then the machines will reproduce the same content. The gathering of cultural data from texts, videos, and audio samples that fully represent a given culture, and which has the potential to be shared with various machine learning models, requires a lot of effort, and significant trust, and cooperation with local communities. The first steps of the Indian startups and AI laboratories have been strong but a considerable amount of work still needs to be done. Given that the core of the next generation of AI systems is the basis, there is a significant chance that the bias of culture will be embedded in these models. If we are not careful about it, the algorithms that will be produced in the future could be much less inclusive than those of today.

Despite these oppositions, the connotations embedded in the above statements/paragraphs carry with them the possibility to bring about something new. The tools that have been blamed for acting as the force behind the assimilation of the human race can all be restructured anew to bring about diversity. For instance, the existing recommendation engines could be converted to not just selecting the most engaging but the underexposed creators and contents to be recommended to the users spread across the globe. We should move forward to employ federated models that absorb local behavior to create lightweight layers and avoid placement of power at one point. Small modifications in the display—like multiple-based suggestions in the search section or trending tab in many languages—can lead to significant changes in what the users are going to browse.

It is not just about content diversity at stake here, it also concerns the online treatment of everyone's culture, language, and stories. Digital dignity, the right that each person in India should enjoy to witness their culture, language, and narratives treated as first-class citizens in the platforms they inhabit, is a deeply rooted issue.

Algorithms, when not observed, will retain as well as give life to the prejudices of their creators. However, if given a proper purpose and close attention, they can become the means of freedomâ€"to the extent of enabling the proliferation of Indiaâ€TMs storytelling traditions rather than endangering them.

When all has been said and done, the question whose algorithm is it anyway is in the nature of a demand for reclaiming authorship. The excruciating fact is that the digital universe, while expressed through computer programming language, must still answer to human values. As the number of Indians joining the online community grows, the stories they see, share, and tell will mold the national imagination for the years ahead. The physical structure of that imagination should not be an unknown place to be left to others. It should be constructed, like India itself, in many tongues, in varied voices, and with the full might of cultural aim.

From Oral to Viral

Bharat, the abounding treasure trove of the inhabitants of the world, the Jambudvipa, this was recorded, not in ink, but transmitted by word of mouth and that too on the person level. The history and religion of Indian society in ancient times, such as the Vedic period, were disseminated in the same way. In those days, the age of oral tradition allowed not only the elders and parents to dominate the lives of their own communities through the vehicle of the hearing art but also history, science, and literature to be passed down to younger generations. As for today, the spoken and sung texts have been rediscovered while a greater audience has been attracted by these lectures and, as a consequence, oral communication has become the focal point for all modes of transmission.

Fast forward to this day, and we find ourselves in a strange situation: the digital revolution has not only conserved oral traditions but has changed them. On platforms such as YouTube, Instagram Reels, Moj, and TikTok (lesser these days), storytelling has gotten its most visual, algorithmic form. The oral has gone viral, but not without side effects. The question now is not just about the content of stories, but how the format itself is influencing their structure, rhythm, and meaning. The moment the dynamics of virality replace the cadence of oral tradition, a quiet yet radical change is taking place: the culture's memory is being redesigned.

Imagine the oral storytelling process in its native environment. It was inherently with the nature surrounding it. A grandmother narrating a story to her grandchild, a bard singing in a village square, a qissa being performed during harvest were all participatory experiences that were shaped by the immediate context. The narrator could easily change the tone, pace, and content in response to the audience hearing the story. It is essential to mention that not only were these stories open to the possibility of change, but also each retelling allowed for improvisation. Local idioms, personal insights, and generational shifts were imprinted on the narrative thereby recreated. This made oral tradition rather than frozen heritage, not only a living archive, but also a breathing one.

What about stories that go viral on digital platforms? Virality is the result of good packaging i.e. being short yet catchy, having a visual hook, being relatable, and easily shareable. Instead of improvisation, there is a process of selection. Instead of modulation, there is a performance for the algorithm. Content is repeated with some changes to suit more viewers rather than the context causing its development. This shift is not all that bad. It does more good than harm, for example, a storyteller in Bastar is able to connect with a girl from Boston. However, it poses a major threat: what will the result be when a culture of retelling and a culture of repeating meet?

More and more, the answer seems to be splitting. While oral storytelling has rich and meaningful plots with subtlety, pauses, and where lines between the protagonists and the antagonists are quite unclear, digital sketches and fashion are farthest from the very story abstractness. Instead of a whole story needing 30 minutes of participation from the community, the same story is now reduced to 30 seconds of the screen. It's a different way of engaging with the content though it's not some kind of objective parameter that affects people's minds, it's the cognition which is changed significantly. Our brain processes a story in rather different ways if we listen to it in a conversation than if we consume it in a scroll. The story of the voice-filled memory is an act of memory, whereas the viral one is an act of memory by a left or right finger.

The world has already gone through an absolutely radical transformation and, in fact, the Internet considerably contributed to this. Yet, this transformation presents an unlikely and marvellous opportunity. With the right intentions, platforms meant for digital interactions can effectively reach out to the voiceless. For instance, "The Digital Sutradhar" project is suitable in this context because it allows tribal elders to retell and convey Gond folktales through the means of local YouTube channels. There is also the story of Padmavathi, a 62-year-old folk singer from Telangana whose performance of Telugu ballads with the aid of a smartphone recorded by her grandson went viral. Many such individuals consider the screen not as a thing to be afraid of but as a means to preserve their lives. Their dialects, which have hitherto been excluded from the pages of mainstream publishing or broadcast media, now have a chance to spread to the very ends of their traditional area and beyond.

However, being allowed to participate is not the same as having power. It is still not just a matter of being creative or of being at the mercy of the algorithmic curation that decides who will become popular and what type of material will be put on the platform. The fact that a tribal woman from the woods singing a traditional song in her dialect may not be as visible as the urban creator who knows the tongue and who lip-syncs to it might create a problem of greater disparity. If the original regional culture is not recognised through its original form and is only through metrical performance, a kind of mimicry loop will be created. Furthermore, the regional metadata, subtitling infrastructure, and linguistic tagging are additional factors that contribute to the problem. The unbracketed nature of metadata has an impact on it in a way that the digital content is indeed visible yet invisible to systems that would otherwise elevate it.

The loss of contextual storytelling stands as a major hurdle as well. Throughout history, every story was tied to certain seasons, places, rituals, or social hierarchies in the traditional sense. In this layout, a story about rain spirits shared in a dry village was not just a myth—it was the weather. When such stories are transferred to an electronic medium and the mentioned references are missing, the content of the stories can also be lost. The viewer realizes just the words without understanding the meaning behind them. If cultural transfer is not a conscious part of adapting to digital media, then the disconnection is certainly happening and is almost inevitable.

Moreover, oral storytelling was essentially a communal event. It was not only the plot of the story that was so affecting, but it was the place of storytelling—the public's joint listening to the story, a common gasp, and the reaction of the community. By contrast, viral storytelling is barely corresponding to this environment. The audience is engaged with the contents of the story without sharing the experience with others, as it is very rarely followed by profound reflection or discussion. Progressing from a societal memory base to an individual consumption era raises the question of what types of values and ways of thinking are favored. Thus, the kind of storytelling that is reduced to content production becomes more of nostalgic commodities rather than relics of old.

The way things are going, digital storytelling is taking new forms in line with the changing times, and they are trying to stay true to the style and feelings of the oral mode of storytelling. Podcasts created in languages that are local, voice messages sent through the WhatsApp group of family, and online storytelling experiences conducted during the course of celebrations can be taken as some of those forms. Features of the oral forms—voice, tone, intimacy—are those that will be brought back into the digital style by these examples. However, they are not becoming genuinely well-liked and farther away from the views of society in general. Still, the websites prefer videos instead of voice, visuals instead of thoughts, and speed instead of the surrounding details of the content.

Less reliance on individual creators and more on infrastructural support will determine how the system can preserve the narratives of indigenous people and their local language. Such support includes financial help for the cultural documentation, linguistic digitization projects, regional creator incentives and algorithmic rebalancing to highlight long-form and low engagement content that serves the heritage rather than only popularity. The involvement of saving the oral traditions is not the work to be left to non-profit organizations and folklorists. It must be one of the key points of the national policy and tech platform design. Archiving the oral traditions in a digital format is an act of the progressive future and not a storage of the past.

At the heart of it, the change from oral to viral is not a simple shift in technology. It is a renovation of how we recall, share, and adjust the idea of who we are. The main task of the people is not to be anti-digital but to digitize it with care and be cautious so that when the stories of our grandfathers and grandmothers are transformed into content, they do not lose their spirit. For the people of India, whose identity is narrated as much as it is taught, this is not just a cultural task; it is also a civilisational one.

Chapter 4
Digital Dharma and the Ethics of Connection

Digitalisation in India is no longer simply a technological adaptation, but a force that has refashioned the core of Indian socio-cultural life. From a nation that has been historically shaped by diverse dharma principles: *mandli ki farmanbardari, sacha prem, janmjati ki ummeed*, and *dharamanusar vibhav*, the introduction of ubiquitous connectivity has introduced a new set of values: digital ethics. What are the parameters of behavior that make a person responsible and ethical in the digital world? Is it that anonymity is a way of individual freedom although also considered as a cover-up to ill actions of the bulk? Or, is it for example privacy a foreign concept or a requirement for people's self-respect in the digital age? These are not mere theoretical questions - they are happening on a regular basis in everyone's daily life - on phones, in law courts, on channels television, and in family conversations. So, our project studies the emergence of Digital Dharma - a term not used by us referring solely to religion but as a framework concept posed to understand how India handles most of the moral issues in its digital transformation.

In opposition to liberal democracies, particularly the Western ones, where the self is put on a pedestal, India is known for being a collectivist society, wherein the members live in harmony and are interdependent. In India, privacy is a concept that has always been embraced as a relationship, not as an absolute state of being. The notion of every individual having the right to a completely sealed sphere of informational privacy is in conflict with the reality of the joint family system, nosy neighbors, big open kitchens, and having a community that works through accountability. This contradiction is also reflected in the online world. For instance, the situation of spouses who share their Facebook passwords speaks volumes about the issue, as well as the scenario of public WhatsApp groups where the screenshots of personal instants become the subjects of viral attacks. It is very clear that the boundaries between private and public life are extensively broken. It is, however, important to note that while the digital medium might adhere to international procedures and codes of practice, its interpretation in India is often influenced by the traditional social structures imbued in its current society. The event of a college student's phone being checked by the parents or the landlord asking for the tenant's Instagram profile is never regarded as just a kind of control over an individual, but it is also considered as a show of cultural significance.

The struggle happens when the legal systems observe one person's privacy while the norms change which silently leads to a more open society. The decision of the Supreme Court in 2017 attributed to Puttaswamy regarding the fundamental nature of the right to privacy. This has received a lot of plaudits globally from those who are progressive. But, the benefits of the judgment have not reached everyone equally. So, practically it becomes meaningless for the housewife living in a rural area who is sharing her phone with her husband or for the street vendor whose financial data is placed on the device of another person. If the status of privacy is on the document, it does not come in the design of a product or in any policy or cultural behavior, that will hardly change the already existing hierarchies, but should strengthen them. In this case, the smartphone changes its role to a paradoxical one, as it looks like it grants the user some freedom to accessibility, while in reality, it makes the user more exposed to unsafe situations.

Besides privacy, the use of the digital realm in India has turned out to be a karma-based economy where the commodities are people's attention, confirmation, and less-obclusion. These days, things that are viral make no mistake but to be aspirational. At the moment, the one who has gone viral is the one who believes that he/she is on the map, is recognized, and his/her existence is acknowledged. For an urban creator of content, it might be a chance for him to make money, or it could be the gaining of influence he intends to have. As for a rural artisan or dancer, he/she might realize that it is the moment, where he/she is able to leave that mud of the unknown. But for the majority of people, they perceive viral phenomena as an agreeable return-- they are, thereby, spiritually validated. By this very act of others recognizing them, digital platforms have become the very want of modern karma. A video of (what looks like) feeding the poor, a tweet standing up for the nation, a reel displaying devotional behavior in a temple—these happenings, when conducted on multimedia and further shared, translate into a stronger and favorable person via moral patronage. The digital community shares its likes and shares through online blessings; retweets are equivalent to a collective view.

The fusion of platform logic with karmic logic has led to the emergence of newer kinds of performance, some of which are authentic, and some opportunistic. When ethics changes to a quantified dimension, the demarcation between a good deed and virtue signaling becomes less apparent. The acts of morality, charity, and patriotism performed in public are now mostly for the feed and less for the field. This notwithstanding dismissing of such performances as being only with the surface would be reductionism. The electronic space has become a site for moral creativity, specifically among custodians of various identity positions like the younger generation of Indians. Whether it is an Islamic woman's Instagram shout-out of pride in hijab or a Dalit poet's interaction with his audience on YouTube, the act of going viral is no longer an administrative activity but a political and spiritual one. It is through such acts that respect is accorded individuals through their being seen and heard.

However, the digital dharma of India is time and again put to the test by a plethora of public moral panics. The story of TikTok being banned in 2020 to the regular crackdown on adult websites, from influencers' often alleged uncivilized behavior to the increase of vigilantes in ruling online ...

However, these meltdowns have a silver lining too. The same social media which make the worst of human behaviour viral also can reveal small fights against it too. The Hathras rape case in 2020 is not an example of a crime made known by the state media but independent digital journalists and social media users - whose pressure led to the caste-based violence being in the focus of the whole nation. Likewise, when the farmers' protests were highlighted in a wrong way through the traditional media, it was through the apps that are similar to TikTok and the influencers who use the native language that the rest of the story was told. They are not the only examples, they are the signs of India's digital future that will be determined not only by engineers or regulators but also by the country's moral citizens. That is, those who realize that every like is a value choice, every post an ethical act, and every share a signal of what we think deserves to be seen.

The issue is, therefore, to encourage a digital system that is not anti-moral nor moralizing. India does not want a pure and too bright internet space what is governed by sentiment or censorship. It asks for a conversation around values to unfold – what builds a connection worth our time, what content is deserving our trust, and what community are we creating public with every click. The connections' ethics should not be given to the bots or the foreign companies. They should be handled internally by the people, arise from the Indian social environment, and take into account the global human rights levels.

This unit is not trying to promote only one answer or like that give the moral code to be followed. The focus is on delving into the gap between those customs transmitted from the past and the emerging behaviour, between the community's responsibility and individual dignity. Thus, it tries to bring forth the interwoven issues on the one hand a need for the ethics of dharma from ancient times and on the other the urgency of being a digital citizen. When India transforms itself at various levels statuesque from its identity and economy to religion and representation, it also has to rethink its moral direction. In the digital age, the element of your interconnectedness is also your conscience. And just like any system of ethics, digital dharma will survive if it continues to be discussed, revised, or is done in practice.

Surveillance as Seva?

A lady residing in rural Chhattisgarh receives an SMS that her subsidized ration has been dispatched at a local fair price shop. She goes to the shop with her Aadhaar card, authenticates her fingerprint, and returns home with her necessary food items. She may not be aware that her data has passed through many servers, is kept in the store of the government, is recorded for reviews, and eventually could have been linked to more databases, such as her mobile number, bank transactions, and health records.

Who can say it if she has not been informed about how her data will be used/has no access to the privacy policy and therefore has not been asked whether she agrees to something or not?! However, the service has been delivered to her despite this, and this fact alone can bring some Indians a sense of empowerment which they might not have felt otherwise. It is indeed ironic as therein lies the essence of India's data economy: surveillance is made to seem like a durable part of the system and not just an invasive act all of a sudden; it is the foundation of the country's data economy.

Such talk about seva is not a coincidence. It is rather thoughtful and is an attempt to gain people's support. In the Indian context, where paternalistic governance and collective welfare are deeply rooted, the word "seva" which means service without self-interest, has a moral weight. Political leaders often use this language to refer to digital ventures, ranging from Direct Benefit Transfers (DBTs) to COVID vaccine registrations, that resonate with the citizens through numerous channels.

The state becomes the custodian of the people's interests, and the dispenser of technology that facilitates the administrative process, without any middlemen or loss of self-respect. However, self-respect, according to the philosopher Martha Nussbaum, is not just a matter of entitlement; it is also about having a voice in the process. Nevertheless, in such a manner that the individual's consent is not obtained, dignity becomes exhausted.

India's association with surveillance has historically been more about the variation between, rather than symmetry in, dominating power, language, and understanding capacities. Trusted sources claim that Indian society, by contrast, puts comfort over the rule of being the ultimate power, and at present, the convenience is actually worth more than the risk of being monitored. If a digital service is efficient—-could be a chargeback of LPG, pension disbursement, or a lightning-fast UPI refund—it confirms the locals' belief in good governance thus, the myth becomes even stronger. The data policy of the nation is the citizen's basis for economic development, which gets universally accepted. Now, she is not offended that her face is recognized, or her location is being monitored because it is felt that it is no longer a violation, but rather just payment for quick delivery of the service. But this perception of surveillance-as-service does not necessarily mean people are indifferent. It is more a result of the rewards given, framing, and digital literacy being limited.

The framework that outlines consent in India is not robust, is ambiguous, and it is more often seen in symbolic form. In order to use most digital services, the user has to tick "I agree" to a description of terms, which they do not know being in a language not fully understood by 90% of the population i.e. English. The main reason someone picks "I agree" is not because they feel knowledgeable about their decision but because it becomes a formality, they have to do the same as when signing a government form. Additionally, the basic infrastructure of the platforms passing through the Aadhar-based PDS system, health databases, and mobile eKYC is done via data centralization where the user's data is disseminated among state ministries and private enterprises. The issue of consent is fragmented, and so it's not granular. They can't tell the system they don't want different data pieces they are using, nor can they challenge the data that's been misused.

One good example is the National Digital Health Mission (NDHM) that claims to be the nation's health marker and to enable more or less free access to medical records from all the hospitals to the people. Although the goal of the mission seems to be great, its carrying out raised many doubts.

People from rural areas were signed up even though they did not clearly get what it meant to them. In some cases, health workers in the field pre-filled the consent forms to achieve the set target. To this end, citizens were given the added allowances or bonuses of fewer quantities of food. Not real involvements of coercion but there is also no meaningful choice involved. The situation of the state's ability to gather and relate to the data of health, finance, mobility, and welfare has become a kind of an ambient surveillance ecosystem where there is continuous visibility and consent is seldom original; it is only performed.

The message here is that not all of the Indian citizens are apathetic or ignorant. A very opposite process of surveillance fightback is happening alongside the Indian population, albeit mostly through cultural and tactical channels. Acts, like joining WhatsApp groups that share privacy-conscious fintech practices, holding meetings where CCTV cameras are being covered, and also the turning off of the location on government apps, are small-scale rebellions. Though they are very rare. The majority of the discussions in the society concerning surveillance are still polemically covered in one way or another; it's either that they are emotionally driven by trust in the power of technology and innovation or they are the result of fear-driven moral panic. India has none of the framework of an articulate public discussion of data dignity, and we are now speaking only of data protection. The new Personal Data Protection Bill has not managed to change the situation completely. The idea of the citizen as a "data principal" still remains present. However, some of the laws were revised. The citizens' rights are now shared between them and the data fiduciaries. The latter idea is part of the framework of cultural ethics talking about issues of data dignity.

The danger of seva is not just a mere concept. It prevents surveillance from being questioned by the use of the word "service." Digital collectivism-based countries may look promising on the surface but the requirements that people need to meet so as not to misuse the technology must also be addressed. But when the state is just a donor and the people not only the owners of the projects, then the approval of citizens is only a formality and the process of transparency a show. E.g. If an AI employee of a facilities management company was allowed to lay down the rules for smart energy use and additionally for participating volunteers, how to be rewarded, after which power would no longer be visible?

But that's not all the stakeholders – without a doubt, the corporate also treat privacy invasion exclusively as something positive. Film and music production platforms monitor app user's movements in the city, to learn about their habits and reactions and the least frequently available item on the delivery may be noise-canceling earphones. On the other hand, behaving in such a way when the purpose is not apparent means that the inititative is manipulative. The AI technology provides data that can prevent fraud in financial transactions and can predict health issues, yet at the same time that data can be used to support the w concept of abusing human rights. For example, the eye-tracking software the student had to use made sure nobody cheated on the tests and did other things that were not acceptable behavior. However, matrimonial apps that mine social media for individuals with common interests in order to find a suitable match is no longer an ambitious plan. These are all mostly automatic and are outside the jurisdiction of the government. All for a good cause you say? Superior matchmaking services. More convenience. Better quality.

The Indian citizen is, in essence, wrongly in the middle of a circle of imagined comfort. Each provision of the data is being justified as a method of achieving the greater good: improved governance, better urbanization, ecological visibility, as well as quickness in rebates. But who sets the conditions for dialogue? In what areas are the exits? Who makes sure that from service it does not turn into servitude?

There is an added layer of complexity: the spiritual and symbolic dimension of Indian public life. In a society where being answerable to the higher power is often positioned as moral obligation to the aged, the country, or God, a notion of disobeying digital surveillance is not a natural one. A request for the annulment of the data order might be taken as selfish, unthankful, and even as a non-patriotic act. State ads that describe it as desh seva (service to the nation) when people download an app, have the same effect as well. Surveillance is then equated with self-denial. But surveillance free of resistance is not the same as submission; it is yielding, which cannot be the ground for digital democracy.

If ethically resilient data society is to be envisioned, India has to rework its story. Seva should hold within its meaning the privilege to disagree. User-friendliness should be matched with user knowledge. The design should be that it speaks more to the people who are on the fringes of the society than to those who are fully into the digital world. Similarly, data without consent is control, even if it is well-meaning, as the case of welfare without dignity is paternalism. The citizen should not be dealt with as a passive receiver of algorithms, rather be present as an active participant in the state's moral engineering.

To bring this to fruition, there are three transformations to be made. Number one, the policy needs to enforce explicit, multilingual, and graduated consent systems - whereas collectives share their information with whom and how long. Second, civil society and media must provide access to digital literacy as a social and political right, not as a technical skill. Consent may start and evolve only when understanding exists. And the third one, the ethical standards of design both in the public and private sectors should be a matter of course, embedding opt-outs, transparency dashboards, and accountability audits as a standard practice.

India's digital world of tomorrow has no need for complete surveillance rejection. It should take back service and not as an askance to power, but as a pledge to freedom. Let Seva not imply only compliance in silence; it must rather mean the respect that both share. The respect that will initiate not from the gathering of data, but from the acknowledgment of humanity.

Joint Family Culture and Privacy

A girl in Jaipur, who is in her teenage and using the cellphone of his brother, is the case in point. She is watching the videos in incognito mode, after which her search history gets deleted, and she closes apps immediately when her mother comes into the room. Elsewhere, a woman recently married to her husband also happens to have a joint bank account, phone, and is the holder of a Facebook account jointly with her husband. In the two laid out situations, one's life is not the outcome of one's own choice or decision but an act of negotiating with the parties involved. In the West, 'privacy' is associated with an individual, yet in India, such a right is enjoyed mostly as a privilege resulting from the availability of space, and assertion. Therefore, although privacy is not totally unavailable, it is largely malleable, affected by the environment, close relatives, and all the social customs. One of the situations where these issues are obvious and conflicting is the Indian joint family system, it is this basic Indian culture that now struggles to adjust or even merge with the digital technology and the culture of individuality.

Privacy, as practiced in Indian society, was never a solitary affair. Primarily, it concerned the right to be selective about one's social contacts and not the right to keep others out. In families where numerous generations live together, there are no distinct walls. Meals are communal. Financial, marriage, education-related decisions are group decisions. The joint family is not a mere housing pattern. It has always been an institution of intimacy surveillance. Even though there is a genuine feeling of affection, the potential for inquiries, advice-giving and intrusiveness is also there. "What are you doing on your phone?" is more a form of friendship than an act of distrust.

The cultural template may be in the digital space but it does not have to be wiped out. It is a common practice in India for one device to be used by several people, for them to share passwords, or to have multiple accounts and it is not because they are really so open but rather out of habit. The notion that each and every person should have a private identity in the online world is still unknown in various social situations. A rural housewife, for example, might have been signed up for a WhatsApp account by her son-in-law. Or a migrant worker might have used his employer's phone number to get himself registered for the state's social programs. These are the ways digital natives are onboarding the elderly to digital life, as well as the examples of practical adaptations of one person to a specific technology. Finally, these are the actions that correspond to the fact that the boundaries between the personal and the public, as well as those between individual and collective, are in reality constantly changing.

Very often, the technology platforms do not take into account the existence of this multifaceted zone. They are programmed on the assumption that the Western view of a single person who owns a device is correct and that one login means only one user and, finally, the biometric authentication can be relied upon to connect only with the real person. These suppositions about the Indian families with their multiple people scandals on only one phone are the ones that divide or create privilege. In general, the women are the ones who become the most affected group. Research has presented numerous data that even though the number of cell phone users in India is on the rise, among them, women are still regarded only as second-tier-electronic-devices users—those who are allowed only a supervised or a limited access to devices, quite often under the rule of a male.

To say that people of India do not care about their private life would be an incorrect statement. Their relationship is a significant consideration for their understanding of private space. In fact, the thought is, "This data is not just mine, you also have the right to read it, but only because I trust you." Trust and not a form of control is the price which talks of a privacy status in the Indian way of thinking—privacy that is gained from trust. This aspect is very important. It can remember everyone of the reason why it is immoral for your friend to read your WhatsApp and why no one thinks it strange to entrust their device to a family member. Then again, this becomes the explanation of why state data programs, while having the welfare entity, do not usually clash with the people. Aadhaar, for example, has not only been taken on by the public but also has been widely used in the government despite fears of being surveilled, as its promise of seamless service was more often resonant than the lack of the necessary information.

This cultural orientation voids digital policies in India. Laws are developed with the belief in the individual rights that do not exist due to frequent loss of the self in the crowd belief. As an example, the proposed Digital Personal Data Protection Act insists that the "data principal" is the sole person who can give consent. For every instance of data flow, the social exercise of negotiation becomes quite difficult of the consentor, especially if the latter are elders, spouses, or employers. How are the rights of a young girl being taken care of as her parent is the one spying on her mobile device? And where is the voice of the woman who is being facially scanned by her employer at the entrance gate without even a single word of explanation? In the case of a big family, privacy is not only owning the key to one's information, it is about power, the permission to use and silence.

The picture becomes even blurrier if we also include the perspective of gender. Privacy in India has always had its specific gender implying particularly in the digital world. As far as men are concerned, the cell phone is a thing of expression, while women see it as a place of order. Parents habitually check the calls of their daughters, restrict the usage of apps, or even make having the passwords they require. A 2020 report by the Internet Democracy Project outlined that women who voice their demand for digital privacy are often wrongly accused of being secret or disobedient. The very gesture of looking for a private zone was imagined as suspicious. The ethical framing of privacy—as indulgence, as defiance—leads to societal outcomes. It controls the power of women to get knowledge about their reproductive health, report maltreatment, and express their views without fear of anything.

This control is found to be multiplied when a group of several family members are responsible, by their nature, for deciding what to share. Technological resources are considered household goods, and thus the family members are free to undertake full vetting processes of these possessions. Surveillance is not framed as an imposed action from the outside. Rather, it is understood as it is embedded in the caring that takes place. Checking her grandson's browser history is not considered as a surveillance action in the eyes of the grandmother – she is trying to ensure the safety of her grandson. "Managing" a wife by her husband in her facebook settings is seen by the latter as "guiding" her, and not as a violation of her freedom. The above-mentioned rationalizations are not the result of malicious intentions but the result of the creation of the notion of relational responsibility deeply into the culture. Yet, as malicious as it is, the outcome is the same: the victim has to waive the right to privacy and what is more, enjoy the situation.

Digitalization also doubles up as a billboard for any silent protests. The youngest group especially ones based in semi-urban and rural India are in the core of the research on the use of cutting edge techniques for claiming private space. App lockers, clone apps, alternate accounts, or Instagram Close Friends are the most popular tools among the young for achieving communication privacy. Their privacy is a kind of a formal compacted by the government but a creation of the people themselves through the use of methods—ways to either grow visibility or shrink it, exposure, indistinguishability, and exerting absolute right under any conditions.

Thus, designers, legislators, and educators should begin working with a multipolar approach, which is not confined to the opposition of privacy to openness, control to chaos, and the state to citizen. The complex Indian culture calls for a multi-layered approach to understanding. But apart from teaching privacy it is very crucial to let the technologically advanced citizens know that they are entitled to their digital space invasion-free in their communal area. How can we develop interfaces for shared use that do not infringe upon personal rights? In some cases of privacy, relationships are interdependent while not violating the integrity of privacy. Questions that are not just imaginary, as they are serious design challenges, are the kind of legal obligatory laws as well as the moral issues that we are confronted with.

Think about the government apps where one family member can handle the affairs of his kin to avail of the services. On the surface, it could seem quite practical, but in reality, there is a parallel risk to the deactivation of the very rights that are supposed to benefit people. When a pensioner who does not see well receives an SMS and asks their son to read it for her, although her son's assistance is very praiseworthy and helpful, she does not acquire digital empowerment. Evading the real problem, thus, one example of this could be a woman who gives her phone to her husband while they are bonded at home, and in her absence, she cannot make phone calls to the center for domestic violence even if it is a toll-free number. There is no agency in this situation, and claiming it is full of falseness.

The way to surpass this obstacle is not so much about considering privacy as a Western concept but more about redefining it like, for example, our logical thinking of its necessity in India. Namely, the place here is to create the situation and to make it suitable in the context of the environment, and this includes the facilitation of local languages, voice interfaces, and the users' consent. The extension of the discourse should reach from such figures like lawyers and engineers to those of anthropologists, community leaders, including users, thus concreting the idea that privacy is a right sans fear of losing the real value of Indian family relationships it is rather than the cog for it, the wheels to the car.

India is moving ahead, respecting the principles of privacy is long overdue in both "-" is the idea that the state is bound by society's mores, values, and ethics and, in this connection, which is moral, the privacy of individuals is in their hands. It does not show us that Indian family values will lose authenticity when a person retires from any relationship. It strengthens the relationships instead. Being connected does not always mean having to give up our personal limits.

India, while reshaping its digefespect theferent assumptions about privacy. Privacy is not synonymous with individualism and therefore not your typical trait of selfishness. The society in question is a place where we share our joys and pains with everyone. Privacy that rejects a close-knit society where individuals have no private space is a sign that one is not selfish but reverent. The essence of Indian culture, even if obscured, is privacy, the essence of privacy, not individualism. By providing the right to open up everything, we do not mean giving up everything.

The Virtue of Virality

A very clear example that illustrates this is a video showing a rickshaw driver singing a classic Mohammed Rafi tune that goes viral overnight. In a few days, the news is seen on the national TV channel, and in a few weeks, he gets a recording contract. In the past, it would probably have been a matter of years of tireless effort, reputation-establishing, and off-putting various gates in the industry. However, now it is all a matter of shares, likes, and a suggestion by the algorithm. However, behind the grandeur of the sudden fame lies a question that is much deeper: What is it in the viral nature today that gives the feeling of validation, even seems sacred, to the common Indian? What can be inferred about how this behavior reflects Indians' fight for visibility, recognition, and the quest for moral worth in the digital society being created?

In a country where religion, ritual, and karma have long been principles that have both public and private life in their orbit, the process of growing a video of a rickshaw driver into one that has gone viral has taken on the aspect of something that's almost holy or spiritual. The phenomenon of being visible to others has already gone beyond the numbers inquiry and is now in the process of becoming one's social boon. To be seen is to be acknowledged. To be liked is to be affirmed. And to go viral? That is digital darshan—a kind of common witnessing that is a source of relevance, legality, and, for the lucky ones, a temporary form of being immortal.

The event which is spoken of is something that one should understand in the background of the Indian cultural basis. Traditional Indian thought puts a lot of value on becoming visible as a prerequisite for understanding. The gods are not worshipped in a vacuum; they tend to be visualized, bejeweled, and seen in public. The darshan—this act of seeing and being seen by the divine—is the heart of religious experiences. Also, social status goals have traditionally been tightly related to the public role, family tree name, or caste identity of a person, all of which work on the basis of being recognized by others. According to this background, the viral nature of the Internet does not imply only a new cause, it can be considered as an integral part of the people's behavior related to social visibility, attributed to one's network of fellow citizens, now found in the form of an algorithm.

However, in the digital world, the term "virality" functions more like a karmic scoreboard. On the one hand, religious karma was considered to be developed over lifetimes, whereas algorithmic one is instantaneous and could be measured. One viral reel is able to exchange obscurity for fame instantly; one trending hashtag can overtake structural disadvantage. This phenomenon is at once liberating and confusing. The old respect-building methods—education, seniority, etc—are no longer valid; a new currency is entering the power dynamic: attention. A 21-year-old meme creator from Indore can today have greater cultural impact than a 60-year-old scholar from Delhi. The rules of the game have been modified and now they reward not the old-fashioned virtue, but the new one, which is resonance in the digital world.

This reshaped mindset has led to a transfer of energy towards ambition. The youth of India, particularly those from the smaller regions, are now open to achieve wider goals than becoming just a doctor, an engineer, or a civil servant. They are not only after acquiring a job, they want to make themselves visible. Also, increasingly, the place where they intend to seek acknowledgment are digital platforms such as Instagram, YouTube, Sharechat, Moj, or their WhatsApp statuses. Fame is no longer the privilege of media houses or film studios; it is globally accessible, an added value gaming experience, and of course, mobile-first. However, this shift has a darker facet where spontaneous absence means nothing but disaster.

Expect these powerful implications to surface with individualism. This is going to be how Indians create identity, express opinion, talk and listen to each other over the internet. Most content creators are no longer focusing on building an intimate relationship with the audience or hosting a dialogue, their primary concern is the reach of the message. Be it a wedding dance, a devotional chant, or a street-side food review, people not only see them as expressions but also as offerings made to the platform, to the audience, and to the gods of virality. The aesthetics are generally devotional with deep respect expressing themselves in the form of folded hands, poetic captions, background bhajans. Moreover, the algorithm also likes this kind of content. The performance of genuineness becomes a power move choice. Appeal to emotions is converted to the click so that the content becomes more popular. Belief and passionate support intermingle.

What we are observing is only partially new as Indian mass culture has always been characterized by the so-called affective economy—Bollywood tears, mythological serials, celebrity worship. Nevertheless, the change has happened in the agency source. Previously, the emotional content was sent to the audience, and now the audience is the one who chooses, manages, and arranges it. A young girl from Chhattisgarh can achieve TikTok star status by miming devotional songs. A father in Gujarat can see his sincerity post about his daughter's graduation go viral. These acts are not necessarily insignificant—they are also the telling signs of the individuals' pride, happiness, and belonging. But more than that, they are also the signs that the algorithm understands that someone is there, that somebody wants to be spotted and promoted.

Unfortunately, there is also the other side, a much darker perspective of the economy of visibility. It is a fact that as fame can spring up overnight, infamy, or what is known as the dark side of fame, can appear equally fast. The same jury that raises to the stars a mere vegetable seller who also owns a blissful voice lowers from grace an innocent girl who became the subject of a ridiculous meme. Public shaming is a spreading phenomenon, outpacing good manners that appear in public. The digital mob more often than not is not an altruistic one. Ethical outrage, encouraged by the layout of most social media platforms, turns good people into bad guys and vice versa very promptly. In the present structure, it's the impact that counts rather than the purpose. Moreover, the judgment is done by the same crowd which mostly makes up the public.

Such a situation is, at the same time, a stressor, especially for young people. Each like and each share one gets act as a kind of authorized mark indicating his or her value. To users, what becomes of value is what causes a stir, where every happening is important for their existence. The Indian situation is definitely not isolated but still, it has its characteristic touches in a culture where it is human relationships that vastly comprise the main distinction between shame and honour. The idea of being ridiculed over the internet is not just an insult to someone - actually, it is deemed to cause shame and is a disgrace to one's kin, tribe, or society. To be given a go-ahead online, however, is tantamount to glorifying one's collective identity. It's a clear indication that the rise of the so-called viral Indian videos is a result of the explicit references to regional pride, religious fervor, or family values that they make. It is also to be noted that what is personal for me can be political for the whole society, which, in turn, can even take a further step and become algorithmic.

Nevertheless, the subject can not be reduced to a narrative of worry or manipulation because a lot of Indians are spreading virality to change the biases which seemed unchangeable for a long time. Dalit poets, queer influencers and rural artists are finding their place in the digital dialogue only by their truefit which forces the message of the conversation to spread by itself. Regional language creators usually have more interaction with their audience than their English-speaking friends. The reasons for such preferences in video genres are not just about changing the taste but also about changing the power within the culture. The act of getting viral is far more than just tricking public into entertainment, it contains the truth, and rebukes. It brings the eternal and the social together in the new domain, that is, the digital world.

The spread of Bhakti content on YouTube, Instagram, a nd other social media is a good example of this phenomenon. The former took the shape of a social media post and the latter an audiovisual one. The increase in the spread of devotional music by sharing on YouTube and Instagram contributed to a new way of engaging with Bhakti in a digital era. Due to the change of the technology, religiosity did not disappear; it has become really popular and diversified in it. When you look at most of the content creators on these platforms, they do the great service to the god by spreading the word, one share at a once. They do not count views, but rather count blessings. They still have the followers, but their followers are those who are in satsang.

Regarding the digital Bhakti happening, it's not just something you can part with. It reflects the way in which members of Indian society are moving closer to the divine in a more technology-driven manner. When viewed in the Western context, the idea of virality is often associated with superficiality or even godlessness. The Indian scene, on the other hand, allows for a far more complex interpretation of this phenomenon. The inclination towards virality in this context doesn't aim to stoke our vanity; it seeks to present itself as virtue, in principle, it is the knowledge, consent, and collective welfare that are deeply embedded in the culture of the Indian society. Nevertheless, it is a fragile kind of virtue which may be susceptible to market incentives, corporate algorithm, or even collective mentality, which indicates the necessity to keep its moral potential without submitting to its most disastrous effects.

This involves reshaping the platform structure. Not just should the algorithms increase engagement, they should take into account cultural subtleties. Community rules should show that they are not against differences in culture by defending local diversities and not the carefully selected moral codes. Furthermore, the awareness of digital literacy should encompass not only safety but also discussions on dignity, identity, and agency. Going viral should be like standing in public square, that is to say, a little bit dangerous but a respect-filled place at the same time.

Nevertheless, it also requires all of us—designers, educators, parents, policymakers—to think about what type of virtue we want to be rewarded by the virality. Should virality be the one at the expense of noise or be the one that is a result of having to dig deeper into an issue? Should we make young Indians aware that they need to attract attention, or should we guide them to look for substance? And, can the two even coexist?

Until then, the smartphone again retains the title of both the mirror that reflects our nature and the altar where our desires reside. Its feed is a scripture in motion, updated every minute, to be judged by the crowd, and to be kept safe by the cloud. It is in this refreshing relationship with oneself and the community where the will to become viral is not a trifle. It is the desire to be something—to be visible, to be shared, and to be remembered. Thirst for immortality? Not exactly. But in the era of algorithms, it is undeniable that popularity comes close.

New Tech Moral Fear and Ethical Opportunity

Earlier in 2020, the sudden Indian government's banning of TikTok by citing the deepest national security concerns was more than just a geopolitical move in the eyes of various people—it was considered an act of moral condemnation. Some folks regarded TikTok as a platform of vulgarity, low-brow content, and social degeneration. The others saw it as an oasis of structure with Dalits and vernacular creators, a source of empowerment -- by the same reasons, a channel that may be reaching the unreachable parts of the media universe. The menace was not only a policy issue but a social catastrophe, one that revealed all the underlying cultural tensions in the process of executing digital sovereignty in India. Which moral principles should govern the behavior of participants in India's digital public arena? And who will be the one to rule out?

India has been known for moral panic, not only recently. History can give us such examples: the time when Nehru was Prime Minister and cinema was the subject of censorship and the case of the protests against cable television in the 1990s, where the development of every medium was accompanied by both a sense of satisfaction and fear. That which is currently identical is the quickness and overtness of moral responses in the digital domain. The controversies proliferate on online platforms real-time and lots of users are actively taking part in them. EDM, hashtags, trolling, mass mailings are only some of the means through which they regulate their society. Conversely, unlike traditional institutions such as legislative bodies, courts, censors, and clergy, platforms do not have the single gatekeeper--they are fluid, chaotic, and often self-contradictory.

In this environment of constant change and uncertainty, morality is the central theme in the battle. In 2015, when the government prohibited access to more than 800 pornographic websites, claiming that they had a strong moral stand and the action was taken to fight moral corruption and crimes against children, free speech opponents slammed the decision. Nevertheless, those who lent their support for the ban were not only the predominant number but also quite remarkable in their arguments that only these visuals threatened the existence of social establishments such as family. The majority from among those unconcerned about pornography justified their support based on cultural reasons: "Why should we let the Indian youth experience the westernized depiction of sex and intimacy?" From the very beginning, the real question was not just about access, it was more about the kind of society that India wanted to be.

These are not new tensions but digital platforms have sharpened them due to the dissonant nature of Indian society, which is fragmented in terms of morality. There is no single consensus on morality. Urban liberals, rural conservatives, the youth who are moving up, religious communities, caste-based groups, and regional identities often have different views about "good" conduct. Contrary to popular belief, digital platforms have not helped to merge different groups but rather to accentuate the differing positions. A case in point is a young woman who decides to post some videos of herself dancing in a hijab, with some sections of the society celebrating her while others being against her actions. A meme from one's consciousness to speak truth to power in the most legitimate way may inspire anger and become a source of trouble for others. The instant matter at hand in any of the cases is how the moral narrative in public life is being managed.

Though moral panics are typically repressive events, they also provide a window of opportunity. They are indicators of the societal community's concerns and what topics the community is ready to fight for. Often, the anger against trolling on social media platforms has led people to reconsider their opinions regarding gender, safety, and liability. A typical public response after the well-known journalists, activists, or celebrities get threatening e-mails on rape or abuse online will be that the concerned citizens come forward to talk about the challenges to Indian society posed by misogyny and caste brutality. Digital moral panic converted by society with foresight can lead to moral revolutions.

India's changing policy on digital media is where this dual nature—peril and encouragement—is the most straightforward. On one hand, the government has been the most active player in the moral high ground, claiming the need for "decency," "national interest," and "public order" with increasing frequency. The tools to achieve this are various: the Information Technology Rules, the issue of platforms to take down a specified content, or legislative proposals for modifying content are examples of this, and the actions indicate a rising trend in the demand for cultural governance through algorithmic means. The situation is, however, that the citizens are not taking it lying down. The normal practices of digital negative rights, which are quite popular today, through flintstones, new systems of resistance in digital media.

An example of this is the group Agents of Ishq, an organization that creates sex-positive, culturally rooted content in Indian languages and combats the voices that are creating a moral panic. Persons using Dalit Camera produce multimedia and video, and social media has become the bearer of their subalternized messages to the people, as they are often attacked and excluded in the digital domain. These activities stress the point that the reaction to moral panic should be neither by moving away nor through silence—it can be the product of creative and ethically-based counter-morality over hasty reaction.

The politics of content moderation inject an additional layer of intricacy into talks of the matter as well. Social media platforms are seen as being impartial but the algorithms and policies utilized by them reflect the implicit cultural values that are often Western, liberal, or sanitized for advertisers. For example, not infrequently are entries on topics such as menstruation or caste injustice not approved for public viewing as they are marked as "sensitive," whereas at the same time, hate speech in the form of humor is not censored at all. In the case of India, if political power and religious sentiments are interwoven, this asymmetry poses a threat to society. Deplatforming decisions, shadow bans, and the position of the content on the screen are not only technical changes but they are moral decisions that directly influence the world.

This has led to a paradox in the sense that some users demand a platform's action to eliminate inappropriate content—e.g., rape threats, fake news, hate speech while others are worried about the misuse of this regulation to stifle dissent. The same technology that is designed to cut off the transmission of bad-enough comments can also be used to prevent the expression of the marginalized voices. Any form of moral control in the digital space should not be seen exclusively as censorship versus freedom of speech. Instead, it should follow the norms of ethical pluralism, procedural transparency, and social accountability.

The public's response to TikTok also serves as an additional indicator of such effects. Rural, lower-middle-class, and non-English-speaking groups in India represented the platform's main users, thus making it both a huge challenge to the established cultural norms and at the same time, a source of social, technological, and economic progress. Its aesthetic style—natural, emotional, and sometimes kitschy—was totally in contrast to the urban Instagram's slick, curated ethos. It gave women from peripheral regions a chance to make a splash in the entertainment industry by posting humoristic affiliations, dance, and everyday activities without being challenged by the elite. However, they also became louder in their criticism as TikTok grew in power. Charges of obscenity, cringe content, and moral degeneration were usually excuses for the elite to mask their prejudices against the poor. The final ban, despite being officially about the infringement of data privacy, was nothing else but a reset in order to reduce the cultural power of creators from the margin.

In their very nature, moral panics may seem clearly and surely irrational; however, they carry very rational features. They are a way for society to identify the edges between "us" and "them," between the sacred and the profane. In the digital era in India, these borders are continually being discussed, remodelled, and challenged. Be it the conversations on the time kids spend on screens, the wrath of people against the influencers, or the conflicts on political propaganda, in every argument, the issues here are ultimately the deeper uncertainties regarding identity, agency, and authority.

But, panic is not a one-way street, as it also has the capacity to awaken society. It begs the questions: What sort of digital society are you shopping for? What are the values that should be visible in your online communication? And who should be the police—a government, a corporation, the communities, or the individuals?

These types of questions are neither rhetorical nor metaphorical; they are very right now, very burning, and very foundational. The emergence of troll armies--often as highly coordinated, politics-centered groups--become the topic of crucial discussions on psychological warfare, radicalisation, and online anonymity. On the other hand, it has been instrumental in the platforms' reconsideration of security standards, the political party's addressing of cyber ethics, and the users' recognizing their complicity in digital violence.

The fact that legal excesses have been the ones to spur the growth of healthy public debate. People are now able to respond to the proposed repressive measures by filing lawsuit after lawsuit and debriefing the public. New partnerships of technologists, lawyers, educators, and artists so that they can support and promote fair, humane, and diverse forms of digital engagement have been created.

To go through this changing environment, it is wrong to call the noise generated by the sensationalism of the situation nothing but noise; such noise is to be taken as a signal—a signal of values, fears, feelings, norms, and so on. India is not only involved with the internet. Rather, it is biochemically processing it through a cultural digestion of the highest complexity. And this process is certainly not smooth and undisturbed. It is characterized by outbreaks of indignation, periods of reflection, and spasms of change.

The morality in digital India is still far from being pure. It needs moral ingenuity. The challenge is not to stifle moral discourse but to raise it—to go from panic to principle, from prohibitions to a better set of norms, from fear to ethical creativity. This revolution requires a wise approach to public regulation, culturally sensitive platform building, and, most importantly, the more liberal moral education among the people.

We have to tell the users how to protect themselves on the Internet and how to behave morally on the Internet and we should do this not by force, but through dialogue. Not with imposed codes, but with shared responsibilities. Because a moral panic that is a result of repression ultimately undermines democracy. On the other hand, a moral opportunity that is the product of dialogue eventually strengthens democracy. And it is exactly this that maybe can be regarded as the most promising approach to the discussion of India's digital moral dramas—not as the symptoms of degradation, but as the signs of the ethical boiling in a society that learns to connect its values with its screens.

Chapter 5

Bharat Goes Online—Stories from the Margins

The digital transformation in India is often spoken about in terms of engineering marvels, start-up successes, and financial platforms. However, if we go beyond the news, there is a revolution which is not so obvious. This is the revolution which does not occur in business salons and city campuses but is everywhere in the humble mustard fields, roadside dhabas, and crowded bastis. This is the digital story of Bharat, not India. Not the urban metros but the rural, the subaltern, the culturally plural. And it is here, in the margins, that the internet is performing its most complex act: not disruption, but recalibration.

This change is something that the denizens of the core would first have to unlearn, as they are accustomed to regarding the margins as a label of passivity and voids waiting to be filled with broadband or benevolent handouts. Contrary to these beliefs, the margins are really energetic environments with their unique logic, their own collective memory, and a rhythm of their own. The interaction of technology with these habitats is not a matter of assimilation, but rather an unpredictable, almost magical mixture, which is purely dependent on the context. This means that the margins do not lose their identity rather they add new shades to it and affirm it through the process of interconnection.

Imagine the example of the farmers in Maharashtra who started to pilot drones in order to check the condition of the crops and to detect the soil stress. These farmers have always been the enslaved to the monsoon seasons and market manipulations. They were the ones with the knowledge of touch—the with fingers deep in the soil and eyes searching the sky. Today, their field wisdom is associated with AI-fueled agritech dashboards and satellite imaging tools. But this is much more than a double-edged sword where the first side is efficiency and the second is productivity. This is about the farmer. If the farmer's produce is being efficiently managed, all the problems are resolved, the environment is clean, and then the farmer has no complaints, and on the contrary, new land, plants, and lands are shown as evidence of the farmers' knowledge, the knowledge no one can argue with. The experts in this case are the scientists who are the first to respond to the changes. Certainly, what the evergreen image of the farmer effectively intended was this aided process which suggested cleaner land, plants, a, and a new spot no one would contest! I hope I wasn't necessarily wandering overly far from facts, nevertheless, the point still remains that a drone isn't an alien gizmo—it's an accessory for human wisdom.

Equally powerful is the tale of India's hijras—more specifically, their use of social media such as Instagram and YouTube to fight against the social exclusion and economic marginalisation spanning centuries. Traditionally, hijras have been the traditional answer to many a cultural event: the midwives and musicians of life's key events. The modern system of education, employer-employee relations, and the financial world cohort have so far, always kept them out. But online, they have been the creators, the most influential ones, the idols, the local economic movers, and the globe's citizens, and we are not exaggerating, no, indeed, the local economic or key actors, and the globe's citizens, and we are not exaggerating, no. Through their range of followers and their video clips that can attract millions of viewers globally, they create a wider network and higher gratification. However, personal integrity is more important than the figures. A well-thought selfie is not merely a vain indulgence, and a viral dance video is not simply an act of fun. On the contrary, it should be viewed as a powerful step of lesbians who proclaim their voice and visibility in a community that has been a mute spectator of their suppression. The channel now becomes a reflection of the people, as well as a peek into a new form of citizenship.

Moreover, the vast nomadic groups of India—Banjaras, Gaddis, Nats—form a lifestyle characterized by movement. Oral epics, folklore, and the collective memory have been held by them for many generations. However, their own displacement, the criminalization laws, and the state's indifference have become a challenge to preserving their memory as a nation's heritage. Present members of these tribes, who are the vanguards, are now recording stories, and publishing songs through the use of mobile phones, audio recorders, and cloud storage. For them, the process is not just facing the technology; they are intentionally weaving a future. For communities traditionally excluded from the maps and the voter rolls of the state, this digital inscription is the ultimate solution when it comes to being and self-representation.

What these instances have in common is the fusion of technology with authorship. People who are not just 'customers' of new technologies. They take what already exists, rework, and reframe it according to their needs. It is like they are multiplying those tools to use them in different aspects of their everyday lives. By doing this, they on top of it, destroy some of the digital discourse clichés such as urban-rural or traditional-modern or literate-illiterate. A farmer with an app that monitors soil health, the hijra who has a ring light, a nomad with a podcast microphone—all three of them are capable of challenging the view that people who are really sophisticated in terms of digital know-how are those who have completed their formal education.

In a country of such diversity as India, this new definition is more important. In India, very often, the narration of the Digital India program coming from the government reduces the nation to be merely the source of KPIs and dashboards. Yet, it is clear that migrants in and out of urban areas are still the ones who drive the development of social businesses. The phrase "number of connections" is not synonymous with "quality of connection". Before we consider logging in as one process, we need to dissect it in various dimensions such as those of caste, gender, geography, language, and lineage. For instance, a tribal woman in Chhattisgarh who has a phone in her possession technically may be able to use it only partially, i.e., not with the full freedom of speech by authorities and family members, after a few words spoken in the local dialect, or without social barriers. In such a case, if she takes the initiative to go online, she can look up a local herb, discuss her problems on a WhatsApp group, or make a voice recording of a folk song, she is not only online but also transferring power.

In order to bring out these stories effectively, one must not ignore the role of infrastructure. The differences in broadband accessibility between urban and rural parts of India are quite significant. For most people living in rural areas, however, 4G is out of reach and thus still a luxury. The power supply is very unreliable and far from stable. For some reason, not even network towers are evenly distributed, and digital illiteracy is rife to the extent that it is now a caste and class issue. Yet there is also the identification of the creativity and resourcefulness of rural India. In Jharkhand, young locals prepare and use YouTube videos recorded in the local dialects to describe the right application of the ration benefits or how to resist land eviction.

Camel herders who come from Rajasthan managing milk cooperatives through voice messages and missed calls. What has become more obvious is that in the days before an electronic digital era, the digital age was substituted with a culture that was always compulsory and still exists today. The new technologies did not bring about these changes—they only helped facilitate and streamline the old practices. Evidently, the deficiencies seem to embrace the status of design adaptations. The people who keep up the alive, functioning, and changing culture of the world and on top of that breathe life into it are the best designers of the present and of the future.

The chapter is not one of these idealized stories. It is the problems — huge ones. In these areas, surveillance is something that is not easy to understand. The definition of the consent framework is not clear. News that is incorrect moves swiftly, always disturbing, and is rarely corrected. And digital exclusion, not less, is a constant reminder of the existing caste, gender, and regional hierarchies. Nonetheless, there is the most important fact left unstated: the disabled parts of society are not voiceless. The technological advance is making it possible that they now can communicate more than they ever did.

The stories' larger meaning is purely epistemological. Who fits the innovation bill? Why do we put up founders with startups in Bengaluru on a pedestal while we do not even acknowledge that cattle-health tracking apps were created by farmers in Nashik? Why are the offline-English-lesson episodes act as antiques and the digital tribal songs stored in Google Drive called local classics? These answers do not just show one side of the story, but they also expose and question the opposite. A digital culture that does not see the innovation in the margins is non-reasonable and non-righteous.

India's digital revolution is not only about speed. It is more about quality; it carries its logic, its rhythm, and sets its ethics. The needy part of society such as the farmer, the hijra, the nomad are not in need of your help just like a needy person wants charity. They ask for tools that are adapted to the knowledge of their environment. They need respect, not salvation.

While you read about the stories below, kindly open yourself to the possibility of paradigm change. Let go of the old-fashioned idea that the margin is just catching up. In a lot of aspects, the margins are the ones which are taking the lead—bearing fewer burdens from past tech, more open to experimentation, and living more in harmony with the technology used while the legacy remains. They tell us that the web is not only a marketplace or an amplifier of one's voice. Sometimes it is a sanctuary, a knowledge keeper, a theatre, or even a barrier.

Bharat would rather use the internet as a tool to become visible in its own right than just another India, and in that declaration lies the future of a truly plural, deeply digital nation.

The WhatsApp Warriors of Bundelkhand

The source of this information was not a protest rally or press conference, but the very first message about a ping. A message on WhatsApp sent at 4:52 a.m., which was written with the sender's exhausted fingers, and a felt moment of urgency: "गांव में स्कूल में मास्टर दो महीने से नहीं आया। बच्चों की पढ़ाई बंद है।" The owner of the phone isn't a politician, journalist, or NGO worker. She is a mother, a farmer's wife, a sari-clad sentinel from Bundelkhand—armed not with a loudspeaker, but with a ₹10 recharge pack, and a borrowed smartphone. And she is not alone.

Throughout the dusty lanes and drought-stricken fields, a digital silent revolution is taking place. In a region that is one of the most underdeveloped and neglected parts of India, groups of women—many of whom have no formal training in journalism, governance, or technology—have created a strong bond using the most easily available tool in the digital world of India: WhatsApp. These women do not regard themselves as activists. But their phones tell a different story—one of awareness, resistance, and radical care. This is digital activism, re-shaped by the rural rhythms of life and the gendered survival mode.

One cannot comprehend the value of these women's groups if one has not first grasped the environment in which they exist. The Bundelkhand region that lays in the states of Uttar Pradesh and Madhya Pradesh is reputed not for its connectivity but for the water scarcity, the constantly crying dry lands, and men's privilege. Public institutions here are not regular in being serviceable. State facilities are most of the time either delayed or absent. The lack of a voice for the women, who are being oppressed in twofold ways, by their castes, and by their gender, is an everyday occurrence. It has been institutionalized in the daily.`,

bread of common life.

And still, mobile connectivity began to seep into the region, and women not only saw the use but the potential in that—absolutely everyone saw that. However, not only for communication solely, but for cooperation also. With the smallest resources and the greatest courage, these teams were the first to come up with the idea to utilize WhatsApp for gathering information about problems at the village-level that had to be addressed—unused anganwadis, bribed ration dealers, cases of domestic violence, sexual harassment at the workplace. Pictures, videos, voice notes, and typed reports, which were the means of communication, were being exchanged in the groups and were also the material which the more experienced members who were moderators helped verify, adapt, and elevate in the group.

This was no passive reporting. The whole process was not limited to the actions of the people who did the witnessing; the community has demanded that people become witnesses to those who are a constant source of negligence and are potential sources of abuse.

Suppose the local hospital is engaged in the practice of overcharging patients for medication, then a subtle move from a patient with the camera on, could shoot a video of the specific situation. Or if there is a government scheme but the very people for whom it is intended are the ones denied the benefits, it is an example of a situation where a person can upload their Aadhar card and bank paperscreenshots to a so-called "evidence" group. After the details have been taken care of, i.e. among themselves they find the best option—some of them go to the block officials, others write the letters, and only a few of them get in touch with the journalists at the district-level. Through the continued insistence and efforts, most of these micro-campaigns have been known to produce not something else but direct action from the officials. But at times, it is the perpetuated piece of misinformation that leads to the result of a school being closed. But at other times, it becomes the cause of the land being reassigned to a different corrupt official as a result. The action of bringing the matter up in itself goes in this way along with them and it becomes a form of public pedagogy, which at that moment, teaches individuals in society of their worth.

One of the most significant features of this model is its redefinition of the roles of a reporter, a reformer, a digital citizen. Viewing from their perspective, these women did not depend on social media platforms for their voices to be heard and issues to be known to the public. They established their own networks of influence using the language of the locals, their credibility earned in the community, and personal relationships. Their content is not going to be a hit on social media platforms making each of their campaigns a talk of the town, but most of it is created to make them or their locality accountable. On the one hand, they do not expect their content to be spread far and wide, but, on the other hand, within the confines of the closed-loop of their digital community, each message gains enough momentum to be effective.

Surprisingly, these women blatantly refute the stereotype that rural India is technologically backward as they boast advanced digital skills. The women have the awareness to save and hide data, go under the digital radar, and even manage the situation by using features like disappearing messages. For an illustration, besides the women, there are a number of ladies who have been catching up on their basic mobile phone skills by taking part in WhatsApp training classes—a service to neighbors and daughters-in-law, the majority of whom only use smartphones for the first time. However, the education is essentially more than technical—it is tactical. People don't just describe a function as just a function—they understand the implications of the function.

Imagine the genius that is the choice of voice notes over a written one. Voice is a uniting factor for the unschooled for instance the senior citizens who can't read nor write. Talking is the better option—it is warmer, requires personal interaction and cannot easily be dismissed. One can gloss over a typed message, but it is a crying mother's protest of her child's midday meal deprivation that won't be easily brushed aside. Similarly, the trick use of emojis is something incredibly sophisticated—it's like using the symbols representing softness but actually means criticism, or using the symbols as a code for a message, all entirely honed from a lived experience of negotiating with authority.

The gradual transformation of WhatsApp groups offers a glimpse of the complicated ways in which digital trust is built. On platforms like Facebook or Instagram, people do things for show and the content is mostly politicized, rather than in these groups which are nurtured by an authentic sense of belonging. To join a group, it is necessary not to just simply follow a link but also to act accordingly, being reliable and consistent. The ethics that guide the groups may be unspoken but are very clear—do not spread rumors, do not add anything superfluous, make sure before you send. This in many cases is what professional sites can't achieve and they are the ones trying hard, while this group is community-run and is truth-centered.

However, the women have put themselves at risk. Enabling women to speak their minds provides them with an opportunity to understand they can be potential victims of reactionary authorities, as well as from their families and the communities at large. Some of the women have been intimidated, humiliated, and in some cases, they have been physically beaten for bringing up or getting involved in matters they are not supposed to. Even to the point, they have had to sacrifice their digital devices—phones, SIM cards, and data packs. Due to this, the collectives have found alternative ways such as covert backup reporters and using the cell phones of their husbands or kids for a short time, or by rotating the leadership of the organization to avoid overexposure. What we behold here, therefore, is not really a tech-utopia that is clothed with the latest tech gadgets but a tedious uphill struggle for presence in the digital space.

They also raise the question of why most of the groundbreaking online work is produced by people invisible in the mainstream. For example, the official campaigns initiated by the government like "Digital India" exhibit high technology products like big data dashboards, and smart city pilots. However, in contrast, it is these low-profile, underprivileged women wearing saris who carry out the entire task of creating accountability from the bottom. Their WhatsApp chats are not exhibited at tech conferences, but they are reaching out and influencing even more people than some of the famous start-ups can claim.

People should realize the significance of such groups not as unusual alone, but as part of a larger transformation in India where women are reclaiming digital spaces in the image of their sociopolitical needs. Cases include digitization of ASHA workers in Bihar saving their mother's health data in the form of apps, while Dalit women from Tamil Nadu run campaigns through Telegram groups to fight for their right to own property. The story is not new, but the aspects of region-specific details emerge. At the core of the event is a transformation in the concept of technology from something consumed to something that is used as a strategy.

The WhatsApp warriors of Bundelkhand are other than the conventional type of activists. They do not start campaigns with hashtags, do not give TED talks, do not go in search of NGOs to sponsor them. Their case is innovative because they have ceased to be the quiet ones in the place where silence was taken as acceptance. The message they sent, the blurry video about a broken handpump, every voice note asking for an FIR, is nothing if not an affirmation: We are here. We are watching. We will speak.

The story of digital India is incomplete without a call made by women through the rough patches on their ₹1,500 smartphones and under the shade of a neem tree. If we look for the true indicator of digital empowerment, it has nothing to do with the number of downloads or dashboards but is more about the woman in Bundelkhand who once was startled by police shear now telling people to file RTIs through WhatsApp

that wasn't only their way of being uplifted. It was also the oppressed, who, without a sound, without much attention, just the way the Indians often do, managed to raise against the status quo. And it was evident in their everyday lives, their collective and quiet struggle

Drone Farmers

In the aftermath of Vidarbha's desolate and sunbaked earth, accustomed to agrarian despair and distress, a different picture has emerged. At the time of the first light of the day, one can see a man in a faded Nehru jacket, with a tablet in his thick hands instead of a sickle, who is looking at the drones flying in the skies. After that, he looks at his phone and adjusts the flying machine. Despite the fact that no one could have staged such a video in a documentary setting, the film was set in a government headquarters, it's still happening

in and around Maharashtra. The region that was once the focus of some of India's most grievous farmer suicides is achieving smarter and more efficient agricultural practices through AI-powered soil diagnostics, multispectral drone imagery, and real-time agri-analytics and that's not all but the platform that technology services in the agrarian zones.

All the upheaval of late isn't just some superficial facelift—it's civilization-changing. The Indian agrarian has always been technology literate in a pragmatic way: things like the rainy season cycle, the types of seeds, pests, and unplanned irrigation, have been passed down by older people through many generations as their very foundations. However, the methods of development were conflicting with this livestock-like intelligence of the Indian farmer for a couple of decades, because they were mostly based on standardized or one-size-fits-all solutions: subsidies without return subventions, seeds with no more than that, and apps giving advice unilaterally. What we are witnessing now is a correction that had long been overdue. The point is not to make tradition vanished, being replaced with digital still the living issue but to make tradition and digital to coexist smoothly—Maharashtra is an example of a successful project.

Currently, technology, such as Yavatmal and Jalgaon drones, is used by many smallholder farmers for better spraying. Drones spare ecological problems, since the technology being is not only assisting the farmers in having a precise target but also not exposing the users to chemical fumes. In addition to that, the speed and efficiency that come about with relying on the drone, as well as labor costs being significantly reduced are quite noticeable. Even more interestingly, these devices are not some foreign devices from an advanced country; they are actually redesigned and customized to serve our needs. Current drone libraries have been set up by farmer-producer organizations (FPOs), cooperatives, and different self-help groups so that these groups can have a tool to be checking it out just like flock members could resolve when borrowing or returning the borrowed technology

At the same time, the hardware is just part of the solution as the greater change is the mental one. AI-empowered soil health apps are now being used by farmers, who, in this way, know their land much better. These platforms through their advanced functions which are an amalgamation of a phone's camera and the detailed nutrient maps produced through the analysis of soilstamps not only plant oil but simmer the seeds which in some esteem is something unheard of In addition to this, the apps also give advice on the choice of good sowing dates and also the same crops but different sowings, they can go to the extent of predicting different possibilities of yield to the farmer. The decision-making solely based on the traditional way of generational habits passed from one farmer to another now gets leverage from hard data, thus allowing resource-poor farmers to take their most treacherous bet—the planting season—down the scale.

The change is massive in itself. For many years, farmers have been in the hands of intermediaries and priced at the control of mandi. Although they were the main suppliers of the food, they were passive without any possibility of being active. By using digital tools to new capabilities like forecasting the demand, following pests migrating, and making direct connections with online marketplaces, the farmers are starting to be content as the providers of the data too—information on which economy is also based. This new interaction element is far more powerful because it is not imposed from above but literally a side-by-side concept. It is based not on the approval of the state apparatus or the use of multinationals' apps; it is carried out via informal tech WhatsApp groups, vernacular YouTube tutorials, and peer-to-peer mentorship across talukas.

Let's illustrate it with the example of Sangram Bhandare, one of the cotton farmers from the Buldhana district of Maharashtra, India. A couple of years back, he hardly used his smartphone for texting and cricket updates. Now, after his visit to a regional agri-tech mela, he has become a member of the drone service co-operative and a user of AI soil scanner, which he operates through the Bhoomi AI app. He states that his fertiliser expenses have been minimized, his cotton yields have gone up, and most importantly, he is in control. He remarks, pre- viously we did our work based on our guess. But now we are doing it with data. She helped him in his business a lot. In the past, farmer's apprehension of data has been a major challenge, leading to a lot of problems during the transition. Making sure the farmers have equal access to the devices, the training they are getting through the programs they are enrolled in, and the prices of the tools remain the biggest challenges for the broader acceptance of the technology. While farmers' cooperation will likely grow well, the technological ecosystem is still not interconnected. Application programs are mainly not earmarked to date with regional dialects, or they cannot be supported by the lowest bandwidth rural sites. Realize that there are still those sources that will still collect data without asking for the permission of the farmer, or, the farmer is still not going to be given the benefit or the information that he was supposed to be. On the other hand, farmers are now producing data, and therefore, the risk of opt-out shifts from local middlemen towards opaque digital intermediaries. There is no challenge in this process just for adoption; it is mainly a challenge of agency.

Most times, the techno-optimism that is always presented by the agri-tech start-ups does not highlight the deeper philosophical truth. It is not just an economic act that farming is but a cultural one too. Those tools which are not aware of local seasonal changes, eminence of a caste around land inheritance, or the holiness of some practices (not ploughing on festival days) may be a success in theory but they do not work in the fields. Therefore, the headlines of Maharashtra tell only about the realism where the digital forces changed their method of thinking according to the soil and not vice versa. The drones that are seen to be effective are those that are not the fastest or the most complicated but those whose suppliers know how to talk to a farmer who has never used Google Maps in his life but is aware of every corner of his ten-acre plot.

Another area that deserves a mention is the aspect of gender. Consistently overlooked in agri-policy discourse, women farmers account for over 30% of the agricultural workforce and are usually not included in the training and access channels. But there, too, we are seeing a change happen, especially in Maharashtra. The women-run FPOs in Beed and Osmanabad are gradually merging modern ways with their operations. They are approaching digital tools to perform activities like keeping track of the production of the farmer, joint management of the cooperative accounts, and the negotiation of the input prices. In such situations, technological progress is no longer only a disruptor but more of a means to their dignity. They are now in a position to bargain with the establishments that have never imagined them knowing anything about that sector. Therefore, a message with the voice and yield proof, an image of the drone evidence of pest attack, these cannot be dismissed but only considered if the system that did not think of them as valid items.

And thus comes in the new spirit to overthrow a system that heirs-managed for centuries. The same spirit that for years has been compelling the farmers to automate their way of living, used to the fact of being more efficient, more businesslike, and therefore more predictable. However, the tools given often have not of the farmer's thought. The farmers of Maharashtra show us that only a continuous transformation is possible if digital systems are used in co-design—when the technology is not "for" farmers but "with" the farmers. Here the drone ceases to exist only as a reflection of the dreams of the creators of Silicon Valley; it becomes something more—a modern version of the trusted, shared and embedded plow.

The outcome of these stories of the farmer also shows India as a vibrant and dynamic place that is not resistant to technology. On the contrary, it is a story about survival and success. Establishing technology as basis and the freedom to allow agility and local innovation are the essence of what they are doing. These very same individuals who are creating intelligent agricultural models are the last to resort to saving themselves by teaming up with the government or the business world alone so they are..."

They are not only principal players in policy matters; they take an active part in restructuring the agrarian intelligence of a new era.

Stories propagated by the fields of Maharashtra as India seeks food security, climate resilience, and equitable development are not only appealing — they are also informative. It is conveyed that digitization in agriculture from the bottom up rather than a top-to-bottom digital revolution is future farming and the insight, instinct, and strong infrastructure-based agriculture (source: bottom-up fusion of insight, instinct, and infrastructure). It is also probable that the villagers of rural India — of the present — do the most striking job with a completely different task since maybe more oxygen ... This farmer is now the visible one — someone who gets the news from the drone that watched, scanned, and understands the soil: "You are not just seen. You are also recognized."

Hijras on Instagram

The Hijra community in India has for ages been living on the periphery, being visible but marginalized, feared but made fun of, simultaneously accepted and rejected. The transition to institutional acknowledgment has come very slowly, social integration—the latest, and active participation in the economy is still hampered mainly because of the stigma that is deeply ingrained. Responding to public perception, hijras have been mostly subjected to ridicule only: they are usually shown either as playing a spiritual role during a birth ceremony, or they are depicted as insolences at traffic signals. Seldom are they seen to have any influence. On Instagram, it is gentlemen of designations, and with the help of digital friends, they are the ones who tin-- the others outside of a circle--create the means of support and thus, it could be the most revolutionary. It is the people who create the platform, not the platform that creates the people, who change the rules by giving up to them.

Consequently, there has always been this notion suggesting that social media is of inferior quality, and this is particularly true in the arena of marginalized politics. In the case of hijra users, however, Instagram has been their source of infrastructure for them to be seen, and not just a channel for expression. To give an instance, education, jobs, and properties are all historically known to be avoided by the community members. Insta ran counter to this by being not the kind of app in which you are compelled to produce your caste and resume and to speak English fluently, but all that is required of an individual is the skill of storytelling that is touching to the heart. This is where the hijras find their place among those who have been familiar with the oral tradition and who are now, at the sanme time, very skillful speakers during the performances and therefore, they are taking the lead.

Think about the profile of @rudrani_chettri, a transgender activist from Delhi who is using her Instagram account not only to share her life journey but also as a means to empower others, criticize policies, and work with different brands. Or @vihaanpeethambar, a transgender man and the founder of The Transmen Collective, who goes beyond the stereotypes. This is not a single story but an ongoing movement. What was once a secret in the neighbourhood is now shared among people in a much more public way. The number of followers is not only a show-off thing; it is the epitome of one's existence—of being part and being recognised.

However, the narrative does not only show personal growth but also explores the collective. Across Tamil Nadu, Karnataka, and Maharashtra, hijra collectives use Instagram to do crowd fundraising, receive reports on missing persons, disseminate legal updates, and document incidents of violence—something that used to be done only in activist newsletters or NGOs. This platform is the reason for a much more spread-out and not centred mobilisation that is speedy, visual, and communicative. A person who is in a sari and lip-syncing to the tune of a Bollywood song might look like someone who is wasting time until they come to realise that behind the act lies the recovery of public femininity whose holder was denied it on a systematic basis.

One other thing is that hence, the visibility in economic terms is of critical importance. Many hijras have been left with no other choice but to rely on begging and sex work for economic sustenance, not so much by choice as by a system that excluded them. It is only on Instagram, and not elsewhere, that they are liberated. Now you can watch videos of beauty tips, cooking shows, dance steps as they now have become not just creative hobbies but the main income of the persons who are presenting them. So, influencer marketing, affiliate links, and sponsored posts were ideal for the urban class only, but now they are accessible to the transgender community. Some had even gone further to where they have worked with fashion houses, beauty, and skin care brands, or even in local handicraft business. This was a big change as they had turned IG into a portfolio. Thus, the digital platform has turned to a place where one could achieve economic dignity.

And yet these radical changes also cause much friction. Even though Instagram's algorithm offers so much in terms of mass participation, it is still a black box subject to cultural regulations. The marked "inappropriate" is predominantly the domain of queer and trans people and especially those who are less in line with Western cultural norms. For instance, a hijra wearing a backless blouse could be screened but a cis influencer similarly dressed can be celebrated. The community's visibility will stay only if the implementation of said tools would be more transparent and accountable towards their contexts of use which is very rare if not impossible. This condition does not result from any accidental factors as it is the outcome of a structure.

At the same time, Instagram is a place where one can find more freedom and gain self-consciousness, but it also sounds the alarm for harassment. Abusive behaviors such as trolling, doxxing, and transphobic activities are a regular part of Instagram users' lives, most notably creators who are in the spotlight. The reporting system at Instagram cannot keep pace with the local culture's expression as the tool is language blind to Indian conventional demeanors that create a harasser. For hijras who are victims of a society which is already accused of unfriendliness in their life at home, the dream of inheriting the freedom of the spirit from the online world is very difficult. Being seen and heard means strength, but at the same time, it is a dangerous thing.

Many other countries are not alien to this incongruity, but in India, the situation is even more complex. The hijra community lies in a vague legal terrain—though still not recognized in many institutional sectors, they have found a legal anchor from the Supreme Court's NALSA judgment in 2014 where they now get to be considered the "third gender." It is not just the narrative format of stories that is seen in the online display but it symbolizes new legal and cultural practices. The hijras are not just sitting back and waiting for the government to give them legal standing as persons, they are already busy establishing digital micro-nations in defiance and exposure of the same themselves—beyond the parameters and even the time horizons in which traditional bureaucracy operates.

Further, as Instagram moulds the sphere of connectivity, it also doesn't dissolve the traditional social structure of the offline community. Hijra households have poor internet consistency. The smartphones are shared and the data packs are limited. The level of literacy in the house may drastically differ. The most seniors in the hijra community, who get near MyGharaana, are the same people who are not on these platforms, leading to a generational division of digital resources within the community itself. Thus, a girl who is a show-off at 22 years, with forty thousand followers, can be looked at in awe on Instagram yet she still agrees to her guru's physical world powers. Instagram nods towards democracy, giving voice to the individuals but they must have Internet bandwidth to voice it.

The main question is as follows: what is digital empowerment, within a domain where cultural capital and economic capital are not evenly distributed, like? Does virality underpin the empowerment of a group, or does it remain a temporary phenomenon? Or is it rather some other task which is obligatory to undertake by a community that, for centuries, has had to perform for its survival? The answers are not straightforward. However, it is clear that Instagram's hijras are not technology users—they are strategic analysts of it. They use the platform as a kind of weapon, not just for things like adaptation and the like, but to oppose, invent, and recover.

The language is also redefined. The traditional jargon used by the hijras—feminine tone, meaningful gestures, and equivocation—formerly spoken only on dholaks and in the ears of the initiated, has now taken a new playful form in the captions and reels of Instagram. Cultural rites, whichever they are the rites of guru-chela or the preparation of the make-up before the celebration of a festival, are not only solemnly but also stylishly logged in. These virtual exhibits are not extraordinary exhibits nation-building because they do not aim for creating consciousness via other people but they are expressions of one's own worth, authentically and by own rules

What we see now is not a media trend but a major change in thinking. A long-oppressed community censored in the official census, excluded from the movie, and drawn in public speech is now finally revealing its stories—vivid, intimate, funny, angry, and proud. And in addition, they are also making a statement about the very idea of Indian identity by being authentic, that identity comes not from following the popular line and that the taking of identity which is enough is just one of the many ways of the resistance, earning and beauty.

To completely understand the digital shift of India, we have to go beyond broadband penetration and smart cities. We have to see a lady in a saree in a digital meeting with the Creator doing her light, hair or make-up and who is living in a rented room in Bhopal. We not only ask the technical but also who and why questions. The hijras on Instagram declare us that just being able to reach out is not the same as having the power—but when the power comes, it's never quiet. It's vocal. It's dancing. It's smiling. Most of all, it's demanding a visibility.

Passing through with Pen n' Pencils

To the average Indian urban dweller, "nomad" sparks a romantic picture: camel caravans on the fringes of Rajasthan, folk musicians, moonlit storytellers, and snake-charmers. However, what are the more salient points behind this kind of picture? The tribes of India that can be classified as nomadic or denotified are wandering persons that have no permanent address, ancestral land, or the recognition of the state—such people are the most extremely culturally rich and at the same time, the most institutionally invisible in the country. They are usually one of the minorities that are recorded in the broadest possible terms during the census and thus, their numerous differences are not acknowledged as they should be. Over the course of centuries, they survived by employing such oral traditions as song instead of the written word, memory instead of maps, and the elderly as teachers instead of textbooks. Just as urban areas swallow them up with great speed and the state is in the process of creating a stationary image of citizenship, these verbal lineages face the extinction of the oral lineages. Their vaults were not those that one finds in libraries. They were inside the speakers, survivors of the death of oral language.

Recently, there has been a quiet but extraordinary shift that has led some nomadic tribes to opt digital means of communication tools instead of the old methods. The term "Nomads with Notebooks" is not quite a metaphor. It represents a literal push towards a new trend among those upholding the traditional values of storytelling, bards, and craftsmen who through the use of smartphones, voice recorders, Google Docs, and YouTube are now expanding their cultural legacies, that is, languages, rituals, epics, and genealogies, being passed without any outdated intermediaries. The function of these materials will get more central with each use due to the fact that they are more credible locally, and they will cause further social activity in accumulating and transmitting knowledge. The function of these materials will get more central with each use due to the fact that they are more credible locally, and they will cause further social activity in accumulating and transmitting knowledge. They are not just content curators but also changing the base of what is accepted as knowledge through the liberation of the oral forms of traditional knowledge.

One such example is the Pardhis, a tribe criminalized for the Poona Pact that were once widely known for seeking information about animals, birds, in the forests of Maharashtra, and Madhya Pradesh as well as the past. As they became victims of the incoherent forest policies and marginalized because they were out of the social circles, there was a lot of worry about the elder Pardhi's stories being lost. However, the situation changed greatly after the NGOs at the grassroots encouraged the youth to take up the new challenge through various digitally literate projects. The youth have adopted the idea of recording in audio the communal stories in various dialects which by a little margin do not fit in with the linguists' classification. These recordings are often translated, subtitled, and shared on community YouTube channels and/or among the family members as part of the WhatsApp groups that gather the migrants around the world. Oral culture is transitioning to digital not because there is no other choice, but as part of its adaptation strategy.

This self-archiving process is not about romanticizing the past. It is rather a matter of owning up to the fact of the knowledge that has been erased. For India's new development model that depends on the visibility of the population through land records, the maintenance of a permanent address, and the Aadhaar card, there is no space where knowledge and mobility can meet. However, digital technologies are not the antagonist but the aid in unlocking this dilemma. The smartphone is the voice of the rootless youth who aspire to have a say in their own lives and culture. The smartphone is not a passive tool - it is a tool for cultural revolution.

Now, among Gadia Lohars—alternating blacksmiths wandering through Rajasthan and Uttar Pradesh to manufacture ancient farm tools—teenagers have started using Google Lens for translating signboards, finding ways, and recognizing settlements of related clans. Yet, they are not limited to TikTok (before the government ban), Instagram reels, and Facebook videos only; they are also broadcasting folk songs, making long-distance kinship ties, and awakening the youth in urban centers and Diasporic Gadia Lohars of India and the Gulf. A wedding shot on a no-frills smartphone, say, in Agra, can travel to cousins in Ajmer or Ahmedabad within minutes, enabling rituals to be re-embodied, and participation thus could occur in real-time. It's digital literacy not from the top, but digitally driven.

The most important aspect here is the role of the language. A lot of the spoken and unwritten nomadic dialects that have no standard scripts, so far, are still in danger of extinction. More recently, language has seen the tide turn i.e., with the help of voice-to-text tools, audio transcription apps, and cheap cloud storage that turns into the source of dialects' recording in a manner that can survive even after the speakers. What makes this different is that the languages spoken are not necessarily translated to English or Hindi. However, it is used to preserve the language within the community. Bhantu speakers narrating Bhantu stories for other Bhantus is a clear example of the lateral preservation movement, something that teachers can do but not for the display of academics. The aim is to preserve the local culture by passing the language and tradition from one generation to the next.

The situation, however, is not as rosy as it might appear at first glance. Even nowadays, there are still a lot of areas where there is hardly a signal. The people living near forests are not able to use their phones since the network is not stable enough. There is a blackout by electricity most of the time. In many communities that still have the image of frequent criminals, the stigma remains. According to the label, these people can be nomadic people who were previously criminals. Even local police still use this label. Therefore, if nomads are seen with phones, they will be suspected of stealing those phones. So the police have the right to detained those they suspect without justifying what they have done. The young men who are detained under these circumstances are often released at a later date without any reason. Sometimes there are also elements of a societal group that detain these young men. They are sometimes released some days after the incident. There have been times when young men were harassed after release, a serious problem indeed. One evidence of this is that some young men are harassed even after they have been released, a time when the situation becomes quite a headache. In some cases where detained youths are not released at a later date, they suffer from uncertainly brutal treatment. According to the prosecutor, if the crime is proven via the presence of a "suspicious" device, the "wandering tribe" is the prime suspect. This is like banning people from using the internet and the police overlook how the local economy is of benefit. Net-connected mobiles are not the terror tool that they are portrayed to be. When a group e.g., bandits or undocumented people, is referred to as "habitual offenders" crimes are often committed with the fiscals' knowledge. There is a spin. Officials could perpetrate crimes on the people. Maybe these crimes are just self-committed. Nevertheless, the truth is that these hooligans want and need the internet in their business. There are some other signals of misconduct in addition to these findings,

Even in tribes, internal hierarchies can stop people from participating. In more than three cases of nomadic groups, women are not only excluded from the oral knowledge and digital access but they are incapable of acquiring them. The situations in those remote areas with no internet or mobile phones are very hard as the men still hold the phone the only phone available for them on the land and then give to the women who mainly use it for business and education.

Nevertheless, it remains true that a certain action of self-documentation is a change in the logistics of the research process. In a time gone by, the research could count on the compliance of the objects of the study, the so-called "natives," as they collected "native knowledge." Naturally, a host of young nomadic Indians is discontented with such a neo-colonial set up and opt to establish their own data banks which are frequently distributed in their kinship units or user community network, thereby resisting the standardization and curation aspects no matter what the academia or NGO circles demand. The digital is not merely about the obstacles a person may encounter in a desire for structuring platforms but this individual creates own ones.

The metamorphosis is likely most significant at the level of epistemology. In these societies where a written word has a more long-standing validity feeling on the field of human knowledge, the communities are introducing the new standards of definition of "knowledge." A lullaby that was once only folklore sung by an old lady has now become an online resource once it was recorded, geocoded and put on the family cloud. On the other hand, a tribal narrative that was retold during a burial ceremony in olden days is now an educational media evaluated by kids in the diaspora who are watching the ceremony from their homes in Dubai. The oral was considered by many as being mere words and songs which would get lost soon.

This shift in the way of life is also significantly affecting the relationships between children and the older generations. No longer the young nomads who were out of the habit of out of shame or necessity together now, the oral history projects they have started have awakened new interests. Hence one can see that the older people who were left out in their families with all the gadgets have now become very important; they are the ones who are interviewed, they are the ones who are recorded, they are the ones who are consulted. A youngster who before could not stand yet another long speech from his grandfather now requests the old man to tell him the tale "just once more time" so as to make a clear recording. The digital space becomes not only a storage medium but also the actual means of reuniting with the particular theme.

On the one hand, the position of the state in this process makes it a bittersweet one. On the positive side, the latest official undertakings are still approaching the subject of moving tribes with a view to restoring them, not empowering them. On the contrary, India's new Digital Scheme has already made even the remote villages vibrant with new smartphones which the local people have at their disposal. The ironical side of the situation is that while on paper the Indian government very often decides not to take these people into account, it is this very government that has unknowingly caused the whole thing to be blossoming online. The young man in the tribe rather than the charismatic lawyer has become the person who updates the national archive if you like.

We must be cautious not to get carried away with the romance of digital transformation. Not all tribes have access to the digital platform, not every story gets saved in the same media, and people rarely get to say what they want. There is no doubt about the very real phenomenon of digital erasure that is happening, especially with the tendencies of the algorithms to put style before substance and the social media platforms to publish only that which is of high commercial value. The traditional narrative told in an audio of poor quality may not have hit the roof in terms of going viral, yet the value of that narrative as a cultural good is immeasurable. By no means should we agree with indigenous knowledge if we only examine it through the prism of engagement metrics.

Ultimately, we are seeing a reconfiguration; previous archaeological communities, who were seen as objects of the research, are now becoming the makers of history. Their traditional knowledge, which was once ipso facto limited to a particular place, is now spreading through USB sticks, SD cards, and encrypted messages even across the globe. They may not be a part of the government's "development" project, but they are the ones who are real architects of their own change. They are doing this not by abandoning nomadism, but by enriching it--from highways to fiber-optic networks.

India's journey to digital has not only IT centers and startup founders but also the narrators of the past who still tell stories through uncostly handsets in open skies and under trees. It must be willing to allow the unsung heroines of forgotten dialects to sing their songs. And the readers should know that getting in touch with the web does not always come as a performance of utility or trade. At times, it's about existence. At times, it's about saying: We were here. We remember. And now, so will you.

Chapter 6

The Digital Family—New Relationships, Old Values

What happens when a culture that was defined by cohabitation of diverse age groups gets in touch with a technology that is personalized for the individual? What if the emotions in everyday activities, such as lighting the evening lamp, reciting shlokas, and sharing dinner from one plate, are replaced by devices like smartphones and streaming services or the cloud? The 21st-century Indian household, previously characterised by a group of people living in proximity to each other and based on a pattern of cultural continuity, faces a new challenge: they must protect their traditional values in a digital world that rewards novelty, speed, and individual expression.

This chapter examines the ways in which Indian families are adapting, rather than merely reacting, to the digital age. It is not a story of severance, as is the popular belief, but of a fruitful process of developing as a couple. Instead of a confrontation between generations or a dilution of the culture, the reality observed in homes across Mumbai to Mangalore and Meerut is one of continuous accommodation. A grandmother who uploads her bhajan lessons on YouTube, a millennial who arranges an astrologers Zoom call for his wedding, a parent from two cities away who shares the WhatsApp stories of how they put the kids to sleep are all examples that do not happen only occasionally. They are signs of a cultural system that changes its form without breaking.

Very likely, the most underestimated actors in this shift are the elderly in the country. Even as a society that has traditionally revered age is now increasingly shifting gears at the speed of the younger generation, the older adults are not stood on the sidelines of the digital transformation—they are found in the midst of it all. Take, for example, the various types of religious content that appear on YouTube quite all right and many of them uploaded by people dwelling in their small house in the towns of the second and third order—still a very significant part of the country. The elderly, across the nation, in addition to the live Ramayan recitations or the aarti performances that are being so carefully produced, have turned the camera into their own tool of expression and communication for the divine. Again, we should clarify that these are examples of a form of digital devotion that has no commercial purpose, and still, thousands of people come here to pray, and like-minded people are not scarce of a genuine believer expressing their opinion. For these creators, their brand of spirituality is digital, and they are not merely broadcasting their content rather they are ensuring continuity. It is by way of the device of the smartphone that they have found their place of worship in the world that never existed as a real temple of God. (mobile).

Beyond the spiritual realm, technology has also advanced the visibility of older adults through unique digital projects such as cooking YouTube channels, embroidery reels, and Instagram poetry accounts. Not only do these online platforms allow for artistic expression, but they also give back the recognition that these elders only got before when grandkids showed them how to use a mobile. Respect, once passed on, is now certified by algorithms when a seventy-year-old lady is getting more followers than her grandson. It is also important to note that digital validation is becoming popular among elders, so instead of criticizing this trend, we should encourage them by asking—why not?

Furthermore, technology has reimagined the practice of rituals in various ways. In the beginning, livestreamed funerals only served as a temporary solution during the COVID-19 pandemic, now they have become a virtue among diaspora families. A length of a 'remote' grihapravesh ceremony is confined to the time spent on Zoom. Despite all odds, modern platforms have shifted even the least likely things such as providing for the modes of shraddh pujas, priest booking, and others to be done from any place in the world. This idea of spiritual outsourcing can be seen as a negative aspect, but it also demonstrates a rekindling of human relationships in an age of digital transience. When the physical presence becomes impossible, participating in the virtual sphere becomes one's way of practicing emotional responsibility.

The current alterations in religious practices bring up various questions. Is the essence of a ceremony lost when it is performed through a screen instead of being there in person? Can a recorded mantra be as holy as one recited in the very place the mantras were recorded? When AI bots create horoscopes for humans and an algorithm is used to determine if two people are indeed compatible for marriage, are we putting the decisions of spirituality in the hands of machines? How do we differentiate between spiritual faith and our love of convenience? These issues of conflict are lived through banter in WhatsApp groups about Muhurat timing, the feedback forms fans use, and the inner turmoil some encounter while conducting sacred rituals under the bright glow of studio lights for an audience they cannot see.

Parenting is one of the most "hotly-debated topics" in the world. Parents in India have for ages not just been about providing food and shelter but also about sanskriti that involves transferring the customs of the culture. When more choices and pressures enter the online world, the question turns into: can sanskaar be made into the digital form? There are apps for Gita teachings, ethical stories, and Bharatiya culture quizzes galore. The story of Panchatantra is sent to children in the cartoon version via Telegram by parents and family members organize cultural trivia debates through Google Meet. No matter how things are done, they are all still ineffective. Do children get influenced by screen-time repetitiveness in terms of moral values? Or does the teaching of morals lose its appeal if it is taken out of the narrative and the embodiment? What makes a value traditional is not only its content but also the eco-behavioral in which it is learned.

It is mainly in nuclear or diasporic families with no grandparents that the tension becomes even more real. The online family has, in a variety of ways, become a type of prosthetic joint family. The older generation is still able to be a part of the family from their location. Virtual technology is now used to keep the family tradition alive. Plus, not only the cultural etiquette... discipline too can be done through the use of smartphone monitoring. And though, on a broader spectrum of usefulness, this model of family is seen flexible in terms of logistics, it sometimes fails to deliver the learning experience that is rich and that comes as a result of being part of a natural adult conversation or being quietly led into a ritual. Digital sanskaar is usually specific, performative and well-timed while traditional sanskaar, on the other hand, was continuous, and the environment was calm, and it was part, not away, to be observed

However, it doesn't mean that everything is bad and we should lose hope. In several houses, the use of digital tools has helped in constructing families which were almost extinct. Children who have never been physically together before now bond with each other by creating joint playlists by Hindi film classics. Uncles located in different parts of the world join in the same weekly satsang on Clubhouse. Grandparents make storytime enjoyable with their grandchildren through video calls, broadcasting stories that capture the young listener's interest. These cases may not reproduce the traditional family—it is more of a makeover. The metaphor changes, still, the intention remains: the main goals are identity-building, memory-keeping, and love.

However, such new-look family arrangements don't necessarily eliminate all the strain. The differences in the behavior related to screen time, internet culture, and cyber boundaries can lead to new cracks in the relationships between generations. According to the parent, it may be quite normal to forbid the child to use Instagram unreasonably, but at the same time, that parent sits down watching back WhatsApp stories at midnight. A grandparent may feel that their teenager is misguided by the content of the TikTok video just as they themselves are filming the bhajan for YouTube. The examples are neither hypocrites nor do they reflect the fear of losing control. Rather they are the choice of one generation without the need for consultation with the others and the creator.

Furthermore, the issue of digital authority is becoming more and more important. Who should determine what "appropriate" digital use is? - The youngest one, who is well versed in technology, or the older one, who is the gatekeeper of values? With changes in consumer behavior, we also see the transformation in power relations. For example, in a family scenario where the child is sole manager of the YouTube channel, but the content is provided by the grandmother, authority becomes cooperative. Mutual respect is hence generated and not forcefully commanded.

An Indian family has always been not only a community but a value system, a place for teaching, and, at the same time, also a network for social relations. Currently, it is even a media world. All the celebrations are photo calls, and we share the recipe as an illustrative video. Then, we associate every milestone with a hashtag. While this trend gives rise to concerns about the facade and business of affection, it, on the other hand, and more importantly, confirms a deep and held belief that the most tech-saturated India family is still in love with, and hence obssessed with memory, sharing, and continuity.

Throughout the chapter, we'll get to know the impact of digital tools on family life in India from urban to both non-residential Indian areas as well as WhatsApp groups that span continents. We will see how elders walk through unchartered territory with digital innovation, how rituals are done in another way over the Internet, and how families redefine sanskaar in an era of screens.

No tech-induced family story in India should be told without the family being seen not just as a technology user but as an arena where new cultures are formed, challenged, and resisted. This story is not about losing traditional values, but about new values being developed. The family of the digital age is not the end of tradition. On the contrary, it is the most unexpected continuation.

The Screen Between Us: Smartphone as an instrument that changes the relationship between parents and children, spouses, and even the institution of arranged marriage

In essence, a smartphone is a tool whose only function is communication, information, and entertainment. But in the context of Indian daily affairs, it has changed into a special device symbolizing much more: a translator of emotions, a validator of generation power, and, most recently, a source of the expectations of love, duty, and individuality. To comprehend the lately observed technological expansion, one should not concentrate only on regulations, social networks, or the infrastructure level. One must be a participant in the home, where the display mostly prevents children.

The smartphone is the most important and probably the only thing that a person in most Indian households touch every day. That single fact, however, is not culturally relevant if we miss the following fact: the device is sneakingly but essentially transforming the family structure. It not only affects the communication but also clearly the idea of communication that we have. It is a situation, which is not only ...

The transition most conspicuous among all is the parent-child relationship. Indian parenting has usually covered rather close proximity—emotional, physical, and moral. As long as children were at parental homes, the parents were to seriously monitor not only their behavior but also keep a watch on their values, social circles, and in some instances their thoughts. Basically, the family was the first identity filter. However, today's kids, who live in a world of the ...

This change is not always the case of the children rebelling. In a lot of the situations, the children are not reject their parents but they just do things on their own. A child, who learns dance routines from Korean pop stars, still might kiss their parent's feet in the morning. But in between those acts is a gap that cannot be bridged by the only ceremonial way. The smartphone works to introduce ...

Surprisingly, out of the same group of people, a lot are very well acquainted with digital media. Mothers share health tips on WhatsApp. Fathers discuss on Facebook. Grandparents do Zoom bhajans. However, the way of using media by the different generations is extremely contrasting. The mobile phone, in the case of the seniors, is the tool of continuity, that is the old traditions are just changing the media. By contrast, for the kids the phone appears the way of finding oneself and being independent. What results is a sort of a conflict between the two parties: both are connected but very rarely is it in the same direction. The child swipes up to go upstairs, while the father scrolls down to go down to familiar things.

Moreover, this demographic conflict comes to the fore where the question of discipline is concerned. Is it possible to have control over the time a teenager spends on the phone when you can't stop forwarding WhatsApp videos to your friends? How can parents set a rule on going to bed early when they themselves have to do their bit to meet their online world's demand for the day? Clearly, a smartphone only spreads its tentacles and, in the midst of which, boundaries become cloudier. In a large number of households, the one who leaves the child, keeps the spouse entertained, and deals with the discomfort of the confrontation is the smartphone. Indeed, it's way simpler to escape to a gadget than to start a tough talk.

Marital power structures are no longer the same. Indian marital traditions have, for a long time, especially those that are arranged, been built upon getting to know the other person more and more as time passes. Silence was permissible. Emotions were often hidden beneath layers of responsibility. However, the coming of smartphones has led to a novel emotional economy. One in which affirmation is instant, affection is mostly received through the media, and comparison is an everyday occurrence. Now, one spouse may not necessarily be comparing their partner to a neighbour or a relative, rather they may be comparing their partner to the lives of influencers and celebrities. It is these strangers who hold the expectations of love.

This digital intimacy recalibration is not a practice that is only being done by the younger generation, even middle-aged couples have been observed doing this. An example of romantic couples' silent and quiet companionship during an evening tea time is usually replaced by each being busy scrolling their gadgets. The altercation is caused by the blaring sounds of notification and thus fights are being started. Love oftentimes is defeated by distraction. It seems, however, that people are still standing next to each other, they are emotionally far from each other, or in simple words, they are not united but instead, they are the slaves of the screen.

This in-effect can form into a mild form of distrust as well. The digital footprint that includes messages, likes, and following becomes the space where trust and disloyalty will be equally staged. In more traditional or patriarchal societies, smartphones are perceived as the manifestation of the fear of too much independence. Who is she chatting with? What's the reason for him staying up late at night and being on his mobile at the very same time? Formerly, the home was not only charge on sight and also sound, but nowadays, it is under digital-family surveillance. Couples are no longer checking the partner's phone for safety reasons, but those are inquiries for seeking consolation.

Interestingly, quite a lot of couples are at peace with the idea of smartphones and consider them to be some sort of a sanctuary. Such a type of marriage where a woman is not allowed to be free may unfortunately lead to the woman's isolation. A man with communication challenges can use text messages to communicate the same message of love that he cannot put through verbally. Good communication means between couples are the possibility of working in tandem the muscle of connectedness, even over long distances, and also the solidarity of a relationship ignited through sharing memes, playlists, or having late-night discussions. Following the last point, the screen is the problem, but it's also the solution. The primary direction of the technology is to transfer information, but at the same time, it is enabling human interaction.

The complexities most apparent with Regards to match-making and permanent marriage bonding through arranged relationships can be seen through all the sunrise and sunset phases of digital applications in the matchmaking realm. The earlier ways of arranged marriages that involved families, close-knit communities, faith groups for some, and the services of local matchmakers have now been switched to the internet, with platforms like Shaadi.com, Bharat Matrimony, and Jeevansathi leading the charge digitizing this very ancient institution as well. This transformative practice does not only speed up the process of pairing but it also profoundly refashions the entire concept of matrimony. Profiles are compiled to look exactly like CVs. The compatibility test is nothing more than electives: birth, education, salary, height. Filtered down in a twinking of an eye will be the probability of meeting the right partner, with 5 minutes only being the average time it takes to screen each profile before the final decision is made.

What once was a social negotiation between families is now transformed into an exercise in self-presentation. The excitement of getting ideal profiles with edited photos, and presenting oneself in the best manner is what happens nowadays. The conversations that people had with the beginning of shared rituals started to replace with emoji-loaded chat in the period, the transition of which has positive as well as negative effects. That is, on the one hand, it increases human beings' power—women, in particular, now have a chance to decide by themselves, interact directly and dictate terms of operation. On the other hand, it creates a shopping experience that can not only be time-consuming but also be saturated with a lack of patience, or be without the heartfelt nature of relationships.

Additonally, the involvement of the family in the digital courtship process is really a strange thing. It is a common thing for here in Nepal where the parents to create and manage the profile of their sons or daughters and also to communicate to the would be partner on behalf of their children. The problem is that the image of autonomy is only an illusion, and as a user, you are fully controlled by the administrator. Someone might think of having a private conversation with a potential life partner, then after a long period, he/she may come to know that it was his/her parent or uncle who was talking to him/her. Curation makes authenticity disappear.

These practices do not only affect matchmaking but also have a spill-over effect on the marriage itself. More often than not the couples define their ideal marriage from communications that are through narrowed virtual channels and are yet to jolt with a reality check through the ordinary necessities of living beside each other. The source of the conflicting situation is the difference of personalities, of course. But also, the main conflict area may emerge when the online persona and the person's character do not harmonize. A man who was gifted with a silver tongue during his WhatsApp chats might turn sheepish when having to showcase his vulnerabilities in person...... A lady who was light-hearted online might show traits of fundamentalist behavior. The screen, in such cases, serves as both matchmaker and mask.

However, the focus on dysfunctions only would suggest that there is more to this issue than meets the eye. The mobile phone is not an adversary of the Indian family, rather, it is a new participant in a centuries-old drama of changing and dealing with the changes. Indian families have traditionally been harmonious with the technology that has been introduced to them—whether it was the radio in the 1960s, the television in the 1980s, or the internet in the 2000s. Each phase of the technology revolution was seen as a threat but, on the other hand, it has introduced people to a kind of intimate communication and consequently, societal change.

What has changed now, however, is the scale of the impact as well as the close personal nature of the transformation. Unlike the TV, which was in the living room, the cellphone is something we store in our hands, our bedrooms, and in our pockets. It is not a common utility item but a personal gateway. Therefore, its influence is very specific, very invasive, and very emotional, and it affects not only our behavior but also our feelings, not only for us as individuals, but our families, and our futures.

The smartphone will be the most reflective when the past-changing course of Indian families is surveyed, a mixture of symptoms and causes (or agents). Its scope is the most prominent in the forefront of the technological change that will be a dramatic shift in the values of the world—choice by the individual, freedom of expression and identity that is flexible. However, it will also cause conflict: of personal space with no facility of privacy, distraction caused by overconnection, and change in spontaneity and rituals. The problem is not to disallow the device simply, but to know where it is located and the interactions that take place—the part of the device being between us and around us and now in a growing number of instances within us.

Elders in the Cloud: Looks at India's older generation going digital—and their surprising embrace of platforms like YouTube, where many are creating devotional content or cooking channels

The classic picture of India's digital change is very often about the youth – tech-savvy, meme-literate, agile on social media. Such a description depicts a large group, but apart from it, there is a deeper and more meaningful change happening behind the scenes. Senior citizens in India have shown a new face of surfing the internet – they are not just using it, they are changing it. Whether it is the case of a septuagenarian who uploads bhajan recitals to YouTube, a retired homemaker who shares traditional recipes with subscribers across continents, or a grandfather who runs a meditation podcast from his living room in Kanpur, India's elderly are going to cloud — not only as passive users but also as makers, curators, and digital anchors of cultural continuity.

On more than one level, this evolution is putting a wrinkle in assumptions. The first is technological: that digital fluency belongs only to the young. The second is cultural: that elders are anti-digital and they are happy with the activities prevailing from the analog life. The third is generational: that the internet has made the gap between the old and the young even wider. However, what we see today comes as a rearrangement of rather than a total overturning of these assumptions. Elders' previous role of merely being spectators in the digital economy is now replaced by one of active participants.

To fully comprehend this change, one has to delve into what the internet brings this demographic and why their bond with it is not just a matter of functionality but also deeply emotional. For many seniors, especially those who have given up their professional duties or have lost their traditional social roles, digital platforms don't just distract them from being irrelevant, they actually become their lifeblood. It allows them to put themselves out there even when it seems that, generally, they are invisible in society, not a burden yet somehow oppressive. More than just hobbies, now the internet gives the chance to collaborate, educate and safeguard the culture, and, importantly, to receive the information.

Let's consider the case of Shanta Devi, a 68-year-old from Nashik, with a YouTube channel named "Amma's Vrat Recipes" which has, till now, attracted more than 300,000 subscribers. The videos are as it were not scripted, rather they are taken with a telephone camera by the grand-aughter and narrated in colloquial Marathi. However, the production value is not what makes videos from some people, who watch them in Canada and Coimbatore, stand out. The quality that attracts them more is actually the truth—the author's detailed information on fasting ceremonies, her calm sense of humor, and the closeness of the kitchen that makes you feel the place is unchanged by global culture.

The online media are not just a part of her economic existence, it also represents a social circle where Shanta Devi communicates. Today we call her not a modern content creator, but a person who saves culture in the digital world. The business model is changing, so Shanta is carrying on her cultural mission online, now through the screen.

The content that tends to talk about or is a hymn of praise on a wide range of topics is mostly the one that attracts the most people. A large proportion of those channels on YouTube that are all about devotional songs, hymns, dialogues on spiritual topics, and the hosting of home worship puja live are the work—and the food—of aged people. And there's nothing spontaneous about it. The practice of India's religion has always rested on verbal transmission, collective efforts, and a lived-through experience. Since the pandemic has prohibited physical gatherings, and the nuclear family is breaking down the traditional worship pattern, the elderly have taken it upon themselves to lead the technological advocated devotion at home. Commuting the memorized shloka from the manuscript and live-streaming aarti are no longer just technological activities; they are a forward shift of ancestors. To know the generational translation.

However, this is far from being a foolish affection. A lot of the older people are very careful about the way they navigate their way on digital platforms. They don't need to be computer whiz kids to be able to do (or run) some things online. They may not be able to do the coding or configuring, but the duty they perform with love is this of the curation of their family's art well. They do not only read comments carefully, but they can also spot trolls, deal with the monetization of the threshold for the number of views that can be recorded, and even grow the influence of the algorithm over time. Members of the generations read, on Facebook, Whatsapp, give and take advice about lighting through the thumbnails of YouTube, even about the platform launching. In this respect, the stereotypes of the elderly being not digitally savvy are not true. Instead what we witness is the generations pick up just as much technology as they need in order to transmit their heritage.

The adaptation of the scenario also presents a side of intergenerational cooperation which was previously hidden. In many situations, grandchildren would repair, modify, and market the channels of their grandparents. The whole thing is very educational: youngsters provide the technical gadgets; the elders give them the stories. This way, the laptop screen ceases to be an obstacle and acts as a facilitator instead. The family bonds are often greatly resurged through such partnerships to the extent that the mere static normal conversation doesn't have the power to do. A girl who may be well able to endure her grandmother's advice physically may still find it burdensome, but she may view the situation from a completely different perspective when the same thing is through a YouTube frame, and thousands of people watch the video.

The social media phenomenon also has broader implications in society. In India, the number of elderly people is steadily increasing, and a considerable part of them have substantially better educated, healthy, and aspirational characteristics than the generations that preceded them. They have a sense of financial freedom that propels them to start their journey into the online world without feeling the desperation which often characterizes the younger generation of creators. This kind of freedom is what inspires their sincerity. Elders are not interested in trend following or getting viral;

they are more involved in doing what they know best. Their content is not fashionable; it is timeless, and this is ironically what gives it its worth.

Nevertheless, the situation is sometimes tense. Some of the senior citizens may not be very comfortable with the showy nature of the social media landscape. The notion of 'likes' as a form of recognition might not be received well, as it is usually associated with juveniles. The requirement for 'interaction' with the audience, adjusting thumbnails, or even using the tools of the platform may sound foreign or be tiring. Furthermore, the perils of either exploitation are not completely removed as a concept, let alone as a reality. Unprincipled characters have taken advantage of senior people's trust to mislead them into content structures that they are neither understand nor benefit from. There is a lot of evidence of family members taking control of monetized channels for themselves, of management firms charging hefty commissions, and of trolls attacking the looks or mannerism of older women. Thus, digital and any kind of empowerment, for that matter, faces this issue and needs a strong protection system in place to ensure such things don't happen.

There is another deep conceptual tension that arises from the inversion of the usual roles. Earlier, the grown-ups used to be the knowledge keepers and the youth the knowledge seekers. But on the internet, the authority is distributed. A 22-year old influencer may be followed by a million people; a 65-year-old person, who has a much deeper understanding, may not be able to achieve the same level of followers or even to be less than the former. This is not only uncomfortable but also confusing. It is a normal situation in the case of the elderly that respect comes with their age whereas the new information-addressing the generation disparity-often proposes the superfluousness of age. Navigating this change takes a sense of humility that is often not found in their generation. Yet, those who are successful in this area often manifest just this quality: the willingness to learn but without an inflated ego and, to teach but without condescension.

Additionally, one must pay attention to the broader cultural implications. Given India's urbanization, the increasing use of mobile phones, and the infiltration of the media, we can see that the existence of varied regional languages, food, and religion is being threatened. The old generation uploading stories in Awadhi, bhajans in Kannada, or recipes in Konkani are not only entertainers but archivists for the digital world. They are the ones who are keeping the torch of one's culture fueled. They are making the otherwise forgotten culture alive via the internet.

The world of policy and platforms has yet to catch up with such a dramatic demographic change, however. On the one hand, digital literacy programs often do not consider older people thinking that they are not interested or competent. Monetization models almost always depend on the frequency of uploads which mostly is heavier and the size of the audience which in most cases is not small. The systems created for content moderation are found to be inefficient, especially when it comes to protecting the elderly from being bullied or harassed. Still, even UI/UX design for the elderly is being designed from the viewpoint of younger hands and eyes. If the digital future of India is to be inclusive, the entire infrastructure of participation must be overhauled--not just ensuring access but also gaining confirmation.

The storyline behind elders in the cloud stands for something else than innovation. We can draw parallels with the modernization through tradition. It points out that the internet can still be a platform that nurtures tradition despite the breakneck speed at which it operates and the glossy finish. It insists that a grandmother's lyrical cry can exist together with a viral reel. The cloud can not only transport data, but wisdom as well. That is to say, digital transformation in a country with as many layers as India and as many generations is most effective when it is not just top-down or bottom-up but inside-out; it means it is there in the habits, the hopes, and the artifice of those who have long been thought to be offline.

The old people are not the ones who are bringing the internet to the brink of change. They are securing it. In acting that way, they are turning India's digital future not only younger and swifter but also wiser because the country's wisdom is being stored online as well.

Ritual in the Age of YouTube tackles the changing nature of religious observance—online pujas, AI-driven horoscopes, and livestreamed funerals

Long ago, it was a given that the sacred and the digital were opposed realms. The former was associated with the divine, and the latter was obviously the setting where permanent upheaval prevailed. This assumption has been proven false. Today ringtone dongs in smartphone temples, astrological charts are whipped around on WhatsApp, and in the case of a cremation, the teaching is done in a foreign country through the speakers of the phone. YouTube - so that until now pop culture and how-tos are categories of YouTube, now there are also songs, astro chambers, and mourning grounds. Religion has not been displaced by the digital—it has been reconfigured by it.

Everything is crystal clear. Aarti live streams from Shirdi and Varanasi are now attracting millions of views each month. After these examples, it is not a surprise that temples have also started offering online puja. Today a notion of online astrology powered by AI has emerged: AstroTalk and ClickAstro not only provide instant janma kundali readings but also no-matchmaking, predictive algorithms, career counseling, etc. The absolute digital package is on offer: from receiving death certificates to streaming the antim sanskar via a secured video link adorned with the necessary audio (chants), video editing, and respectful camera angles. The rituals are not becoming extinct, they are becoming digital.

To feel the weight of this transformation, one has to keep in mind that Hindu ritual has always been the marriage between the place, body, and sequence. The presence of a Brahmin priest, the smell of sandalwood, the symbolic touch of fire or water—these are not just for the eyes and ears of the people present, but they are also the basics of religious meaning at work. Taking the activities of these mutations online is an upgrade in the interface of the rituals and the environment that is full of questions of the theological and the socio-cultural. Can a puja be effective without physical presence? Does an image-made flame hold the same paradisiacal effect as a flame generated in a brass lamp? And who will control that the act of worship remain efficacious after the digital transformation?

A WhatsApp group of the practitioners is divided on the issue. There are those who regard what is going on as a practical adjustment to the lifestyle we are living nowadays—especially for the case of those of Indian origin who live abroad, or the urban nuclear families, which have been separated from their original communities. For such people, the digital way of worshipping is for them a piece of their own continuity. A young couple in Singapore can schedule a Satyanarayan katha for their newborn with a temple priest in Pune, selecting the time slot online and paying via UPI. The priest does the rite and the couple watch, tranquilly, their hands folded in front of a laptop. A man of sixty years in Delhi logs in every day to see a live aarti from Rishikesh, where he thinks it is spiritually enriching, though in the form of a virtual darshan. These rituals, held through a medium screen, if not the technology and the detachment, have repeatedly been described as genuine, perhaps close or intimate. For most of the people, the platforms are just that; the actual intention is what sanctifies the act.

On the contrary, a lot of people are anxious about it. According to them, ritual is not only about faith but also about doing the embodied discipline. The texturalities of the lived religion can neither be downloaded nor simulated. They fear the commodification of the sacred as it would provide convenience at the expense of conviction, thus turning devotion into consumption. Further, they claim that the logic of the platform, such as the way it operates (views, money, and algorithmic visibility), is not in agreement with the ethical beliefs of a person paying attention to his/her inner; hence does not support the purpose of living by a personal morality. When a YouTube priest tells the audience to "like and subscribe" after the prayer section, is it still a ritual or has it turned into spiritual theater?

AI, both with faced with awe and looked upon controversially, has found most of its tension in the likes of astrology. Automated platforms have made it so that a period of instant kundali generation, match-making algorithms for marriages, and daily predictions that are made based on machine learning models can all coexist at the same time. These tools assure people of accuracy, consistency, and speed -- all working areas that traditional astrologers often lack the capability of doing. However, what is left inadequately covered of this problem is the interpretive wisdom of the astrologer who acts as an advisor, a consultant, a figure, who is an indication of the devotee's life moral and emotional situation. An algorithm may be able to find the right information about a planetary transit, but it might not be able to moderate human uncertainty with the delicate touch of symbolism. By changing the astrologer with a program code, it is possible that the ritual is no more than the use of a product.

Nevertheless, the accumulation of these services does not fall to ear to. Platforms such as AstroYogi, InstaAstro, and GaneshaSpeaks have millions of users subscribe to their services and these are the majo... few being the professionals who are young. Not only price and access become the factors that drive users to these services, but also AI perceived rigidity, seen as an against of bias or mistake. This, then, is what we have witnessed: a generation of religious people who share in the continuity of religious traditions that are both traditional in content, digital in form and transactional in the experience of contact. Whether this model of religiosity is deeper or shallower to the soul does not rely much on the technological aspect but on the cultural scenarios that the trend adopts.

This transformation is not restricted to the domain of the living. Death has also been shifted to the digital world. During the COVID-19 pandemic, transmitting funeral services live came into being as a melancholic necessity. It is, however, a fact that practice has not gone away with the emergence of the emergency. Now, families opt for the regular live transmission of the last rites of a loved one who is far distant or cannot attend. Additional services of after-funeral video recordings, digital obituary pages, and memorial slide shows are also available. Some people may say it is a bad practice or a commercial factor, while, on the other hand, others may argue that a wider grieving community can emerge, memories can be preserved, and modern realities can be appropriately honoured through the dead for the dead. Much like the life-cycle rituals, the digital here becomes a substrate for continuity -- not a means of bereavement remembrance itself, rather, it goes as a communicative medium of sharing the sorrow of others.

In addition, this mutation washes women into its normative features. Digital rituals have served as a tool in most cases to position women in roles from which they had traditionally been kept aside. In more traditional environments, the performance of special pujas or chants is usually a male privilege. Virtual non-man devotees start to conduct veneration sessions via YouTube, groom populace about mantras by using Instagram reels, or share faith texts and provide their interpretation on Facebook Live. These acts often do not directly subvert the orthodoxy, instead they subtly readjust its balance. The authority now comes as a result of the number of people that watched the presentation, the clarity of the message, the veracity of the mood towards the devotion rather than the license of the institution. Notice that the digital temple becomes more inclusive than the temple that is made up of bricks and mortar.

Although, despite the above, these shifts uncover social inequalities. In general, the equipment used, the speed of the internet, and the know-how in the digital field stay unevenly accessed, particularly at the caste and class levels. To be able to perform satsangs and bhajans on Zoom it is presumed that not only faith but also the working knowledge of the platform are present. The poor, who are unable to afford digital means, not only pay data service charges but also fees charged by platforms, or they have to buy mobile phones if not already have one to be part of the . Some local priests, as supplanted by platforms, are experiencing the hardship of being left with no source of income without finding an accommodation in the digital economy. Just like other technological transitions, the digitalization of rituals leads to the emergence of new communities as well as to the exclusion of others at the same time.

Of great importance is the fact that the process of innovation we can witness is not exclusively shaped by users—platforms are no less involved in determining them since they are driven by the commercial motive. In the case of users of YouTube or Facebook, it is the engagement level that determines the success not the submission level. An algorithm has no preference as to whether a video is devotional music (bhajan) or a prank, as long as the video is kept in mind by the audience. What it can do is to encourage sensationalism in religious content through things like sensationalist posters, dramatic titles, and the transformation of controversies into debates. In a bid to become visible, religious content could degenerate into a mere entertainment sector while capturing attention. Here the outcome is not secularization; instead, it is a kind of spectacle that causes a ritual to shift from being a deep affair to being drama.

Still, it would be too simplistic to call these changes negative. These digitalized religious rituals can still be called rituals, although they are now influenced by urbanization, migration, globalization, and generational shifts. The question is not so much whether the online can be a sanctified place; it can indeed. What is of real concern here is how the digital infrastructure is to be designed in a way to enable authenticity, belonging, and the richness of the religious experience. This does not only imply to upgrade the good sides of the platforms but to change the way we are currently dealing with the access and the applications of the connection.

It is more like not the end but a renovation. Each of the examples presented above is a proof we are in the era of tradition re-telling through digital technology. Young boys, for example, can learn about God through grandfather videos. The widow in Kolkata got the husband's annual ritual live-streamed with a priest from Varanasi. University girls seek learning for the first time. We are therefore the witnesses of the updated not the lost concept of the tradition that has been transferred to the new medium.

The way the circle of religious life operates in India it has never been in a static and stuck place. The trajectory of the shift from the age-old palm-leaf manuscripts to the advent of temples, and from there, to radio, and later to TV and finally to the skyline. All this was a historical journey of the Indian religious activity. The emergence of the telecom fiber was just a part of the sequence, almost at the end yet not dead, the route that is to be followed is critical and should be done with the utmost respect for the intention, for the values, and by the consistent pursuit of relationship with the divine, beyond the material, even through the media of digital technology.

Digital Sanskaar: Unpacks how Indian families are trying to instill traditional values in a digital-context and whether it is working:

New generations are faced with the problem of continuing the legacy. For digital Indian families, the situation goes beyond just a change in time and is also a major development. The traditional wooden framework that once made the core of the people's lives - joint families, neighborhood temples, bhajans on Doordarshan and long table conversations - is abolished and maybe replaced with modern tools such as algorithms, speed, and global information flows. It is not the issue of whether children are exposed to the values, but from whom those values, through which channels and with what consequences, are the issues crucial.

Sanskaar, which is one of the words that provides an all-encompassing definition for the word the "values" and/or the "way to culture refinement", is not only an ethical ideal but also a way of practice whereby one cultivates it – that is intertwined with the language, the dress code, rituals, and communication with other people. Earlier, children in India learnt sanskaar through more ways than just one teaching. But, they learnt it when they most stood next to the seniormost people of their society. It was only by seeing a grandparent to be patient that the child mirrored the same person and got that virtue. How respect was taught-no talk just using hands, quiet sitting during a dominance act, low voice in determined places. Here, sanskaar was an example of a behavioral norm and not of a set of aphoristic features.

This way of teaching our kids the principles is now facing a hard task. Through different ways, such as the evolutionary process of alteration of social patterns, changing the family's basic structure, both parents out for work, and the small screens eating up the significant part of the home, it has become quite difficult to disclose to the children the real motivational sources. Today, a 6-year-old child might have more of his time watching YouTube in one week than the time he spends talking with an elder. In the case of a teenager, it is possible that they may be getting their first knowledge of identity, achievement, or gender roles not through the stories shared by the family but from global players who have not the least care about cultural context. Parents are not only dealing with the task of saving traditions but making that transfer into a language that comes across to digital natives (their children).

Families in India are coming up with new ways to deal with this situation. Some of the parents make religious music playlists on Spotify, watch mythological series like Ramayan or Mahabharat on Hotstar, or send daily shlokas on WhatsApp to the entire family. Some people buy apps for their children that can teach them good manners in the form of games, and some others subscribe to YouTube channels which offer Indian mythological stories with moral endings. Instagram accounts such as @roots_of_India and @vedicteachings draw a large number of fans by combining colorful pictures with old sayings. Even Amazon's Alexa is used to read Sanskrit slokas that are recited during prayer rituals. Even though the medium is different, the need to retain has not disappeared.

On the other hand, the measures seem to throw up a mixed bag of results. While a devotional playlist is playing, in the background, the child may be seen scrolling through reels. The forwarded quote from Swami Vivekananda may lie forgotten between two memes. with the child hearing from the teacher. Fourth, moral instruction has to take more than mere exposure, in the modern era it involves incorporation of personality.

There is a marked increase in the uncertainty about the "traditional values" in a world that is changing. What should be the characteristics of sanskaar? The values or critical ability? Gender roles or gender balance? Should we have the characteristics of either reverence or questioning? Families are in disagreement, which unsettles the consensus on the issue of what is the right thing to do—there is diversity not only in terms of generation, but also in terms of the regions and social classes. In a particular home, the usage of digital sanskaar means one or both parents set the child's screen time and influence the child to speak in Hindi at home. In some families, it is about Mahatma Gandhi's moral education via YouTube's tutorial; while others, however, it is employing social media as a tool for social equality movement-related tasks, for instance, donating or participating in relief fundraisers conducted online. The term sanskaar no longer refers to just one particular classification but is rather now filled with various contested opinions all trying to find a place online.

Digital environments also present moral development issues. Parents' best efforts might not be enough, and digital spaces could bring new agents of influence who serve a different purpose. Usually, while parents are trying to promote humility and restraint, teenagers are getting exposed to a wide choice of cultures like celebrity culture, consumerism, and carefully crafted images of beauty, among others, via Instagram. Some influencers with huge reach are the unseen principal gurus who either contradict or in surprising ways reproduce family values. For example, a fitness vlogger could be an example of good discipline, a fashion influencer could represent confidence, while a crypto investor could be here to talk to his followers about financial independency. The internet valley is full of different values—a place where values are not absent, but many.

Here, moral pluralism is often taken by the conservative families as a signal of being less meaningful or an actual danger. Talks about "Westernization" and cultural erosion seem to be the main concern around the issue of children's screen use. However, still, there are those who argue that digital channelism provides a new base for moral development. Indian psychologists' YouTube channels are educational, dealing with issues like consent, emotional intelligence, and stress management which were not part of the grown kids' education in the past. Podcasts for kids mix mythology stories with narratives of mental health. Not only do these persons influence the young generations but also give a reason why Indian thinkers such as Gaur Gopal Das or Sadhguru are so popular among the youth: they do not just assume the role of religious leaders but make it funny and accessible to others. In the context of secularism, the era of getting the distinction between secular psychology and sacred philosophy is more and more cloudy, and the youth are much more aware of spirituality than usual.

Meanwhile, there are specific families who have recourse to well-defined digital devices to instill moral principles. Services such as Kutuki, Baal-Sanskaar, and Indic Today Kids have made it their task to deliver the information via language juggling, conducting moral stories, and teaching cultural education through a variety of interactive games to kids. Online lessons organized about the wisdom of Vedic, yoga, or Indian classical art are to offer guidance to parents who are convinced that their kids are not devoid of sanskar. Additionally, some of the summer camps are conducted via Zoom and involve the kids learning the Bhagavad Gita or being part of the Ramayana classical drama. Mostly, the urban middle class in India starts the actions and motivations run through the need to bring the past and the present together. However, the most critical element for success in the use of these materials is that they must be used on a regular basis and parents themselves should be the role models and not just the information alone.

On the one hand, digital sanskaar is a paradox in that it reveals the inner conflict between control and autonomy. In the past, the value systems were primly built on the hierarchical pattern and all were supposed to follow it. However, the online platform provides grounds for self-expression, experimenting, and even opposing. At the same time, young people might still continue with some traditional practices, such as the festival of Raksha Bandhan or bowing to older people, but they will still voice doubts about other aspects, like community roles.

Despite this, the main point of the paragraph, the dynamic of digital role-modelling, seems to be the most convincing part. There, it is very usual that children copy exactly those things that are only doing it orally-and the question of the role stick and others can rightly be considered a very important issue. On the one hand, if parents talk about limiting the screen with the children, at the same time they winkholes on the one hand, if the parents preach the content of the program, they also binge-watch series.

So what we are witnessing here is the rise of a hybrid education consisting of moral stories from classic Indian literature and Disney, hymns, and K-pop music, and receiving values from cultural, contextual, and digital sources. Likewise, it is important to psychologists that this is a dialectical process and not confusion or breakdown of tradition.

In this light, for parents, the main issue at hand is not to stick to their old formula. The key is to understand and then offer the possibilities for the realisation and presentation of their ideals to the children. Therefore, admitting that one can indeed use the Instagram image of seva (service) or share real situations available on various virtual platforms, one can appreciate the point that the author was making.

It is not the question of whether digital sanskaar is a possibility -sanskaar here refers to the conscious nurturing of the child's imbedded heritage and principles, whereas the latter stands for a way of life shaped by the technological advancements.

Admittedly, good values (sanskaar) can't be uploaded as a file and you can't stream them like you do a bhajan. It is just not practical at all. Here it is meant that sanskaar values exist and are to be experienced by the people. Further, the expression of such values in acts or life experiences is what is referred to as adaptability and interpretation. It is clear that digital tools only have the ability to help in this but cannot be the actual replacements. The enabling of reach, variety, and innovativeness is allowed a digital tool. However, being the promoters of values are still people's task that they must do faithfully and consistently. This is a dual challenge faced by the Indians to preserve the cultural heritage of 5,000 years and cope with the 5G technological era which having to strike a balance. Is it possible? The answer is yes, many people, albeit with mistakes, and in a lot of instances, through their creativity and love are already doing so.

Chapter 7

Education's Reckoning

Education in India has never just been about the conveyance of knowledge; it has been the pursuit of culture—a blend of the intellectual, the moral, and the social. With the rise of digital modernity in the country, the nature of the enterprise is being constantly transformed at speeds that outpace the collective capability for reflective thought. Digital India, in the education sector, has, besides anything else, been the promise of open access, individualised learning, and scalable quality (Bharat, A., 2020). However, the delivery of this pledge is now nearing its closure stage.

The pandemic prompted e-learning, allowing for a swift transition to education, which resulted in a significant leap in investment, innovation, and ad-hoc adjustments by all stakeholders involved. Formerly, school assemblies transitioned to Zoom meetings, tablets became the favourite gadgets for teachers, and YouTube became the new virtual tuition centre. Unfortunately, when the screen medium replaced the need for resource persons and classrooms, cultural and pedagogical misunderstandings deepened. Urban children with improved internet access through fibre optics could do a lot of work, but their rural counterparts often lacked connection or Internet data sharing. The application of Artificial Intelligence (IBM Cloud, n.d.) in education has reached its peak, after which the market has been bombarded with edtechs introducing different language learning programs by gamifying them and incorporating personal adaptive technologies, claiming to continuously support flexible, anytime, anywhere education (e.g., Essays). However, the real challenge in the educational discipline was still not addressed, and the monster in the dark was, "What setting these digital models catering for the variety of human intelligences will be conducive to? Whether we are creating it or they are becoming merely a consumer of the material."

By no means does this chapter fail to usher in the discussions about the "gamified gurus," apps, and platforms, which blend the features of animations, interaction, and performance metrics into a new form of instructional design. In many cases, for the first generation of learners, especially, those who are in tier 2-3 towns, these platforms are not only the first but also the most popular instructional sources in a language they are most comfortable with.

The spread of the local language in education cannot be underestimated as it allows knowledge to move laterally, outside the English medium domain's monopolistic control. However, with these good signs, come the best. The way of using points, badges, and streaks to maintain children's involvement becomes an instance in which the intense stimuli of social media are echoed—pleasant for a short time but might have no solid basis. Several applications are proactively promoting the speed in which knowledge is received and the memory or context flexibility has been lost. When schooling crosses the faith over the side of entertainment, the borders between real engagement and time-wasting will start to blur.

With this bright side of technology is the fact that more and more people are getting worried about the certification craze. Anyone with an Internet connection, a bit of time, and a credit card in theory can access the tools unlocking a new set of digital skills within 30 days. Thus, a "full-stack developer in 30 days" YouTube tutorial or online courses that issue a certificate for watching videos in essence signify the beginning of a new educational economy. This is an economy where the appearance of learning is still accepted as a substitute for its existence. Already, employers are pointing out the tremendous discrepancy between the traditional credentials the labor market provides and the digital skills the work structure requires. In sum, carefully reading a résumé with five digital badges certainly sounds good initially, but if the person bearing the résumé fails to be able to argue, collaborate, and present these badges lose their power. The Indian job market, which has to keep up with the dramatically accelerating automation, informality as well as structural unemployment, is not in a position to copious the ubiquitous tags and yet deliver fewer skills. The situation is not just limited to the issues of access to education and the use of technology, but it is more of a question dealing with the episteme: what do we consider as knowledge and how can we be sure that someone has learned?

Teachers are the key players in the process; schools and enterprises merely generate policy and finance. Educators, usually the silent voices in the e-learning change, have broken the withdrawal mould and are the ones primarily responsible for the de-homogenization of the current state of e-learning. Some of them, for instance, are integrating the latest technologies trend with their work or making use of platforms such as Instagram or regional OTT channels. Others are creating a database of people's stories, which supplement their teaching, while others are using traditional frequently asked questions of the community to demonstrate the idea of a scientific inquiry. E-learning teachers currently are not against tech; they are, in fact, the focus of the former but the latter is quite skeptical of all the technology education through technological communication since they are not sure the platform can be able to give their students other dimensions further enhancing them from the point of only being consumers of the services provided.

This is not a case of mistaking pedagogy for nostalgia. It is merely showing that judgment, emotions, and ethical issues cannot be replaced by the machines in the educational system. A machine can help with the grading of an essay, yet it will not have the capacity to feel a student's discouragement. The application can be helpful in checking vocabulary knowledge but cannot interrogate a child in order to understand what the word means in his grandmother's dialect. In most cases involving learning, the process should involve dialogue, doubt, and discomfort—all of which are inherently human.

Fundamentally, the situation at its core embodies a real conflict of cultural forces. In India, educating people has for a long time been a matter of a fight between two ideologies: mere accumulation of KNOWLEDGE (gyan) and gaining wisdom (pragya), rote learning or UNDERSTANDING, school education, and LEARNING. The revolution in electronic devices did promise the world a way of solving these problems, but, at the end of the day, the divide was only made more profound in less obvious ways. In a world where examination preparation apps are the primary educational median, this leads to a possible situation where education is only outlined as information management. The global aim of forming individuals who are reflective, resilient, and responsible begins to shrink. It is no longer the issue of the pedagogical—democratic principles and the need to critically examine them are in just as much danger. A society with a history of being full-time exam-takers does not always automatically transform such a society into a think-tank of members.

The main idea of this chapter belongs to technologies that ensure success in the educational process, depicting it as the present and the future as well. The author defends the view that digital tools should be used in a more enlightened, moral, and local way, to paraphrase, the school should use the tools that course through everyday learning. Imagine technologies that were created with the goal of sharing knowledge rather than replacing the teacher or investing her wisdom in the cloud. What if learning had platforms that included, as mandatory, local arts, history, and ecological knowledge in the syllabus—instead of them being relegated to mere decorations? What if the students' education was not only about the code they know but also about understanding the moral and social consequences of it?

India has an education system that is diverse, complex and spread across a wide area. In essence, it is the room wherever the child comes across a teacher, who will be their anchor while they are trying to make sense of the world both virtually and in person. This has been and continues to be an area which, regardless of the level of digital intervention it undergoes, still has to consider the trust and context. Actually, it is the place where the most subtle and powerful psychological strategies that help in the development of beliefs and attitudes are respectively used and preserved as such. The author's intent by discussing these paradoxes, opportunities, and disputes of India's digital education boom is to challenge the readers. In this process, readers are exposed to the lively debates, self-critical reflections, and provocative arguments that India's education system is undergoing internal transformation; the new era is torn between broadening and deepening, data and wisdom, and platform (technology) and person.

We are at a turning point in the development of educational technology in this country. The coming years are likely to see an emphasis on pedagogical catch-up rather than technological catch-up, especially given that we have just emerged from a period where learning technologically seemed to be what it was all about.

The change is in progress. The fragility or the strength of the result will be determined not by the capability or the financial resources, but by the extent of our ability to reconceptualize learning as something very much human—a digital support enabled but not determined by digital technology.

Indian education has always been regarded as something beyond a house of education. According to Indian beliefs, education was a way of not only getting a job and sustaining the family but also of learning about oneself, keeping social accord, and understanding the cosmic order. The gurukul system, a system that was in vogue thousands of years before, was the one that best exemplified the first sentence about self-knowledge, social harmony, and cosmic order. It was definitely not transactional. The learning process in the case of the students and the teachers was always intimate, intergenerational, and mostly, it was oral, and context-concentrated, besides content-based. The knowledge was not to be capitalised upon, it was kept sacred ... Knowledge was not transmitted in a curriculum but through experience, discussion, and apprenticeship. The teachers were not information spots but were the ones who were responsible for the safekeeping of the character and the moral values among people as well as truths about the real world. This age, however, is characterized by education-technology unicorns, syllabi curated by algorithms, and tutoring apps on a subscription basis. Gurukul has become Google, and now the Indian educational system is no longer just a historical path, it has become the 'existential' dimension of the country's life.

The Indian edtech allure is very strong: a larger scale, increased access, individualization. However, these prospects very often rely on a more general set of assumptions that are worthy of skepticism. The idea that technological tools are apolitical, big data-based learning is the best, or that technology conquers education intelligently, as an engineering would do, are all so wrong. The purpose of education at its highest level is the one that allows the individuals to be safe in the world, not only economically but also ethically and emotionally. This mission cannot be described using only dashboards and games. If one is only taking education from a platform, it always brings the risk of not just disconnection from the teacher, but disconnection from the subject matter.

In order to understand the present, it is mandatory to know how we arrived here first. The gurukul system, although quite good as an idea, still it was not an egalitarian system at all—on the contrary, it was so unjust, and it was primarily based on caste, gender, and lineage. The British rule did reform the Indian educational system in the way that it was suitable for them and through this mode, they intended to create the necessary clerks and not necessarily the creative people. It was through the minute on Indian education given by Lord Macaulay in 1835 that the transition was permanently fixed. The replacement of Sanskrit and Persian by the introduction of English, the devaluation of the indigenous knowledge systems, the uniformization of the curriculum through the bureaucratic procedure, all these were the points that Macaulay addressed in his speech. The new era represented by the government of the newly independent India brought about several efforts at education democratization through the institution of public schools and the constitutional provisions, however, the icing on the cake was missing the core of the situation, thus it developed into a paradox wherein much of the policy implementation was forgotten due to the growing population, inadequate financing, and widespread neglect. This period was later occupied by private tuitions, coaching factories, and lastly by the digital bureaus.

The present surge in education technology has assumed the title of being a disruptive force, yet, in truth, it is often the digital copy of societal disparities. Educational technology that is hailed as the best in India misses the ship by not serving the poor. The rich are the customers who buy the product of these most popular edtech companies, those rich that mostly reside in urban areas. In addition, many edtech companies charge subscription fees that rival the private schools and market themselves to the elite preferring instruction in English that is meeting competitive exams' requirements. The appeal has a contemporary design, but the theme is as old as poverty. Accessibility to the content doesn't ensure access to opportunity, especially when the content is designed to maintain the old pattern of mass producing programmed minds, measuring individual performance, and promoting individual advancement over collective transformation.

The field of education has several serious issues with the way some of the startups and companies have combined the idea of learning with the words of content delivery and the next part tries to highlight these issues. The learning that students receive is not only contained in videos and other media but also includes the coming face-to-face with their fears, questioning the decisions and eventually failing, as these accompany the whole learning process, and also dialogue. But this is not given the full attention it should get in the current edtech models. A teacher was an iconic figure in the Indian pedagogic scenery and was always at the heart of the whole process of carrying out the duties of an educator. However, his status has changed somewhat, as he has become just the talking head on the screen, being totally eliminated to avatars and AI tutors, that look like they communicate with the students, but in reality, they do it only in the appearance of cooperation. The teaching, which used to have a personal touch, now, in the absence of the essence of the teacher-student contact, has become cold and has lost its connection with the students. The human aspects of the education such as the basis of the relationship friendship and confidence, guidance, and role modeling, become insignificant and are discarded for the sake of "efficiency."

Yet as much as edtech is another restriction generator, it disrupts the gatekeepers as well. The platforms that offer learning in the local dialect, skill-oriented training, or open access materials are creating new forms of mobility especially for learners in non-metropolitan India. As an example, the local Dalit student of Bihar can easily sit in his room and watch lectures from the prestigious Harvard University or coding tutorials from Bengaluru. It is however likely that this frontier of accessibility will vanish soon. The students will need to meet the requirements of a proper environment, the infrastructure, the equipment, the knowledge of technology, and guidance, which is what makes it predominantly accessible. Information presented without its context can be misleading. If the democratization is not supported by scaffolding, it is not a source of empowerment rather a kind of rejection. Besides, algorithms are not impartial curators but rather they are pattern amplifiers—the existing ones. Once a child looks for a video on a topic such as algebra, the next one recommended by the platform may well pertain to cricket highlights or beauty tutorials, since gaining attention, and not necessarily for the purpose of understanding, is what the business model is about.

The edtech platforms present another dangerous aspect, they drive the formation of new needs and desires. The accent on tech careers, English fluency, and requirements for Ivy League degrees might downplay the local relevance−the local economy, the vernacular literature, or the ecological knowledge that are important to India's future. While pursuing and aiming at global achievement, local intelligences might be removed. Suppose an Indian edtech landscape that was genuinely Indian were wanted? It could follow Python's and STEM's lead and include Kabir and Kalidasa, as well. A kind of online education that could supply not only discussion on Newton's Laws but also the panchatantra stories for ethical reasoning?

On that basis, we have to think: who decides the pedagogy behind these platforms? Nearly all edtech companies are managed by engineers and investors instead of educators or philosophers. Pedagogical design is treated as a secondary aspect to the major strategic aspects like UI/UX, trigger variables, and market expansion. Feedback loops are built on the determinants of "watch time", not on the depth of the comprehension. If a video is skipped after 45 seconds, the system will be aware of that and it will make the video shorter, more attractive but not necessarily smarter, but this kind of identification is not only a technological breakdown but it is also philosophical. It seems we are teaching students a method of showcasing knowledge, not a way of making them internalize it.

It is a wrong move, although, to call oneself Luddite. Technology, indeed, has a strong potential to facilitate learning in such outstanding ways—through simulations, collaborations, multilingual access, and personalized pacing. However, it needs to support a particular pedagogical vision and not vice versa. To be exact, it is necessary for India to have a public debate about the morals of edtech. Who makes the decisions as to what things are relevant? Who ensures that they are taught that certain way? Should education get privately monetized or should it be publicly guaranteed? These questions are neither peripheral nor secondary – they are the essence of our democratic and civilisational commitments.

But we can see some new models as well that are showing great potential. Local learning centers, which are run by the community in remote areas of Karnataka, are combined by the involvement of the mentee offline and the selected online publication. There are small-scale educators who have started to create resources in local languages and low-bandwidth to blend with the homely environment. The governments of some states are also trying out some schooling models like hybrid ones that still rely on the teacher but make teaching interesting through the use of tablets. There is also a type of educational material designer, who on the other hand, has rejected corporate edtech trends in favor of substance, critical thinking, and not repetition. It is not just by accident that they are unique; they show us the limits of what can be done.

The situation in India is a very critical one. The gurukul was a moral and social economy with respect to the educational system; edtech represents a market economy. In the light of the above, therefore, it should be noted that neither to the past, nor to the future blindly is the way forward, but synthesizing the two into an education model that is humanizing, fair, and future-oriented. This, in turn, necessitates us to inquire into the difficult points of the scalability, equity, attention, and motive of the education process. It also requires a group of educators, philosophers, designers, parents and scholars to come together to ponder not only about the creation of applications but also the idea of learning itself.

If education is to be the public good in a digitally mediated world, India should prioritise that the change from gurukul to Google is not a tale of woe. It should be a story of merger whereby technology is used to do the moral vision of learning better, not to make it worse. That is what should be aimed at as the real edtech revolution.

Virtual Reality (VR) and Artificial Intelligence (AI) are Not Just for Entertainment

A girl from rural Jharkhand opens her father's smartphone and, in her mother tongue, Bhojpuri, starts a virtual lesson on the board. It might sound to be a minor learning action if a girl in rural Jharkhand opens her father's borrowed smartphone and a virtual lesson on the board, in the local language for the first time, but this action represents a very significant educational move in modern India: the majority of local, gamified platforms were designed to make localization of programs a reality and to guarantee underprivileged people's access to these platforms. Companies like Kutuki, Dost, and Pratham's StoryWeaver have come up with the idea of working on a new pedagogy that triggers change by not restricting the educational process to the classroom only, in other words, the provision of a culturally embedded experience that caters for the learners' own self... at a time when they are linguistically, visually, and emotionally not too literate. Yet this optimistic perspective also brings to the table the question of content. Does gamification serve as a connector between traditional and modern practice or does it render the culture as a mechanism that only gives c... one of the key components of cognitive richness or just a source of simplicity? But most importantly, are we restructuring the educational system, or is it just a new word given to distraction?

Gamified learning apps have a substantial draw in India because of multiple reasons. The paper's intent is not just to inform but also to explain the fascination stemming from the availability of free educational content that is flexible, and the possibility, with it, of a user's limited phone data usage. This, driven by the fact of the growing number of internet users (approximately 500 million, as per...) and the fast spread of smartphones in tier 2 and tier 3 cities, marks the large demand for affordable and flexible educational content. The millions of first-generation learners, particularly in the rural areas where English is a barrier, vernacular direction serves to lower the wall of comprehension. With gamification, either through points, stickers, A... the learning experience less threatening, especially for early learners. It changes the learning environment from a place of rote memorization to one of playing, exploring, and trying out situations without the fear...to be of curiosity-led learning is, in and of itself, a non-violent change just as a quiet revolution without history, is.

However, engagement is different from understanding. The fact that a student keeps coming back to a certain learning app is no guarantee that the student is getting the gist of the matter. Most often, the dopamine-fueled mechanics of gamification such as the looped rewards and the colored transitions might look more like the addiction features of video games that are reflective education. Furthermore, while giving points and stars can be rewarding, they also train the learners to look for external acknowledgement and not deeper insights. In reality, the matter at stake here is not only a matter of transferring information but also the very way a child will approach learning at the cognitive level: is it inquiry or just a game to win?

Today, respect for educational principles is of crucial importance in the Indian context, where the learning gap is huge and the stakes are high. Over the years, the Annual Status of Education Report (ASER) has been showing that many children in Class 5- the students of fifth grade, essentially- have severe difficulties reading a text designed for the level of a student of just the second grade. Such a scenario may lead to mirror situations where labels may seem as if those shortcuts could offer solutions. But short paths usually miss the reality of depth. A kid may perform an online task of correctly matching an image of a mango to the word "aam" and still, it might happen that the child is not capable of building a sentence using that word. It is very easy for gamification to be relied upon to briefly explain the very surface of a subject but not offer help in the process of new ideas through bringing them together or a result that will be crucial to critical thinking that, however, is only limited to the current moment of engaging.

Nonetheless, one of the most popular benefits of such platforms is the regularization of the languages in their spoken versions. That is the principal reason: India has at least 22 languages recognized as official languages of the country and dialects that reaches hundreds. For quite a long time, it has been assumed that children who speak English as well as those who use this as their language of instruction, have more access to learning in Indian schools. However, by switching to Marathi, Kannada, Tamil, or Chhattisgarhi, apps bring in the comfort level that makes the children feel at home...

But, for all that, localisation is not a cure-all. The translation of content is definitely not equal to the localization of knowledge. So the math problem about computations of the discount rate asked at a Western-style shopping center could confuse a child in a rural village. A good illustrative example is a story of a grandmother who weaves mango pickles or of a father who checks soil moisture with the help of a mobile app. The latter does not only make sense to the learner but also helps to ground his own intellectual capabilities in the real world. The most valuable gamified platforms are those that not only translate but also evolve curriculum, making it culturally relevant. The setting of knowledge must not be applied from internal models of the students' past only.

Significantly, the dilemma of quality assurance is pretty serious. The Indian market has been inundated with hundreds of different edtech products, and many of them are supported by venture capital with aggressive user acquisition goals. As a result, one is usually forced to choose between the growth of given resources and quality. And if the app is user-centred, content curation seems never to come up. Quite often the drive to increase the number of "retention" or "daily active users" happens without being critically analyzed whether learning is echt, developmentally reasonable, or morally correct. Educational researchers are concerned about the direction of this trend: a considerable range of the gamified apps do not seem to have scaffolding, sequence, or integration with them. Thus, a solitary learner may swiftly go from phonics to fractions in a single app without any educational connective means. Although the experience is seamless, the learning is still fragmented.

What is equally bothering is the change in the figure of the teacher. In most gamified e-learning platforms, the figure of the teacher does not appear at all but is replaced by voice-overs, avatars, or computer-generated hints. This may be a rational solution in the conditions of scarce qualified educators, but still, the implications are manifold, meaning not just a new model of education is represented, but a greatly depersonalised one. In reality, the Indian education problem has never been just about the content of education-- it has always been about educational relations. The teacher, especially in low-resource context, is not just an information provider, but also a role model, a person that gives an affirmation, and most importantly, a link between home and the system. A teacher cannot be abolished from the educational setting without diminishing the educational process down to information transfer only.

However, being dismissive of gamification without consideration would be a sign of lack of intelligence. If accompanied by good planning, the use of games in learning can cover a lot of cognitive processes like the visual, the auditory, and the kinaesthetic ones. It can help learners engage with the fear of failure, be open to experiment, and match students with different learning rhythms and styles. Gamified tools can provide a medium for neurodevelopment for kids who are not good learners but not also necessarily from marginalized places who are not familiar with the traditional schooling system but still carry a psychology burden to transition to or back to the formal subject of learning.

Among those hopeful changes is the arrival of community-oriented, open-access platforms. Social projects such as Diksha (a Ministry of Education project) or Pratham's open databases are taking advantage of being free to both students and teachers, educators may choose content and methods that are relevant to the child's native culture, they let parents give support and have the said content in the local language, as opposed to most digital platforms that just download some worksheets to be done on smartphones. The best models also lead to the same natural world that educates the child; it does not lead to the child becoming isolated from it.

Furthermore, a rising crop of education innovators is playing with low-tech gamification, employing such tools as story cards, quizzes via SMS, and audio lessons that are interactive. These offerings are taking into consideration the essence of all innovations—namely that they are fit for purpose. The Indian context gives us an example of where real too much electricity is not available and the amount is very expensive, and the future of gamified learning in simple ways devoid of sophistication would correspond at a time when energy is wasted and data is used sparingly.

As always, the most important question to ponder is: What type of citizens do we want to grow? When education is not aimed solely at creating employable but rather empathic and not just numerate but also nuanced people, gamification has a role to play beyond the simple entertainment of learners. The process of gamifying the classroom should be built on the foundation of pedagogy, should be infused with knowledge of what people can do with it, and should be ultimately communities-responsive. Admittedly, the education sector cannot be replaced by edtech, but it can definitely be complemented by it—thus allowing for a more human and organic learning process.

The first step towards this goal is for India's education sector to rise to the occasion. It is essential that a system of nonpartisan authorities capable of assessing educational applications be set up in the shortest possible time, and these apps, in turn, would be evaluated not only on usability or market size but on the impact they have on students' development. The regulation of educational tools along the lines of nutritional standards for food products is an important step to complete. A multiplayer app may be sold as an entertainment one, but does it also encourage critical thinking? Can it be utilized for the acquisition of a wider vocabulary? Is it designed to relate the learned knowledge to the learner's life? These are not questions of beauty, but questions of the essence of democracy, which implies the access to knowledge for all.

India needs less of the "app for everything" attitude and more of the discussions on the inadequate as well […]"> of the one-size-fits-all apps. That is, the use of gamified methods in education may be established for good if it shows potential to eradicate the divide or reduces the dichotomy in the learning process, while the choice of the design, deployment, and the system regulating is what will matter as to whether it actually happens. The digitized classrooms must carry a message that is not to amuse but to enlighten. And this text just cannot be coded in the form of points and tokens.

Degrees Without Depth

From a global learning platform, a student in Pune receives a digital certificate at the end of a three-month online course in "Business Analytics". He uploads it to LinkedIn, and in no time, he gets likes and congratulations from his network. Currently, he is in possession of six such certificates, representing areas like blockchain fundamentals and leadership essentials. However, when pushed into a real-world project that requires critical reasoning, data interpretation, or teamwork under ambiguity, he is at a loss. This is not a story of laziness or lack of ambition. The fundamental trust is the rising confusion between a title of a degree and its related capabilities. In a system where the indicators of learning are getting increasingly bigger in number, although substance is vanishing.

Through MOOCs and micro-certifications, education has become less complex, faster, and more skilful. These platforms are the source of liberation for millions, particularly in countries such as India, where learners sometimes have to deal with financial, institutional or distance barriers. Players like Coursera, edX, Udemy, upGrad and other local providers boast of social justice through free education. However, democratization of knowledge without a discussion is superficial. The value of a degree is in direct proportion to the quality of understanding that it reflects. But today, the massive expansion of online certificates is overshadowing the growth of intellectual capacity represented by them. The ideal, of course, is not that easy.

MOOCs are flypaper for the masses as they are easy to access. It is possible for any person with a smartphone and the Wi-Fi connection to register for a class at the Massachusetts Institute of Technology (MIT) or the Indian Institute of Technology (IIT). Yet just because something is accessible does not mean it is readily understood or accepted. Online classes presented from a screen with a pre-recorded lecture, in the absence of dialogue, the strictness of assessment or academic teacher's modest hearty, often they become some passive education. The students are mostly keen on watching a lot of videos, i.e. passivity rather than the activity of grappling with content is what is of main concern. The decision is taken, multiple-choice question wins it as the quest for new ideas is seldom heard. Forums are good places for debates, but this is not the case here the structure of the majority of online courses is directed towards speed and achievement but not towards deeply developed ideas and reflections.

Additionally, this tendency corresponds to yet another social development: the metricisation of success that is also very prevalent. Modern society competes about every step of the way from the school register to corporate performance review, it may be a fact the ubiquitous has made us addicted to measurement. The electronic learning platforms are inflicted with this malady too. The "Progress" can be tracked through dashboards, while the concept of "Achievement" has been transformed into gaming by getting a badge. But such numbering puts the learning at the same level as the performance. The threat is not only that we turn knowledge learning into a performance but we may stop seeking it altogether.

While the digital revolution of education in India has imbibed this trend with an overdose of adrenaline, it has not shown any sign of any such facilitation in the restoration of the deep-rooted inequalities present in the traditional education system. Educational technology not only bridges the gap but also it gives the lowest stratum of the society an effective alternative through digital upskilling platforms to develop their skills. With these online platforms, you could, for instance, become a computer professional competent in Java after one month's study, be AI-adept within a week or do product management with the help of a weekend webinar. But it is an inevitable consequence that when the tempo speeds up, only the breadth will be sacrificed for the depth. Moreover, this trend can also be noticed with the high numbers of "placement guarantees" and "industry-ready" flags. Thus, the mentioned platforms transform learning into a kind of consumer goods and subsequently present it in the full spirit of urgency. Consequently, learning becomes more of a hustle than a regular practice.

What is even worse, due to the overinflation of the qualifications and their credentials, the core of the problem is multiplied, making it extremely pestilential to the society. This trend has led to a vicious cycle in which, as large masses of people try to push more certificates into their CVs, the less return each such certificate yields. This has made employers who are desperate for real talent and are left with lots of resumes full of certifications face an uphill battle in this regard. Consequently, some companies are now asking for more credentials as they already find it hard to differentiate the genuine ones from the forged ones, and in this way, the cycle is sustained. The main tragedy of this system is the learners, especially those who come from a deprived background, they are actually spending a lot of time and money in their quest for surface-level legitimacy even though most of them lack the necessary skills to make good use of those certificates and therefore feel the need to abandon them after some time.

This inflation is less about the mere number of items but about a change in what the 'course' means in the educational discourse. Now we can see how the simple 'video lecture with a 'PDF is being called a 'certificating program which is an example of a massive misconception of the issue. The rationale of curriculum development, sequencing, scaffolding, and pedagogy is no longer the primary focus, it is sacrificed for the sake of the high production of the content. The content delivered by the platforms is geared toward virality rather than accurate and reliable information. The outcome of this is the rise of a cognitive fast food ecosystem whereby information is easily accessible, highly addictive, and has a low nutritional value.

However, the problem is not only about technology but also about philosophy. We should ask ourselves what the purpose of learning is. If the only thing that education is good for is a productivity weapon, a LinkedIn embellisher, or a ladder to the next position, then effectiveness will not be the main issue of the situation anymore and it is accepted as one of its good aspects. This instrumentalist view is particularly amplified among India's middle classes, who often regard parental investment in education as the return on investment and degrees as the medium of dowry currency. Consequently, the value proposition of edtech ceases to be a social transformation and is rather about a socially transactional process.

The characterization of e-learning as shallow, however, is completely wrong. Indeed, you can find courses that are fewer in the number but they are of high quality and require the application of slow thinking, peer interaction, critical writing, and reflective self-assessment. Certain educators prefer the old-fashioned way and are working hard to transfer the high-touch, empowering, community-driven learning spaces to the digital realm. As these experiments clearly reveal, we need to be clear that technology is good at scaling information but it is not the same with mentorship, it cannot help it grow. Where real learning occurs, it is still in the process of dialogue, feedback, and struggle.

The process of determining whether a person has indeed learned something is a key issue as well. Traditional tests by no means being perfect for this are still better than nothing since they at least test the retention, synthesis, and application. Numerous digital courses on the other hand completely ignore this matter by only conducting very basic quizzes, using automated scoring, or even using peer-reviewed checklists. We just confirm that a person has only come into contact with the domain, and we are no longer sure about the person's expertise.

Employers could also avoid slip-ups in digitally-enabled talent recruitment. Due to the digital transformation, the HR systems often hurry to enumerate the qualification of potential employees headed by word press rankings and a heap of certificates and completed courses. They, thus, generate such an ecosystem where signaling becomes more important than the actual content. One of the major problems associated with hiring decisions which are fully controlled by algorithms that can scan resumes is that the candidates who have six digital badges in data science seem to be "more qualified" than those who are just the authors of a single academic paper and have nothing else to offer. However, the former usually performs well when handling uncertainty or working in groups or solving problems, compared to the latter. The real mastery of a skill is not just tidy but also multifaceted, it is a result of numerous revisions, failed attempts, and all consumed.

The move towards a more digitalized policy environment is already afoot. Some institutions such as the UGC and AICTE have already set up pilot projects to include online learning in their offerings, but the lack of clear guidelines moderating online learning is still the main challenge. The growing world of non-degree certifications does not include curriculum standards, pedagogical quality, or learner outcomes as these are not yet regulated. An independent quality assurance system based on cognitive growth measures beyond pure completion rates is needed, especially if edtech is seen as a necessary good in the future of Indian education.

On the other hand, there exist some pupils who seem to resist non-verbally. A considerable amount of learners, particularly those from first-tier cities and the top institutions, are now showing signs of disillusionment when it comes to over-certification. Five general modules for digital marketing are perceived as not as important as one project that can be easily characterized which has a big impact. They are, without a doubt, understanding the truth that it is not the learned thing that matters at the end of the day, rather it is what you have understood that matters.

We expect the future of Indian education to be hybrid—combining digital flexibility with human mentorship. But hybrid classroom arrangements should be carefully crafted. To tap into the potential of MOOCs and microdegrees, they must go a step further from repositories of knowledge to idea-generating ecosystems. It is, therefore, necessary to finance not just the building of the platform, but the adopting of pedagogy, the formation of a community, and the stimulation of a critical mind. The idea of open-ended lifelong learning should be recovered and separated from the monopoly of empty credentialism that it has fallen in.

Thus, we have to be determined to convey a new and radical message: the essence of something is still significant. In a world where one is repeatedly rewarded for reaching a goal quickly and more superficially than others, the ability to dive deep—think deeply, question fully, and see the connections between different ideas is a very rare and valuable asset. And the inside structure of this capability, however, shiny and trendy, cannot be created by any certificate.

The Digital Teacher Rebellion

In a corner of sunlit rural Kerala, south Indian students will listen to a retired Malayalam literature teacher of the locality, who annotates, through her smartphone, verses from Bhasa Kauthukam, about which they had not been aware. The teacher is not alone in this pursuit it seems a young educator from Lucknow who dwells on tales and their characters, and who speaks the ancient knightly language of the community while teaching Newton's laws and is seen on YouTube. As a result, the citizens are now getting interested in e-learning. It is through the personal medium and not the globally standardized plan of e-learning that the revolution is being made quiet slow and subtle.

Instantly as the pandemic passed forward the digital shift in education, the main theme that was celebrated was the exponential growth, the fast-acting, and the standardisation. Centralized information sources hastened to digitalize the content—in English in most of the cases, usually, without context and not only universal but also often devoid of the cultural element. As a result, the world of e-learning was like a clone, despite the realization, cities like Bengaluru, Bhopal, and Bikaner, etc., were, the only people accessible to were the ones who were lucky enough to be in metropolitan areas. Animated videos, monotonous narrators or talk-overs, MCQs, and pausing points, all these were main components of the educational platform during the time of study in the online environmentalist at the same time, the process of learning was kept steady and unpretentious. However, in the opinion of the learners, including the ones particularly, outside urban areas, this situation was indeed alienating. At the same time, for most of the teachers, these were rather demotivating. Soon digital even, the digital that had promised to include everyone, turned homogenized.

In the mist of the downsides above, an opposing force came out of educators who saw digital tools as not just one way of delivering but also a platform inviting to creativity. They now started to design teaching that embraced the use of authentic, local, diverse, and emotional contexts. Their experience in the field varied, and they were from sectors like academics, communities, freelancers, and NGOs as well. However, all of them had the same mindset, carrying out the process of resisting, and dictating their terms to education was not an option that they could accept. As a result they taught as if students were humans, not data points.

This revolution is the one more careful and academic before it is technical. They are steadfast in their belief that learning is not simply gobbling up the content. Good teaching is not just a mere process of elucidating concepts with the students; it goes further than that through the use of metaphor, emotion, relevance, and relationship. Furthermore, they are denying the diktat of the industrial logic that says that students are passive and knowledge is just put into them as if they were mere machines in a factory of knowledge. The teacher who has gone digital refuses to limit himself or herself to preparing the ground for the content; his or her role is mainly that of a context creator. They give meaning to the lessons; language, geography, and social imaginations are some of the factors they set lessons around. They are putting up students to feel before they think, to be human-centric before they have a mass of information to be memorized.

Let's take the example of "Bhoomi Ki Baat", the environmental education collective from Madhya Pradesh, where the teachers co-create local ecology modules with the high school tribal students. Field trips to the village are part of the instruction on soil erosion combined with Gond stories about the forest spirits. The village is videoed and pictures are taken by the students on their mobile phones. The videos are later edited using an open source software tool and uploaded to a YouTube channel which is also used for learning the curriculum of the various districts. Money is not the only thing that education channel is; it is the channel of the culture of the people.

In another part of Maharashtra, women teachers form a wave of feminism with civic teachers through the Instagram platform in a program named "Shiksha aur Shakti". The language of the messages on 'Shiksha aur Shakti' is drawn from everyday conversations of students' mothers and fathers in Marathi and the subject content flows the same way, dealing with issues such as periods, gender-based stereotypes, and constitutional rights. Each picture is accompanied by a local proverb, a real-life story, or a conversation starter. Users consist of not only students but also parents and panchayat members. A technology which is not of this unicorn and VC era it is quintessential, repetitive and humane.

People have also shown resistance in respect to the language. The thing is that online learning platforms used in the country are usually in English, and they are sometimes translated into "Hinglish" or standardised Hindi. However, India's classroom—and indeed, its cognition—is far more diverse. The math curricula in Telangana that are written in Telugu are designed with students playing around with the rhymes of the local traditional songs. The Assamese schoolteachers are taking up storytelling podcasts in the Bodo language that fit perfectly with the science topics of the curriculum. These efforts do not only make the understanding better but also make the individual recognize his or her own identity. Language is not just a container for education; it is a source of dignity.

All of the efforts made in this movement start with an observation largely disregarded by the corporate edtech sector that becomes very apparent, namely that education is relational. Students gain knowledge not only from what is being taught but also from the person who is teaching them and in what way. Online learning facilities do not exhibit their teacher's approach, neither do they provide trust, motivation, or personalized feedback like a student's video that shares a screen with him or her. However, these digital revolutionaries endeavor to make it happen. For example, some of them conduct "office hours" via WhatsApp. Other faculty members manage the calls with bands of low data. Moreover, there are educators who choose to send the message through the audio as a way of assisting the young learners who lack the internet. They not only clarify the doubts of the students but also allow time for the students to think about the issues alone. Furthermore, they are making an honest effort not to allow the human elements of teaching to be forgotten.

This protest against digital education is in no sense looking into the past or struggling against technological advancements. Instead, it is quite innovative as it tries to utilize digital platform to make teaching more sophisticated and nuanced rather than less so. There is a resistance to the delusion that knowledge can be created on an enormous scale. All students behave in the same way. A teacher's insight is replacable by a highly produced video. It rejects the idea that the transmission of knowledge can become standardized, de-skilled, or outsourced to AI. The part of the digitization of teaching that is opposing it is not taking a step back from advancing, but they are opposing the idea of impoverishing themselves in the disguise of advancing technology.

The movement is not thermal taken by any means, as it also has its associated risks. Most of these educators are acting without any backup from the institutions they work for. Their content is not of economic benefit to them. Their measurements are not really thought-provoking. They mostly operate without attracting the attention of the important decision-makers who are caught up in policies on digital education which mainly affect the stuff enrolled, the platforms, and performance dashboards. Nonetheless, the movement will move on, driven by conviction instead of obedience. They argue that fair distribution of education means that whatever we do in education must also be done in such a way as to create a just world.

This movement has several significant consequences. Through this movement, we are, first of all, made to think that the term "quality" needs to be redefined in digital education. Would quality in quantity, or in matter? Is it a spread, or are learners interested in using it? Moreover, the question arises about the trueness and adaptability of the materials to the local environment. In the case of India, NEP (National Education Policy) which is more or less devoted to local knowledge and inclusion is being overridden by edtech that is always Persuing scale not improving quality.

Further, it argues that education in the future might not digital, or physical, but may be quite a personalized and place-aware one, no matter what kind of carrier technology offers. Hybrid classes should not just be a hybrid of various forms of learning—they should also be a hybrid of the cultures and morals that those various forms come from. Thus, a futuristic classroom where technology is used to bridge a culture gap while at the same time not becoming an irrelevant gadget seems to be one important breakthrough that one should expect in the near future.

It is worth noting that the digital teacher revolt is a message to all that it is the ethical dimension not professional knowledge that guides the ways of the teacher. But for the reproductive thinking education, their richness reflects a different standpoint. As our educational system currently faces a threat of changing into a market, teachers who support it maintain it as a democratic value. The teachers who rise are the ones preserving the pure essence of knowledge—its disorder, connection, and slow, unpredictable loveliness; and, look at what they have for themselves—less or no recognition and funding at all but their love is all over the place.

We may look at these rebels as highly ignorable cases. Yet, it might be true the educators who go against the grain are just a foretaste of what the next learning age will be if we are ready to heed them, and to give them our monetary support, and most importantly, if we dare not to be conformist. Moreover, if we bear in mind that the best teaching online or in person starts with the teacher being present, open, and loving, then students will be more open-hearted toward their teachers, which is a prerequisite to a developing relationship into intellectual explorations.

Chapter 8

Digital Devotion and the New Public Square

In the 16th century, Kabir, a poet and a bhakti figure, mainly disseminated his anti-orthodox, anti-ritual, and non-distinct sacred-profanity worldview through the means of oral circulation, repetition, and the application of the cultural idioms shared among the people. Through these, Kabir might not have needed a chaupai, if he were living today. A meme sufficed with his message. A thirty-second reel hashragged into its path to virality, dropped into the online world of ordinary people. What once was the mandir or the town crossroad has now become the WhatsApp groups, Reddit threads, Instagram grids, and Twitter timelines. The sacred is the same, so as the civil, the devotion, and the dissent are not things that are gone from public life.

They have been, in fact, reformatted. In this chapter, that very reformatting is scrutinized. It seeks to know in what way the new technological spaces have remodeled our public as well as our inner worlds.

This is not just the story of disruption. It is reinvention, too. There is the way in which the traditional customs—be it the rituals, the mythologies, the morals—get reborn in the digital age. They are re-codified as they get mixed with the viral looks, and are then thrown back into the world, blazed with more power. The digital stages for communication aren't balanced.

They prompt, actually they curate visibility, reward emotion, prioritize speed, and atomize discourse.

Nonetheless, even under such considerations, both individuals and communities will be working within the constraints of the said digital platforms, to find out modes of visualization beyond particularly the power of social media, which may be radical, which may be reductive, and in many cases, revealing –ever so in their disclosure of partial or substantial truth. Let's say a meme now. It is often seen as frivolous by those who dismiss it offhand, but actually, it is one of the most flexible and agile forms of ideological expression in contemporary India.

A well-timed meme on Dalit assertion, for example, is capable of being more reproaching to the piety of the Savarna than a policy paper.

Also a doctored image of a political leader turned into satire could be successful in minutes what street protest cannot be achieved in days of protest.

In essence, memes become transit points of cultural ammunition and moral shorthand. They are the ones that shuttle back and forth transmitting the values, creating the allegiances, and marking who belongs in the sphere of the knowing. Similar to the mantras of the past, their power is usually not the content but the rhythm, the repetition, and the recognition. To be in the light of a meme is to be part of the semiotic tribe.

Nevertheless, the public square we use today is not at all times fully democratic. The architecture of the square, so to say, is mediated by algorithms. Not all voices have the same chance to reach the top. Though a few minorities have successfully exploited platforms to become visible, others either remained down below or became the objects of hate by the virality of hate. Hashtags have proven to be the modern-day counterparts of the ancient slogans and they can do much to promote societal wellness or work in the opposite direction. These are such hashtags as #JusticeForAsifa or #IndiaAgainstCorruption: the hashtags that caused a wave of people to start and join the mobilization for a new-value society and thus draw attention to institutional failures and the guilty accountable. The pattern in both cases was that many people—including both activists and those accidentally involved in the process—participated in the demonstration. The hashtag was the core of the organization, as well as the directed moral impulse. It transformed anger into moral duty, and tears into signs of the sentence. The same tool, however, can have a different effect: it can polarize, victimize, and descript. Through the conversion of feelings into surveillance, hashtag nationalism, which is frequently related to hashtag vigilantism, has become a dangerous form of sentimentality. The new public square is like the old one, prone to demagoguery.

And yet, the fact that these platforms have opened up new avenues and capacities is beyond question. The networks that were once confined to mass media and consequently marginalized and excluded—Dalit rights, LGBTQIA+ recognition, environmental justice—are now being strengthened by online networks. The leaders might not go around in robes or guide armies, but they do alter policy agendas, they have power over language and they hold a whole flock of followers. Social media activism exhibits a moral dimension of more performance than real action. By each share, comment, and repost, one becomes a member of a certain group, and one's act becomes a signal of one's good will in the community. Even when critics disparage it by the term "slacktivism," they often remain ignorant of the simple fact that mere attention or exposure can reshape the rules of discourse. The digital public is not at all politics, yet it seems that it has come to be the politics' driving force.

Admittedly, it is not only in the streets of metropolitan cities that our mobile phones now serve as sacred places. This is not surprising given the virtuality of everything in the midst of the pandemic. Demam is a creative community space in the heart of Setia Alam that redefines Shah Alam as a city of creativity. In most cases, Covid-19's impact on urban space has largely been negative, with people deserting the areas due to the fear of infections and lack of social activities that used to happen before the pandemic. The total death toll in New York alone is more than in some countries. Other popular areas like Birmingham's Bull Ring and Oxford Street also saw a reduction in footfall by 10% and 41% respectively. Once crowded with a density of up to14,000 people per square mile, Manhattan was suddenly empty, and a lot of stores and bars are closed or out of business.

This chapter problematizes the given issues to find out the truth by which it is known, that is the theme covered in this chapter. It follows up on how political discourse, mythic imagination, and spiritual practice are the main objects of digital development. Not like the memes, hashtags, or devotional apps are treated as a way to distract from what is important in life; in the chapter, they make sense of where serious things happen today. The digital world is not somewhere else. There, but nowhere else, are convictions born, kinship tested, persons to be made, and hopes to be transferred. To figure out the new moral topography in India, one needs to consult not only the scriptures and the manifestos but also the trending tabs.

We are going to ask the question: who are the new priests of virality? What type of role do memes play as the modern figures of myths, encapsulating centuries of ideology in the form of pixels and punch lines? When does a hashtag metamorphose into a movement, and when does it degenerate into a mob? Are screens capable of keeping the sacred or are they merely using it as a dollar sign? Do the digital rituals empower the faith of people, or it is just the pretense of it? And what happens when politics and religion start talking in the same algorithmic language?

They are not merely academic inquiries since they reach the heart of the speech India uses to talk to itself—about justice, about divinity, about who belongs. The virtual square is under construction again and again. The languages of resistance and religion, of esse and enigma, are transmitted through the fibre-optics. To be ignorant of them is to miss the place where the meaning is today created and redefined. This chapter functions as a public call to pay attention, to listen attentively, and to be indignant critically to the screens that are the core of the collective moral stage of today.

The Rise of the Insta-Guru

Just a while ago in India, being a spiritual leader was a result of many years of ascetic training, institutional approval, and it was slowly gained through a good reputation over the years. They used to pass on their knowledge in conversations that took place under banyan trees or inside ashrams, through pamphlets, radio talk etc. Today, those very individuals or their successors are the ones that are coming from ring lights, captioning wisdom in 30-second reels, and live streaming satsangs to millions of people. The digital era did not just change the way spiritual knowledge is obtained and spread, but it also significantly transformed the issues of who is listened to, how trust is created, and what counts as spiritual authority. This is where we can see the rise of the Insta-Guru—a new kind of teacher for a new kind of public.

The separative characteristic of this person is not only the subject and contents of their speech, but their training in performance, aesthetics and platform development. In order to succeed in the digital spiritual economies, it is necessary to be as capable of stirring the Vedantic non-dualism as of employing the Instagram functionalities. Many key leaders in today's spiritual intelligence community are carrying out their work on the corner of devotion, self-help, and lifestyle branding. The advice they offer is small, algorithmically tuned, and typically presented in the language of personal growth. They might refer to the Bhagavad Gita while at the same time employing such visuals that are used only in presentations for the TED Talks of the world or, alternatively, a productivity app. On top of that, spirituality is now available on your screen.

This is not a minor change—it reveals more profound cultural and economic shifts. With attention becoming the most sought after commodity in digital markets, spiritual teachers not only face each other in the competition but also have to deal with other things that inhabit the user's scroll looking for the very same attention: dance trends, makeup tutorials, breaking news, political drama. Religious leaders to remain in the arena of public opinion must simplify complicated things, teach in a style corresponding to the tempo of the social media feed, and also make the concept of transcendence shareable. Given these conditions, quite a few are able to maintain their influence. Just to illustrate, Sadhguru has an online following that is almost as big as the one that Bollywood stars or prime ministers have. His YouTube channel is subscribed to by over ten million people; his Instagram page is abuzz with succinct wisdom and wellness techniques. Not only he but others, such as Gaur Gopal Das, and Art of Living's Sri Sri Ravi Shankar have also kept up very well surprisingly, they merge digital attraction with ancient teachings. Their platform is the world, their fans have no borders, and the currency is their influence.

What happens when a spiritual lesson turns into a show? Where gurus are expected not only to teach but also to amuse, not only to guide but to "trend"? The question is whether the incentive structures of social media—that quest for likes, shares, and virality—fit the ethical and contemplative requirements that true spiritual traditions have. There is always a danger that the teachings are oversimplified because of the need to become motivational platitudes, left without their cultural and historical background or philosophical depth. A subtle, complex concept like detachment (vairagya) could easily change into an empty slogan of disengagement. Similarly, the doctrine of karma would be narrowed down to mere cause-and-effect actions. Unlike traditional dharma, the Sanskrit term becomes self-help for self-transformation. The Insta-Guru has to be careful not to be a cartoon version of spiritual wisdom dressed for the attention economy that highly rates the rapidness and not the stillness.

However, it would be too simplistic to brush the movement aside as being only about surface matters or as being purely opportunistic. It is through such channels, in many cases, the first real connection with Indian philosophical traditions is made for the online generation, namely younger people. The Reels on mindfulness, live Q&As on emotional resilience, or stories about compassion and karma might not be a substitute for learning within the four walls of schools, but they are, at least, like an invitation to open a door. They give words to the loss of meaning, guidelines to make sense of the world, and a sense of connection so that the digital life being led feels less fragmented. Additionally, a section of the audience not part of religious institutions is the one that is taking part in and absorbing it more, so to them the Insta-Guru is not much of a preacher but more of a companion: one who uses local language, acknowledges present-day problems, and gives moral support without relying on the ideology.

Most importantly, the digital guru is no more the preserve of a male Brahminical elder in the traditional garb of saffron color. The representation of women, Dalits, queer persons, and diasporic Indians in this space - not just as those who consume knowledge, but also as those who are knowledgeable and creative - signifies a quiet but strong democratization. Examples of this trend include Nithya Shanti, a former corporate professional turned mindfulness instructor, whose talks are a blend of regular life stories and Buddhist wisdom. And the YouTube channel of Devdutt Pattanaik, which is one that has the author interpreting Hindu mythology from a queer perspective, and the channel is so acclaimed so as to reach out to millions. Also, the soaring popularity of Instagram accounts like "Brown Girl Therapy", which in addition to South Asians in a global context utilize their speech to inform their services, infuse therapy jargons with eastern wisdom. The spirituality of today is not just about the digitization of religion; it is about plurality, contestation, and a complete reconfiguration.

Nevertheless, the very process of democratisation brings forward new issues. Who has the right to decide who has spiritual authority while the platforms do not guarantee the content's genuineness? Is it conceivable that the algorithms will be able to make the difference between a true spiritual mentor and a showy imposter? In the context of this new reality where "followers" are both disciples and metrics, what does the responsibility element look like? In this era of selfishness (seva) going side by side with influencer economies being money-oriented, how can we possibly address the heightened ethical space?

Of course, the situation is not easy at all. Several of the gurus decide to use their platforms as a source of income for themselves through various means like e.g., offering online courses against money, one-on-one discussions for a fee, charitable products. At the same time, others are against the idea of treating charitable and religious matters as consumer goods. They refuse to accept gifts or keep their digital activity commercial-free. The problem of all of them lies exactly in the discrepancy between what they say and the means of communication. Now, when they went online, it's also a time when they ventured in a world where attention must be struggled for, startup fake culture is prevalent and where boundaries between spiritual teacher, wellness entrepreneur, and content creator are blurred.

Still, could it not be the case that the digital interface is nothing but a cover-up to their mainstay of their unquenchable demand? The reason why the Insta-Guru enjoys such widespread support might be traced back to the very needs that are aggravated by the pandemic. The pervasiveness of digital spirituality somehow matches the dramatic growth of the anxiety, depression, and confusion experienced by the urban and youth populations. Instagram has transformed from a leisure space into the Land of Promise or in reality, it's the place to which people turn to when their lives have lost meaning, and they are at their wits' end. Hence, the popularity of the Insta-Guru is almost like a reflection of the kind of group orientations we currently have. People interrupt the silence of the algorithm to find yet the sound of guidance.

The potential is great and the dangers cannot be ignored. Spirituality shown on a screen as one of its features might fill the gap that was left by the decline of organizations based on spirituality in society. On the other hand, at the same time, it can be perilous - implying that it will solve problems for an individual which are in fact very complex and lead to a situation that individuals are provided with ready-made self-help mantras. It can even show you a one-minute piece of prey, right, which yes, you will be inspired, but instead of that fast track, it would be the wise, arduous task of being a moral person that cannot be replenished that it is to be mine.

Whether there is such a thing as followers being able to recognize the difference or spiritual influence is going through just another version of lifestyle branding is the larger question. The issue of recognizing or rejecting a spiritual leader will be the crux of the problem left for the followers to solve.

What is still obvious is the complete transformation of Indian spiritual life that the digital age has installed. The ethnic communities are there even though there was an introduction of new methods of teaching, different people, and various digital platforms. The teacher-student relationship over the years has not been wiped out from this universe; it only changed base and became DMs, direct communication with the spiritual leader through comments, and interaction with him through live broadcast.

Creator of changes is today's society that is busy buzzing with hashtags in a worldwide network share goal arena. Silence wants to transmit its signal at the same rate as the swipe signal.

Not only the words mean the future of Indian spirituality, but the method by which they were delivered will also play a very significant part in the future of the Indian spirituality. Also, the gurus did not just turn themselves into digital creatures but they have planted new seeds in their followers' hearts and minds through that digital process.

Transformation of the stage from the real to the cyberspace, and the fragmenting of the relationship between the spiritual leader and his disciples, through technologies like streaming, social networks or mobile devices open up a multitude of opportunities for leveraging the virtual platform. Still, the most crucial of these will be transforming a disciple into a flame carrier, communicator of the teaching force.

True grace is not worn in public space alone, following the precepts. Only the interior conditions, the special onlooker understands, and can shine his torch and direct it where the audience will stick. The continuous presence of such encounter, awaited or unexpected, breathes, feels our human fellowship in the link, a bond in the happening of the sharing of good, cheerful events, of y'unity, love, of grace, and joy.

Memes as Modern Mantras

There is a high probability today that a meme to be used strategically and at the right moment will have a greater impact and reach in the culture than a public talk or a bestselling book. Animated into a few short seconds, made powerful by sarcasm, replayed by repetition and perfectly timed, memes have become an unmatched language of dialogue on the digital platform. In India that does not lack in fables, slogans, and emblems, the meme is not just something fit for entertainment. It has become the carrier of all ideological stances, and the disseminator of new and old stories that are both personal and public, and it has been the driving force of grassroots creation of myths in recent decades. Memes are the reflections and at the same time the roots of the culture of the times.

What makes memes uniquely influential in the Indian context is that they have a very smooth transition from the old forms of communication. The primary means of communication in India, the oral tradition, has in its fold compact, repeatable structures called shlokas, dohas, and proverbs, for example, which they used to convey their ideas. These structures were stayable, carried with them the power of recall and were socially engaging. What the meme does is get to this structure but makes it go viral through the benefits of the digital: virality, multimedia layering, and instant reproducibility. Hence the meme becomes the new mantra not essentially a way of passing the wisdom of life but rather of the collective subconscious.

This new status of the meme as a central figure of communication is a consequence of a number of factors. In the condition of the content being oversaturated in the media environment, the meme still acts as a driver of the conversation by employing its simplicity, sharpness, and stickiness. In a democracy which is a mixture of various backgrounds, the meme finds success in being both effervescent and polemical. Moreover, in the economy of attention, the meme circulates as a piece of information, as a means of knowledge, and as entertainment. Actually, its image plus caption formula often contains a pop culture and religious nexus, which is a vantage point that allows it to directly reach the di

Look at how potent political memes in India have become! The politicians and parties can hardly get people to vote for them by talking up issues. In these national elections, memes are used as political propaganda. Eloquent as they are, they hit a hundred birds with one stone saying volumes of which one is strength, nationalism, divine authority without needing other words. Modi's image, for example, can depict him as a lion, a monk, or both, and will deliver those messages to the audience. And at the same time, the old ones were worth only 20 others throwing sp

Political inclination is not the only front where the battle is taking place. The memes have become not just ideological battlegrounds but a war in every major axis of Indian public life such as religion, gender, caste and economy. For example, think of Hindu nationalist accounts that create memes as instruments of power for the supremacy of the culture through laughter about secularism or liberalism at the same time. Mainly, these memes mix images of gods, scriptures, ancient characters with slogans of nationalism or the thoughts of modern politics. The catchy feature of these memes is the blend of high emotion with laugh lines. Repetition, however, is their source of addictive power. They function, in essence, as a ritual, a daily confession of one's identity, tribe, and worldview.

Furthermore, there is a new species of content creators who act like digital mythicizers. A lot of meme pages nowadays are followed by more people than local newspapers have. Not only are these pages not just collectors of jokes but also active predictors of the future of culture. The distinction between satire and propaganda is easily lost. On the one side, the power is criticized and hypocrisies are exposed. On the other, they can very clearly be seen as discriminatory, reiterating stereotypes about minorities, marginalized sexes, or opposing ideologies. The moral issues involved here are very high because the memes are consumed with the goal to convince not to argue.

Moreover, even the structure of memes is apt for ideological sedimentation. The repetitiveness of templates enables ideas to travel from one person to another without any explanation. A meme that shows "X happened under Congress, Y under BJP" is considered valid proof, however, if this statement is not supported by facts. The visual effect makes it look authoritative: neat fonts, apparent pictures, and the idea of being viral add to the perception of being authentic. Memes give the feeling of knowing, minus the hassle of analyzing. This is not a defect of the format but the inherent character of the format. And, this format is a success.

However, there is a shadow side to this cultural coin. Memes are also a form of liberation, especially when it comes to persons who have traditionally been excluded from participation in elite platforms. Dalit memes, feminist memes, queer memes—are all are very clear examples of memes that do not respect the one-way message structure of ideological messaging.

These memes, in fact, resist, laugh at, and reframe the narratives right from the bottom. Through ridicule, protest, and a fresh framing of the narrative, these digital memes make subversive art, which questions the legitimacy of the dominant narrative. A Dalit meme making fun of an upper-caste savarna that feels fragile is not just a joke but a social act, the taking back of digital space. In these subcultures, memes have turned into a form of oral resistance which is as important as the slogans chanted at protests.

It is a fact that several of the most powerful social movements in India were driven by the power of memes. For example, during the anti-CAA protests, Instagram accounts including @withkashmir and @artisansresist posted visually stunning memes that had qualities of memes as well: emotionally appealing, loaded with ideas, and incredibly shareable. In the farmer protests, the visual memes created waves of mockery against the government for doing nothing and films with farmers as the only ones who resist corporate power. These memes not only served the purpose of informing but also the purpose of organising the public.

Not less important at all, the special power of the meme largely comes from its ability to present serious criticism hidden behind a jest. This feature is especially notable in conditions where the freedom of speech is to a greater extent regulated. Because of the ambivalent character of the joke, judgment, memes can manage to escape public detection. A meme can easily surpass the level of the comment in a column. It is able to mock a godman, disapprove a law, or ironically present a policy theme, at the same time, making people laugh. This indeterminacy that is aimed at avoiding control provides both protection and capacities but, on the other hand, brings about the situation when one has to deal with responsibility.

Furthermore, memes are oversimplifying human expression, suppressing negotiation, and thus they are a threat to modern forms of communication. Indeed, memes are the consequence of human expression that is stunted and that results in simplified, unelaborate thoughts and polemics independent of culture or situation. They do not teach by stating points but rather through explaining that which is already accepted. They simplify to the extent of fascination.

Even in this simplification, there is a certain brilliance. The primary task that memes accomplish is the recording of cultural history in their first editions. They register not only the feelings of a society in the development of a benign sense of humor but also through the cacophony of irascibility, shock, and reverence. There might be a time when scholars will explore meme archives as they did pamphlets or folk songs today. Scarred with digital signals, that is, in a resultant of this, digital folklore will say more than speeches and songs ever could. National mood memes make.

In this respect, memes are ideal for explaining concepts, attracting the attention of indifferent students, and better understanding ideology. Progressives may utilize them to energize social change. Opinion polls may use them. On the one hand, the ability of memes is vast, but, on the other hand, there are many related risks such as disinformation, trolling, hate speech, and simplification. Memes, like fire, bring light and warmth, and likewise scorch and smok.

The importance of India's digital culture without their memes is rather challenging as memes have become the essence and the means of communication and the two together have become the subject matter and the instrument. They don't respond to the public vitriol but are the ones who really shape it. These two are the mutually complementing notions with a lot of interconnections and can sometimes result in the different issues that we confront with. They play the role of new mantras for the people: echoed, remixed, reinterpreted until they cannot be told apart as being ironic or truthful. Moreover, whether they ridicule, mobilise, or create a myth, one thing is for certain— memes are not weak.

Hashtag Yatra was started

The advent of a digital front in the Anna Hazare-led movement against corruption, during the sit-in at the Ramlila Maidan, in Delhi back in 2011, revealed new trends of virtual participation. Traditional placard-waving activities along with streaming live news channels were complemented by a new online movement that was mainly characterized by the use of hashtags on social media. Featured #IndiaAgainstCorruption was one of the first steps that people used to utilize the new powerful tool called hashtag. Such a deep impact it had on the society that nobody has ever witnessed this on the previous several hundred years. As a result, the online hashtags not only showed the public opinion but also changed, improved, or diverted the course of political and legal affairs in the country.

The concept of the hashtag seems to be easily understood: a sharp sound that draws attention to a word or a paragraph. Yet, its significance in the digital public space of India is profound. It serves as an electronic record, a battle flag, and a direction pointer at the same time. Messages like #MeTooIndia, #JusticeForManisha, or #StandWithFarmers are expressions that bring hope and direction. They do often come before the change itself or they do give impetus to it to happen.

For example, let's talk about the unfortunate case of the 2020 gang-rape incident in Hathras of Uttar Pradesh. A barbaric act that was coupled with caste-based violence, and quite likely, the police force's cover-up could have represented a mere shadow of what has happened in regional news. However, #JusticeForManisha not only brought grave indignation to people but also initiated a nationwide tirade against the system. Social media users unified and made their voices heard through the sharing of their personal experiences with the crime, calling for a change in the law, as well as giving the latest updates. As of a few days, the whole matter was reported as the hottest topic in almost all news outlets. The authorities were informing society about the ongoing situation via updates. The police officers and the politicians, even the ones that ignored the topic earlier, had to share their opinions publicly. The local government eventually officially announced the formation of a Special Investigation Team. That was the moment when the hashtag acted as public opinion that the authorities had to deal with: thanks to its continuous presence all that while, the issue was never out of sight for the institutions.

However, it is a fact that not all hashtags have the sad part of life as their origin. A good example of these is #IndiaAgainstCorruption, which is an instrument for wider political organisation. What has made it one of the most memorable hashtags in history is the fact that it has united both the digital and the offline world. It has made it clear that social media can not only provide information, but can also be an effective organising tool. The necessary staff was found, money was raised, and the sites of the protests were agreed upon—all this was done by Facebook and Twitter. The digital flow was the pulse of the revolution. Last but not least, the movement had as one of its key results the formation of the Aam Aadmi Party, which globally was a very rare case. This was where a political party went to the people and asked for their vote by using a hashtag created by a social movement on digital platforms.

Hashtags, although frequently vocal online, are not always the bearers of institutional change. The movement of #MeTooIndia offers a case study that shows the point from different angles. Starting in 2018 and with contributions from various sectors, the movement not only unmasked male domination but also went after the already established hierarchy within the country. It did have some of its positive notes—such as the resignation of journalist M.J. Akbar, who was the major culprit—but most of the demands regarding the establishment of laws and policies in the legal system of the workplace were not addressed. The real achievement, however, was the shift in the popular narrative of the Indian society, where concepts of consent, harassment, and gender dynamics were rigorously debated through the lens of urban India. That being the case, laws were not an output of that acceptability change, but rather a change in language that took place.

Yet do we have the real impact of hashtag activism that goes beyond the virtual sphere? Many consider those who are active online to be half-hearted. Hashtags can be popular for two days, and then we forget about them. The time will come when the phrase "slacktivism" which was invented to describe acts of low digital activity in societal engagement and the danger of liking being seen as leadership, or retweeting as revolution, will materialize. Nevertheless, such a critique risks ignoring the multi-dimensional character of social movements. They are capable of reshaping the Overton window if they are not followed by policy modifications. They can redefine the boundaries of the public discourse. They can change the prevalent point of view from the global informants, the continuously disinterested observers, to co-conspirators.

Furthermore, the trending of topics due to hashtags is not a sign of being shallow rather the phrases are more available. It is a matter to be stressed that hashtags are not the same as the policy papers or protest permits. The hashtags are without an authorisation requirement... They are democratic because they give the voice to the people. Dalit teenagers in Bihar are as free to convey their thoughts as Supreme Court lawyers in Delhi. In a country with the deepest divisions in language, caste, and geographical locations hashtags serve as things that bring in all the diversity and people participate in ... The mobile phone hence becomes not only the phone but a loudspeaker for people.

Still, this visibility can lead to two outcomes. On the one hand, some of the hashtags are received very well while the other part of the hashtags is not so good. For instance, many times in response to a Black Lives Matter campaign, we see initiatives wanting to say that all lives are valuable, which, in effect neutralises the original campaign... As a result of that, different groups share a tag with the same acronym for opposing goals, and a new conversation can be started. On the other hand, the bots that compose posts can be part of a plan to discredit somebody or make odd attempts to unite everybody on the same side. Therefore, at the moment, when one or the other of these two conditions is the case, the hashtag is engaged in an empowerment process but in the latter case, it is a battlefield. A hashtag that is trending can be equally a device for propaganda as for the representation of popular emotions.

This is the point where the big role of the platforms is recognized. Twitter's trending algorithm as well as the news feed logic of Facebook and Instagram's explore tab are all factors that determine the ultimate power of hashtags. The systems used mainly or only to be in the application of celebrities, political, media, or influencers present besides, are more certain to be victorious. At the same time, the campaigns that are hyperlocal or which don't belong to a mainstream category are often on their own in the struggles associated with ... And the platform logic is not interested in anything like since it is in no competition with the general public concern. As a consequence, a movement's digital success is linked to how positive it is seen by the media rather than the clearness of the actions it encourages.

But there is no doubt that if digital fluency and moral clarity converge, the result can be extremely significant. The 2020–2021 farmer protests were a case in point where a powerful confluence of these two assets was vividly shown. Through the use of messaging on social media, the Indian peasants' movement of the past year has not only resonated in the country but has also reverberated globally. Global icons like Rihanna and Greta Thunberg were among those who went to bat for the movement by the use of their power of influence. This was not appreciated by the Indian government, and they had to face a situation of unrest that was very different from the ones they were used to. Diplomacy, police raids against activists organisations and the country's global image were some of the areas actually affected by hashtags here.

Of prime concern, the visual language the movements of the hashtags in India have developed. It was observed that Twitter was not alone being used anymore it was being partnered with infographics, a lot of archive clips, memes that are satirical, and documentary videos. Hash-tagged calls are sent via WhatsApp in such a manner that the message goes in with hymn music or slogans that depict love for the country. The Instagram feature that swipes with legal points in various languages is on display. The protest is no longer one-worded—it is also described, patterned and performed. Though this method widens the audience it also requires more and more media literacy from the people sending and receiving it.

But the latter, albeit strong and resonant, can not fill in for the vacuum of legislative reforms. They can initiate, propagate, stigmatize, and energize the people but are unable to pass laws of the country. The outcome of what occurred after the hashtag stops trending is in fact the real barometer to measure the campaign's success. A policy change? A court intervention? Some cultural alterations? If none of the above, the hashtag is at risk of becoming exactly what its opponents fear it will be: a digital show without any political substance.

Yet it cannot be overlooked how the digital campaigns have drastically changed the landscape. To what extent have the hashtags changed the landscape? First, they;ve introduced new members of society, which have partially destroyed the hierarchical structure of powerful people and in addition, have increased(d) the number of citizens who exercise their democratic rights. Even in a country with over 900 million voters, but with a high illiteracy rate and little knowledge of their civil rights, they have still managed to get the message with the use of hashtags—albeit a quite unstable, superficial, or incomplete message.

India's hashtag movements are set apart by the fact that they are not a sole player but are rather an intersection of traditional community activities. The hashtag does not undermine the significance of the rally, the hunger strike, or the hartal, rather it gives them another channel or track, (and) in many cases an ample shelf-life and span of reach. Right now, just like the azaadi slogans of the Independence movement that went from pamphlets to poems, digital protests take place in the public square via the hashtag. The vehicle for the message has changed; the essence of the message remains the same.

It follows that the subject of Indian hashtags is indeed one of real-time dialogue the country has with its own ethics, culture, and overall public image. The subjects are not exclusively hashtags; they are the very parameters of the nation. Whether they disseminate or shrink in virality, they have to leave an indelible mark on the democratic experiment in India.

In all of these: Words made History

A woman in Pune, at 68, opens Kashi Vishwanath temple's live stream on her smartphone. With the start of the broadcast, we see priests performing an arti, the chants in the background, and the digital flowers drifting across the screen. Simultaneously, high up in a tall building in Bengaluru, a coder is listening to Vedic shlokas. And in Delhi, a young Muslim woman is looking up the app of Qur'an with AI-annotated tafsir (interpretations) to help her understand the verses she's memorizing. Spirituality in India is no more dependent on just a spiritually endowed place or even a sacred place — it lives and vibrates in the circuits of a 4G network and in the click of the fingers.

To see how technology has revolutionized our religious experience, we may look no further than the plethora of faith apps, online streaming of rituals, and virtual pilgrimages. The transformation has been so deep, yet there is little literature on this topic available right now. In a country where faith is often embedded in the social, political, and cultural fabric, the transition to digital religiosity is not just a matter of convenience, but rather a change in the way we think about access, authority, and authenticity.

In the last decade, apps such as Divine India, Shrimad Bhagavad Gita, Islam 360, SikhNet, and Daily Darshan have had a combined number of users in millions. The apps' main selling point is their convenience. Everything is available to the user at any time s/he needs without any obstruction. Aarti can be watched live, bhajans can be watched on demand, and azan and the names of God can be realized for the people going out through the medium of a mobile phone only. Also, scripture-explanation and songs done by Guru with a subtitle in the language have been put within reach of emigrants in the internet age. These are the people who will benefit from the new digital platforms.

Despite time getting lost in the process, digitization of religion is a step change in theology and the arts. Not only are the myriad of ways to access the sacred being remade, but also the very definitions of the holy—the very ideas and places associated with the religious—have been reconfigured. When we looked at the way of living in India, we could observe that it was very much a grounded religious worship ground from a cultural and religious point of view. The mere sight of temple towns, riverside ghats, dargahs, gurudwaras, and shrines helped the villagers in their social life and in ritual practices as well. Even festivals were done in a collective manner and those who wanted to go on a pilgrimage had to go there physically and practice bodily austerities. On the one hand, the present move is enduringly engaging the self and is even transforming the idea of the sacred. For example, one can circumambulate online in a 3D model of the Shirdi temple using a VR headset. Furthermore, one can perform the ritual of e-daan, wherein the priest is not present but the ritual can be carried out through the transferring of digital offerings. The credit for spiritual merit is now trackable, recordable, and even the matter of the game can be gambled or wagered.

Furthermore, the current trend allows the display of virtual pilgrimages as a striking example. When the outbreak of COVID-19 forced everyone to stay indoors, the leaders of the Tirumala Tirupati Devasthanams, Vaishno Devi Board, and ISKCON temples had to upgrade the worship experience of their devotees. So, they organised online live darshans and virtual pilgrimages of deities. Surprisingly, the feasibility of these facilities was not just confined to the end of the pandemic, but they became established forms of worship for some groups of followers. Most worshippers refer to the virtual darshan as a complement or a substitute for physical yatra. Nevertheless, the old concept of pilgrimage, which generally implies acts of penance, physical travel, and communal worship, was now transported into the digital world. Abandonment without a journey of spiritual consciousness is filled with the warmth of continuity. Thus the futuristic spiritual experience is the one that can be easily paralleled, can be undisturbed, and can run seamlessly along with daily life. However, when religiosity becomes so accessible, may it seem incomplete without its revolutionary flavor?

All these things are questions of utmost importance for theology. It was not clear what the effect on rituals would be, translated through secreens. Furthermore, could a priest's singing over Wi-Fi be as effective as using a ton or a brass gong? Can one still gain merit through virtual engagement with God? Therefore, the religious institutions have had to invent a new type of life. With carefulness, they have been trying to keep the traditional ritual ritual untouched, maintaining thus the difference between the material and the digital. They have also been quite eager. They are employing digital teams to run their YouTube channels. Swamis are using Instagram Live to give their discourses. The Sikh centers are accepting online payments for their services. Spirituality is not only telecasted but also marketed.

It appears most strikingly that the far-reaching transformation has occurred in the persons who have authority in matters religious. Over many centuries, the bearers of the spiritual riches have been found in places that are not accessible by the majority of people, thus were dubbed the priests, ulema, gurus, and professional scholars of religious institutions. However, in the present immeasurable diversity of content creators very few of which are formally trained religionists have vast numbers of followers.

An engaging explainatory narrative of the Ramayana in colloquial Hindi by a charismatic Youtuber that appeals to the mass can compete with Hollywood movies in Youtube for millions of views. One of those Islamic scholars with a smartphone could choose he/she charges a sheep in answer to fatwa questions asked through their WhatsApp by those Muslims that they are the imam of.

However appealing this democratization movement sounds, it is not without challenges. The thin line between the genuineness of the followers and the virality generated to enter into it is crucial. Clickbait spirituality is making huge inroads. The religious messages are designed to be catchy and not deep. A well-simplified Gita quote on Instagram may become a viral topic rather than a complicated issue of dharma being discussed. Just as algorithms delight in outrage and spectacle, spiritual topics are similarly transformed into sectarian conflicts or reactionaries. Blessings turn into a propaganda machine. The divine screen becomes infected with the divisive principles of social media often.

For instance, those same digital channels have widened the spectrum of beliefs and introduced novelties. Clubhouse is a place where interfaith dialogues happen. LGBT+ religious groups with a mission of inclusion present their versions on the internet. ShareChat and Moj are sites where regional devotional traditions have their say and make themselves known to others and the rest. Bhakti poetry of Maharashtra, Sufi music from Punjab, and Jain discourses in Gujarati spread quickly. In fact, there are indications that the internet, rather than dismantling, is only relocating India's spiritual diversity.

As a result, digitally-fueled personal spiritual practices have become prevalent. Computer-generated but interactive communication with temple art is one of the phenomenal hybrid forms of devotion. Sattva, a meditation app, has combined ancient chants with biometric feedback. The faithful have the option to virtually light 'diyas' in a digital Hanuman temple and receive push notifications of auspicious timings. A religiously inclined app is following the footsteps of online behavioral tech, nudging, reminding, and gamifying through various devotional tasks. It is true that spiritual life is increasingly being reshaped like a habit-forming design.

Yet, behind the scenes, the most important human desires of all continue as always: connection, transcendence, purpose. No matter if it is by a Vedic chant on YouTube, or by a 5-minute AI-assisted morning prayer, digital devotion is an eternal form of spiritual hunger, only presented through new grammars. The problem is not in whether the technology is able to act as a mediator for the sacred. What really matters is if we are being aware of the way this technology will influence the sacred.

For this, a new type of theological literacy is required—from those involved and from the institutions. If through the code, the reconfiguration of the sacred is taking place, who will be the writers of the code? If religious apps not only select which verses to be highlighted, the rituals to be performed, and the stories to be told but also narrow down the issues, then they will be really exercising strong interpretative rights. Apps algorithms and their logic are not easy to challenge or even to explain to others, thus different from the temple priest, who is of clear choice. On the other hand, who is the one to decide which devotion form will be integrated into the interface and which one will not be?

We must take into account the datafication of devotion as well. Data on user behaviour such as how much time you spend on a mantra, the gods you follow, and when you access the app are being mined by religious apps. The collected data is convertible to money, can be profiled, and ads can be targeted so that you buy more. What is the issue about the numerous data points of extracting out the sacred? What happens when the divine interaction not only is related to the screen but also surveillance-related?

Despite the abovementioned issues, it would not be a wise decision to say the sacred screens are inherently corrupt or reductive. To millions of people they serve as a spiritual bridge. Diaspora Indians use them to reconnect with their lineage and the geographical area. While the elderly use them to shatter isolation. Physically disabled faithful can use them for inclusion. The technology is not substituting spirituality—it is remaking its accessibility and aesthetics.

It is true that there is a new form of spiritual language being developed now, and one of the main features of it is its interactivity. Mass media logic is also one of its shapes. It is not only true that this digital transformation is the same with the dissemination of the script but that the smartphones of today are performing the same function. The acts have no longer the traditional confined space and have become mobile.

Eventually, the belief in the sacredness of the screen does not negate the sacred—it prompts us to rethink where it is situated. Not only in stone temples or at mountain shrines, but also in pixels, platforms, and networks. Not only in the priest's voice, but also in the believer's fingertips absently going through a morning mantra. And a posteriori, this is also religious.

Chapter 9

Women, Power, and the Digital Gaze

A woman in India, when she takes space on the internet, can find herself to be the target of ridicule. She experiences this if she does a video tutorial on a makeup look, gives her opinion, or simply uploads a photo of her without the caption, the reactions can be instantaneous and brutal which could include threats of sexual violence, etc. For Indian women, the online world doesn't just exist as a supplement to the public sphere, in fact, it is the place where they struggle and their mere presence is still a challenge.

The notion of visible but still contested, mentioned in the opening lines: "What is it like for women to live, produce, resist or rule in the face of the digital gaze? How does the visibility of the platforms that are structured, in whose interest? Who is spoken to, who is pushed out, and who is transformed by the algorithm?" is set of the issues raised. We see that digital space is a trap where public opinion controls the subjects and their reaction to the contrast is real. From social media to the startup companies in Bangalore and from troll farms to the girls' windows in the evening, the Indian digital world is being gendered in obvious and hidden ways. Women are the new rulers of the digital age, they not only become the target of the digital gaze; they are also the ones who, by wise using, shape opinions, and reverse the rebelling situation.

Leaving out the amazing features of the modern internet, including that now, the world can be seen as a homogenous entity, that there are no more gatekeepers, and that those who lived on the peripheries are likewise given a voice, the internet has emerged as an entity that is still the mirror image of the society of those that laugh at them. The reason why this is referred to as a virtual pandemic is that it is not an occasional occurrence of cyber-violence against gender, but rather a constant threat against it. Doxing, deepfakes, revenge porn, rape threats, and mob harassment practically belong to the same family--ones allowed to exist through certain decisions that coders, owners, and management of platform content make, such as algorithms, and moderation against nuance and non-western contexts. A woman who is active in any of the fields mentioned (or all at the same time), especially when it comes to caste, sexuality, politics, not only constructs gender but also is the one at the receiving end of all the attacks. Some digital technologies are set to carry inequalities and reproduce them more carefully than before as they reflect and even deepen the logic of current power relations.

However, despite the hostile architecture, women do not hesitate to construct. Right from coding classrooms for girls in rural Odisha to WhatsApp-based helplines for domestic abuse survivors, the digital has helped create game-changing involvements. Projects like SHEROES, Safecity, Digital Empowerment Foundation, and Sayfty are heading by women who consider the dangers of their visibility and yet, decide to counter it with infrastructure instead of fleeing. Their work does not bring up feelings of saviorism. It is a power that is practical, with equity at the forefront, and their approach is very strategic. The work provides them with an array of significant assets that include safety, financial literacy, community, and righteousness. Technology is not... It is for women what it cannot do by itself, but in their hands, it can become the solution to the problem.

The following chapter is built around three sets of dynamics. The first issue is as follows: How digital platforms deal with the visibility of a person is subjected to different kinds of surveillance, punishment, and exploitation all based on that person's gender. A young boy who is streaming a game on YouTube is likely to be treated with indifference or respect. In the same situation, a young woman may face the problem of her video being a target for sexualized comments. The right of being visible is not given to everyone—the one who gets it has to face violence. On the other hand, power is also a part of it: the spread of the video, income, the influence of policy. Thus, women creators, entrepreneurs, and activists must actively learn how to even use and direct their visibility themselves while at the same time be ready for the consequences of this act.

The second tension, which is discussed in the chapter, is about how women-oriented movements are utilizing the digital world not solely as a place for laying down a protest but also as a fertile ground for building the new world. The surge of the #PinjraTod campaign, which started with the revocation of oppressive policies in hostels and which was marked out by the use of Facebook, is very illustrative of the above. The #MeTooIndia case, despite its unevenness but being a game-changer, took place here and there, and Instagram and Twitter felt the reverberation of this battle.

The Shaheen Bagh demonstrations—where women, mainly those from the Muslim community, took to the streets and defended their rights—were broadcasted, tweeted, and even more globally amplified as people uploaded videos under different hashtags. However, these movements were not confined to online activities. Making the pixels turn into pressure was the thing. Petitions were one of the ways the groups used to show the legal bodies their determination. These were not hashtags looking for attention-they were hashtags with a purpose.

Third: how the algorithm has overshadowed the female image and someone who seeks a new identity. Smart systems operating on Instagram, TikTok, and YouTube are no longer just silent observers; they are more like influencers who constantly suggest the image of a 'successful woman' the way she should talk, behave, dress, and operate. They help to generate and enforce the classic stereotype of the lady entrepreneur, the skin color change ritual, or the over-stylized Instagram model look. Those are the things that draw more audience and keep advertisers happy.

Meanwhile, the youths are facing a problem of existence—precisely, teenagers are finding themselves living up to and competing for an invisible set of standards with the measurable instance of likes, views, and relatability. The youth's self-image, productivity tendencies, and romantic notions are all subjected to the whims of these unseen algorithms. The fact is that this is not a vivid marketplace for versatility and diversity—it is a vicious circle formation of reproduction of the stronger and the disciplining of the weaker.

Nevertheless, in the crowded space of the algorithmic world, resistance is spotted; counter-stories are emerging on purpose. Dalit women are refusing to be called victims while fat acceptance activists are taking over Reels by storm. On Instagram Stories, sex educators are educating the people on consent, body anatomy, and sex pleasure, topics that are often neglected, to tens of thousands of followers. Women are creating small loyal followings that are based on genuine care and not consumerism within the algoric bubble—the wind of change. The watchful eye watches, inquires, and reflects on itself.

The mentioned group in the chapter will steer clear of polarized views of technology(privileged glimpse of the future or complete disaster)/The authors prefer a third stance/method/paradigm that does not fall into the dichotomous trap of either loving or hating the platform. They will dismiss the idea of reform with the help of more reasonable legislature or of their destruction. Instead, they will put forward questions such as, what are the ways women can be the creators of their own destiny in the wake of digital conditions despite, and probably due to, these conditions? What are the new pedagogies of presence, risk, and resilience that are producing themselves out of the narratives of women? Can unity of all under the same principles be achievable without the sacrifice of the individual differences? Can we make sure that the virtual platforms we are designing are completely safe without demanding silence?

The stories told to readers consist of moments of courage and code, of abuse and agency, of visibility which is partly a resource and partly a threat. We are going to get a picture of women taking legal action to have the unwanted sexually explicit videos removed. There will be a sketch of creators who are teaching young girls how to encrypt their messages. Analogically the chapter will illustrate how digital aesthetics have designed feminist talks–and how at the same time the feminist discourse has influenced digital culture. To interact with women online is nothing but a revelation of local power, desire, and resistance in India.

Instead, this chapter is not at all about the women present on the internet—it is the internet as seen by women. Their involvement is not a minor or irrelevant narrative of the digital revolution. It is precisely in women's digital lives that the digital revolution shows its true colors. The crucial issue is not just that of the safety of the women's digital world. Rather, how women's digital lives unveil the power structure of the digital world and at the same time encourage us to rethink it from the very basics.

Selfies and Selfhood: Young Indian Women, Visibility, and Digital Rebellion

A young lady in Kanpur expresses a picture of herself on Instagram that shows a beautiful face, a talented singer, and a person who has a sense of humor going through the inevitable ups and downs of life. She has a sad face because she is not with those respected by society. (That is the reason for her sadness—she misses being with them.)

A young woman from a middle class family is busy taking a selfie at home. She makes the image as real and impressive as possible. The picture is a perfect show of freedom against suppression. It is a clear voice to the outside world that the girl is out of the old tradition. (The girl, moreover, does not care whether to be in the old tradition or in the new one).

To comprehend the significance of selfies among young Indian women, the explaining would have to start from a fundamental question: Who has the right to be visible?

The distribution of visibility in India has always been unjust, with women, especially those from marginalized castes, classes, and communities, always being requested to cover, hide, or erase themselves-this happened under the twin weights of family honor and patriarchal control. So, the selfie act is not only about the image, but the modern life's public record—and through the claiming of selfies, these ladies make sure that their image is present in this record. The mobile phone camera is not only a mirror but also a way of making our voice louder.

However, this newly gained visibility is not always safe. There are many women who are trolled, made fun of, or stalked by the people who are induced via the social media profiles. A single picture can open the door to the character assassination, moral degradation, or even worse. All the time the line between a self-confident and a vulgar woman is decided by the conservative norms that treat female self-expression as a danger to society. This gives the situation doubledness: the digital channels that offer women an amazing set of instruments for self-presentation also bare them to new ways of surveillance and shame. To post is to fight against it—but, at the same time, it is to risk being punished.

However, as much as the risk factor of women sharing selfies on the internet is tremendous, the number of Indian women who use selfies as a mode of communication has so far been on the rise. Well, one of the grounds is just the intimacy degree of the medium. While formal portraits or selected photoshoots are without exception those, which are taken by another person, selfies are exclusively taken by the object themselves-at a time, in a way, and with a frame that suits her.

The Indian selfie culture has also gone through a certain transformation in the sense of appearance. There was a time when only fair complexion, sharp features, and western clothing used to be digital beauty. Now, to a more significant extent, women exhibit their own culture—national dresses, indigenous jewelry, and native captions. This is not a step back but a new picture. There is now a coexistence of the bindi and the selfie stick. A lady in salwar kameez does a TikTok filter and writes a Bhojpuri caption. Another woman in her saree does a slow-motion twirl to the beat of the latest Punjabi track that has gone viral. These are not only cultural artefacts but also they are hybridity which deconstructs the system of tradition and modernity, modesty, and boldness, rural and urban. The digital platform is the place where new faces rise and old ones fall.

The social media platforms have not only offered but also shaped this new version of the culture. Instagram, in particular through its filters and stories, provides young women the opportunity to try out different styles and images. Despite the ban, TikTok saw the light of the day and all the while, allowed the beauty of short-form performances and humor to be seen and heard of in regional languages, hence, offering young women a platform they could not possibly have access to in the real world. On YouTube, vlogs made by a girl student from Bihar or a homemaker in Kerala now become a source of subdued excitement for the audience that then fans themselves and that way, they create a new local celebrities and the ones that belong in the circle of micro-influencers. Essentially, these platforms are a rat race where users are pushed and chased by algorithms until they present an idea that is perfect, more arousing or only pleases others. This freedom to express oneself is similar and at the same time contrasted with the pressure to get liked by others and make the content go viral.

The selfie is one of the thousands of faces of female resistance to traditional and patriarchal attitudes. Drawing from reality, a story of a girl who for some reason was not allowed to apply makeup at home but in the end of the day, changed clothes to take selfies with friends still exists. Others have secret “finstas” (fake Instagram accounts) to explore their identities away from parents or relatives. Thus, the selfie is more than a photo—it breaks the patriarchy—it becomes a kind of autonomy that is hidden. The screen is no longer just a space of options but a line that allows one to lead two separate lives: one for the family, the other for oneself.

However, as much as it is important not to glorify this rebellion, it is equally important to make sure that we don’t mistake self-expression for freedom. Some of the young women who improvised that they felt enslaved by the constant need of likes, comments, and followers. The lack of a good selfie opportunity can lead to panic-attacks and the awareness of being less engaged (lower engagement) can affect a person negatively. The gaze is virginally constructed, and emanating from the egg of the social hens; in contrast, the male bird’s foundational gaze is strictly one-way and more often than not, the female is a visible or a gettable target- a visible target who instead of going to the male’s cage will still remain unreachable at the very end of the notion of lizard cheap labor. Initially, a woman may feel victorious, but she may turn it into a case of exaggeration, especially when self-regard is in the grip of the AI software that assigns the Frontier Blood Holatics, a perfect score-

Taboo vibe (as wordings that are not taboo matter therefore they are non-taboo vibe) has generated the enthusiasm of some groups of people who have changed the perception of digital self. The groups of women, in question, are the feminist movements such as Blank Noise and Pinjra Tod that not only support selfies as a form of protest but also use this medium to reform the perceptions of the real; their created place. They have come from advocating to witness rape, harassment, or express the right to their existence without begging. For example, they have done it.

Edition of the selfie realm in an attempt to dismantle the hierarchical structure based on color and cast like all the other movements, the #DaliaAdivasiBahujanSelfie campaign is a public statement of both the Dalit, Adivasi, and Bahujan women. These three communities created a word-of-mouth concept to their platforms where individually and collectively they are venturing into territory of resistance. It was not something that the caste of women did; rather, it was women who did it.

Still, the question is, if a digital self can be made and the limits of the digital self-making process are known. Can a selfie be such a powerful tool to overthrow oppressive social constructs? Is online assertion practically converted into real-life empowerment? However, the scenario is different when we consider that the platforms are unpredictable to disappear in one moment—what will be of the archive of assertion that a lot have already formed? Such questions are not merely rhetorical but they pinpoint the problem of the insecure nature of digital empowerment given the aforementioned limitations and the fact that it stands on borrowed infrastructure and is run by opaque algorithms and is prone to state surveillance and commercial censorship.

Even in the aforementioned confinement, the selfie displays strong cultural transformations and is influenced by females who experiment with the camera, learning how to use it as a protection and weapon. They are well aware of the dangers, and yet they are not the people who will give up. Each and every picture, every attitude, every little glimpse into the camera lens is an act of self-assertion, a small but real cry: I was there. I made my choice. I exist by my rule.

What is really being visualized through all this is a multi-layered understanding of the life unseen in India today. The selfie is more than a photo—it reflects changes in the society in a newly emerged dimension of gender, technology, aspiration, and autonomy. It helps us look into the inner worlds of young Indian women who are not only striving to be seen but are also engaged in the digital remaking of their selves. They are no longer the passive participants—they are the ones who reorganize the screen.

Trolled for Existing: Gendered Violence on the Indian Internet

A woman goes on Twitter to find that her name is trending—not for a success, not for a campaign, not even for an opinion, but because she has had the courage to talk. The inbox is full of rape threats, phone number leaked, and very close family being targeted. She is faced with options of deleting the post, saying sorry, going offline, or simply leaving this world. This situation is typical of behaviors that are being repeated time and again. In the digital domain of India, it is not the law offenders, but the women that bear the burden of punishment for getting visible. The only problem is that women's crime is simply to be visible in the public sphere.

Gendered online harassment in India is a continuation of the traditional patriarchal structure, which remained inert before, and is being spread and altered through the pace, range, and anonymity of the Web. Misogyny used to enjoy privacy but the Internet now provides global coverage. Words that were once kept behind closed doors have become public on the Internet and are being shared even more through social media and eventually, they are being used as hashtags. From caste-based slurs thrown at Dalit women journalists to sexually explicit memes targeting female politicians, the Indian internet has become a place of oppression for women, where they are not just watched but also controlled, not just spoken to but shouted at.

Another terrifying weapon from the abuser's sleeve is doxxing, a practice of publishing personal details such as mobile phone numbers, living addresses, workplace, or personal photographs, wholesale. The aim is to eliminate the line between one's digital and physical safety through the method of doxxing. A tweet is easily converted into a threat to the author's place. This kind of abuse is frequently targeted at outspoken women—journalists, activists, and students—with a substantial percentage of them being people from different marginalized groups. When made public, they face a horde of harassers running various campaigns, which platforms seem to be blind to, despite their claims of free speech.

The problem is widespread and does not spare celebrities. Females from all walks of life suffer from online violence that is not only very personal but also terribly frequent. A teenager in Lucknow posts a selfie that swiftly leads to unwanted sexual comments. A single mother in Chennai continues to run her food blog, receiving offensive messages in her DMs. A Dalit student in Hyderabad puts up her university accomplishments on social media only to receive information that she 'slept her way to the top'. These examples are not just byproducts; in fact, they are modern-day India's digital representation of age-old prejudices made in a digital format, the core of which is cruelty measured in bytes.

The layout of the major social media platforms poses a significant challenge. Algorithms focus on engagement—outrage, anger, controversy—over nuance and empathy. It is common for a post that promotes misogyny and gets thousands of comments to be more displayed. The reporting system is not transparent and it is slow and inconsistent in handling it. The victims who report the crime are often told that the content was, in fact, not in violation of the community standards. In the meantime, the abusers are hiding under various aliases and are secretly mobilizing through encrypted chat groups or private forums. The platforms claim that they are neutral, yet it is very clear that they are aiding in the discrimination of the loud over the fair.

Although the Indian legal system provides clues to the legal provisions of cyber abuse under the IT Act and Indian Penal Code, the enforcement of these provisions remains extremely weak. Generally, FIRs are not filed immediately. The majority of police officers, who are generally not very well-versed in digital literacy or gender sensitivity training, reject the claims or insist on the victims "ignoring the incident". The responsibility of proof falls entirely on the own of the victim, and he or she is the one to bear the emotional, financial, and psychological costs. A few survivors have had to change jobs, cities, or even careers just to escape continuous harassment. In the case of digital violence, the aftereffects are certainly as serious as those of physical intimidation.

Nonetheless, fighting back has started. Women are coming out in the open and talking about their cases of abuse, they are naming and shaming their trolls, and most importantly, they are seeking strength in numbers. Organizations like @IndiaLoveProject, @FeminismInIndia, and Smashboard have come into being as counter-public spaces—repositories where women post materials, experiences, and approaches that have been useful in their online endurance. The hashtags #StopOnlineAbuse, #GirlsAtDhabas, and #MeTooIndia have given voice to isolated individual stories and turned them into a strong collective chorus of demands. What we see is not just groups of people moving; it is a collective message calling to envision a digital public as nothing short of a space of dignity, as opposed to a space of domination.

One of the most amazing features of this movement of resistance is its intersectionality. The digital violence that women are exposed to is not homogeneous. Queer women, Dalit women, Muslim women, and women with disabilities have to deal with various layers of violence that are specific to the community they belong to and, as a result, are usually left out of the general discourses. The example of an attack on a queer Dalit woman is one such case as it is a mix of casteist, sexist, and homophobic language in a very intricate and cruel manner. For us to get a nuanced response, we must first recognize the layered oppressions and not wash them down into a general "women's issue". It is analogous to the digital space acting as a battleground, so the paths to justice also have to be asymmetric.

Feminists also engage in discussions pertaining to digital self-defence that are of great importance. What is key in these workshops on privacy settings, encryption tools, identity protection, and mental health is that women are being provided with technological and mental strength. More and more people are jumping onto the bandwagon of campaigns that demand platforms add more women and marginalized individuals as content moderators. A few journalists are using burner accounts so that their safety is maintained while others are opting for the use of pseudonymous accounts to guarantee their freedom. The permission given to people to be represented online should not entail a heavy financial, social, and political sacrifice.

However, there are deeper issues that demand a more wholesome approach, rather than partial solutions. This is about the total reorganization of the internet's status and the reinvention of the audience. The notion of the internet as a level-playing field without discrimination or biases has ceased to be. As it stands, the internet is marked by a digital hierarchy, controlled by both human and algorithmic gatekeepers. Non-conformist women, those who are different in their views, attire, or identification, to be more specific, are presented as solvable issues and not as contributors to be treated honourably. This discrepancy in the basic position of the situation is not straightened, it is only then that moderation tools and policy modifications become minor fixes to a system beyond repair.

Another aspect of the policy that is equally important is the cultural corrections that should go hand in hand. A large part of Indian digital misogyny comes from offline attitudes—misogyny that is transferred from homes, classrooms, movies, and religious texts. If a boy is taught to see women as vessels of the family's honor or objects of moral control and he sees the same situation in the Internet, he will not react otherwise. The alteration demands that ethical concerns are inserted in the digital realm through education at schools, policing with the input of victims, and questioning the somewhat masculine dispositions that prevail in the internet culture. For online space to be accessed universally, it requires to be renovated with empathy as its technological framework.

The risks are very high. As more and more aspects of Indian life are transitioning digital—the move from politics to education, from commerce to culture staying safe and free while taking part in the digital sphere is not a matter of choice anymore. It is at the base of every citizen's role, the creativity of the people, and voicing their opposition. The offlining of women means the death of democracy. When marginalized voices are drowned in a chorus of coordinated abuse, the society has no means of recognizing itself. And when platforms make money from violence and refuse to take responsibility, the entire concept of freedom of expression collapses.

Nevertheless, among the desperation, there is hope. Women are not only the victims of digital violence—they are also the witnesses of events, they are interrupting, and they are seeking improvements. They are not to be removed. and it is this act of resistance that is changing the meaning of online visibility. They are not just users of technology, but also critics, creators, and repurposers of the digital space itself.

This chapter is not just about listing the harms—it goes further to expose the violence, show where the power lies, and make the resistance larger. It is a question not only of the freedom of tweeting, posting, and commenting but also of the right to be alive, to talk, and to be listened to without any threat. This is not the matter of the platform policy. It is the justice that is at issue here.

India added the freedom of software development to its digital arsenal as soon as it got the coveted title of the world's fastest-growing mobile phone market. However, representation and technological innovation across industry sectors were a different story. The idea of Indian tech that was popular in the media—Bengaluru's shiny skyscrapers, IPOs with billions of dollars, and unshaven programmers that are forecasting the future—has been a story that mostly spoke of, and was controlled by, men. Despitethe social distancing orders and the lockdowns that became a common phenomenon, women in India have been at the forefront of the tech sector and have been changing it. They are the heroes of our country. They are the ones whom not only corporations, both national, and those abroad, but also the grass-root levels, their local groups, the poor tech labs, and for-profit organizations have all been active in creating a new India, inventing a new India, and thus, shaping a new India for themselves. They have given a lot of power that fostering an entrepreneurial spirit powered by technology that has its roots in them and have left no one out of the process, women.

Silicon Valley sheroes' ideology from the US was a mirrored image with western stories. Wiping out the stereotypes, going through the same path men usually did in the business arena of Silicon Valley, and funding their startups from venture capitalists were such tales. Still, this gradually turned out not to be the case. The Indian version of this tale has completely been changed to suit the local experience. For instance, Co-Founder of YourDOST, Richa Singh, a mental health platform, her idea was to be the part of the solution to the problem of youth who are deeply affected by the public health crisis in India, especially students. Also, Ajaita Shah, who spearheads Frontier Markets, an online selling platform, in order to make rural women independent solar entrepreneurs, she has mobilized thousands of them right from the start. Instead of founding business houses, these women are the kind that do not fit in, the ones that challenge who has the prerogative to solve problems, who is marked out as a leader, and out of whose stories success is defined.

Safety, financial inclusion, and education are the three areas that used to be women's issues and now are the ones where women are the drivers of innovation. In Jaipur, Pink Legal, a start-up initiated by lawyer-entrepreneur Sonal Jindal, has launched an education campaign on Instagram and entered into small legal fellowships for women. Instead of waiting for the court system to be user-friendly, she is taking the initiative to make it accessible, using UX design and short-form content to turn passive knowledge into actionable power. Safecity, founded by ElsaMarie D'Silva, is one of the organizations that collect reports of sexual harassment through the use of maps based on crowdsourced locations—thus converting almost every ordinary citizen smartphone into an urban safety sensor. Therefore, they are building an awareness that is not waiting for the state's approval but is instead drawn upon the experiences of people.

Education has been reinvented by women through women-centred models that are different from traditional educational methods and connectivity. Enable India, established by Shanti Raghavan, mainly offers online training for people with disabilities, including women, helping them to get formal employment. This would mean that India is in a process of morphing from the tokenism of inclusion to infrastructure. On the flip side, 17000 ft Foundation of Sujata Sahu brings tablets carrying the curriculum customized for each village in Ladakhi, partnering tech- with high-altitude solidarity. They are not meant to be valued in millions as in the case of unicorns or to be acquired by the likes of Silicon Valley; their purpose is handmade social equity, low retention rates, social taboos, and stressful ecology. Their business model may not be as glittering as the one that is still the dream of investors, but the social ROI is more than necessary.

Despite its issues with precarious work and observation, the platform economy has become a haven for informal women's initiatives. Women have been quietly using Instagram, among other platforms, to turn the attention they receive into income and to avoid the media gatekeepers to the maximum. Joining the digital gig workforce not only brings risk but provides women with a unique combination of scale, freedom, and exposure. It allows them to be visible and to portray themselves in a new light so that they can create communities around their identities and turn the skills they have into money while staying right at the current place, without having to reshape family life, or conform to preexisting norms.

Regardless of the achieved success, it is important to take note of underlying issues that often become a limiting factor of triumph. The unequal sharing of the capital is an ever-present issue in the world of entrepreneurship. In a report by the International Finance Corporation, it is shown that women in India own only 14% of businesses and collectively receive less than 6% of SME financing. Even in a start-up setting where one is set to think that the number of women founders should have grown, the opposite remains to be the fact. The drive that is needed for women to innovate in their respective industries is built on shared networks, mentorship and risk-taking; these ingredients are notoriously rife with inequality right now. Furthermore, online visibility is not only a benefit but also an increased exposure to certain risks. It has been a common occurrence for female entrepreneurs to be the subject of targetted trolling, cyberstalking and related attacks whose main aim is not only to vilify not only their personalities but...

One has to pay attention to the matter of where the technologies come from. Despite creating new platforms, women often have to rely on the technological stack made by men, which is then governed by opaque algorithms and foreign policy regulations. Be it the community guidelines for content, which platforms such as Instagram use or the borrowing and lending algorithms, which apps associated with fintech use, the embedded values in the codes are far from neutral. One of the signs that signify an excellence-driven and inclusive culture is the gradually increasing presence of initiatives built by women that are either open-source or community-run. The model that they choose is not one for hyper-growth but a slower one, referred to as equity in businesses: culturally-led, and not to mention, ethically and structurally diverse businesses.

Of utmost importance, what rejects the notion that female empowerment equates with male success are many such start-ups. The focus tends on not just competing for the same popularity as the next Zomato or Flipkart but, to put it in other words, on care, collective intelligence, and lived knowledge. As an example, SHEROES app by Sairee Chahal, which is a multi-purpose platform for women, does not only offer job listings but also provides emotional support, community forums, a chat-based helpline for women facing any kind of abuse, and even microloans. It gives a new meaning to a career by considering it as not only a job but also self-respect, social status, and digital safety. The same concept works for Arti Khosla's Pure India Trust where they take underprivileged girls as a proactive means to create the first business generation, not via a regular 2-hour curriculum, but by deeply understanding their life realities.

This is what sets apart India's digital sheroes from the marketers for the same in the Western world. The innovation is not always perfect—more often, it is messy, iterative, and hybrid. Most people think that it can only be in the high-speed Wi-Fi zone in cities or, conversely, it must be located in areas of rural dim influence on health; it cannot be both, maybe trafficking are not the only businesses; these are just a few out of many places where the idea of women coders brings empowerment not only through tools such as Python programming language but also through their soft skills in understanding the needs of the people, fighting hardships, and altering their situation illegally. These women are involved in building the future through technology, not only waiting for someone to do that.

If, on one hand, the main dominant narratives continue with Smart Cities rhetoric and a solutionism modelled on an idea of hackathon-style, women's stories will always be the other side. Their perspective implies that the digital evolution is not happening by mere app production for the poor but it is a process of empowering those who are poor by them. The digital initiatives led by the female in India are not just finishing up tasks of the start-up country; these are executed by the women as the darker pages of the economy are being corrected. They also reinforce the idea that the fate of technology and business must not be left to the hands of whom and benefits.

If Indian innovation\'s tomorrow is to be genuinely all-encompassing, it has to go beyond women being just users or beneficiaries, but as architects of the future. They are not supposed to be considered only as numbers or the recipients of awards, but should be elevated to the status of the imaginers of a wider circle—that is, they are where the success does not revolve only on fund raising but on secured freedoms, created solidarities and questioned structures.

When we are talking about Sheroes in Silicon, we are not trying to promote branding talk. It is the recognition of a subtle change that is not about getting the attention on social media but is central to this issue, that is recurring the system for the better from the inside. This represents not an extensive one, but it is an intensive revolution. And that, in the long term, is the deeper disruption.

When a teenager from Coimbatore searches for career inspiration on Instagram, it is not the female scientists, community leaders, or policy advocates that she sees. It is more likely that the platform returns a long list including outcome like lifestyle influencers, fashion entrepreneurs, or crypto trading \"girl bosses\" all in vibrant reels. If she decides to look for tips on how to keep fit, her feed is dominated by highly polished workout routines, diet myths, and \"before-and-after\" transformations that show unattainable ideals self-destructively. No, technology is not happening by chance. The situation portrays the increased power of algorithms to influence the view of aspiration, on the sly, determining what millions of Indian young women consider is their goal or what is within their grasp or even allowed.

The basis that digital platforms provide us connection, information, and motivation is solely our preferences in the algorithm of these platforms. One such market is India, with a population of over 300 million women online, largely consuming digital content in their mother tongue and through short-form material, with the main role of recommendation engines which invisibly regulates the next things which women will come across in their online experience. Women are the ultimate decision-makers on YouTube, Instagram, TikTok, Moj, Josh, and Google search. It is through these media that they receive a string of suggestions that match their lifestyle, popularity, etc., as the success of users is determined. In particular, the representation of women with good looks, visibility through performing, and getting a lot of thumbs-up are the parameters which are focused on women.

The e-commerce of the recommendation architecture supports the idea of the product's most clickable, shareable, and viral-optimized content being the ones to be prioritized over content that is constructive, empowering, or diversified. Young women now have a kind of self-fulfilling prophecy: the more of them there are who align with the goals of the platform (bypassing the norm through being very feminine, blatant clickbait, or aspirational consumerism), the more they will draw attention. Those whose actions signal nuance, discomfort, or divergence are switched off, shadow-banned, or slipped under the algorithmic radar. The qualities that make a person multifaceted are the things that make her virtual self lose visibility in the digital space.

Women in the 2nd and 3rd tier cities of India—like Ratnagiri, Orai, Ramgarh, etc.—tend to see that they have the 'role' to pretty much structure their online content along the lines of what is being encouraged with platforms such as Brave—like what they should wear, how they should conduct themselves, etc. equaling the amount of likes being given to such activities. By the norms of society, women are steered mostly by the norms of society, however, social media very often `get involved' themselves. One can easily notice the pressure of the algorithmic kind when talking about those who are featured in the study. A woman in a small city in India who writes poetry and has just come to public attention will be called upon to "look more polished" in order to extend her audience. A girl who is into coding and lives in Hyderabad is faced with her tutorials having a lower viewership than her reels set to trending music. Moreover, the algorithm subtly controls the flow of the entire thing. Apart from some basic details, which are constantly repeated in different forms, suggestions are clustered under three main areas: self-management of wage disputes, interview stage confidence-building, and ensuring fair pay.

The problem is not merely of the aesthetics of media; it is a question of the structure that determines the rules of digital recognition. A vast majority of the algorithms are trained on behavioral data collected from users of various backgrounds around the world, so this data carries with it existing biases on gender roles, cultural expression, and economic value. In the West, feminism has always been against the objectification of women. Nevertheless, in a society like that of India, where women are still struggling for their access to public space, speech, and financial participation, the algorithm becomes a tool of reinforcement and the reflex effect of an oppressive society in the name of neutrality.

The body is certainly among the places where this algorithmic governance is vividly illustrated. Typical health and fitness content for females often blur the boundaries between wellness and thinness, vigour and beauty, and self-respect and revolution. Slimming techniques, sculpting workouts, and beauty "glow-ups" are major highlights of the content on fitness in both English and vernacular languages. A number of young women confess to the development of nervous disorders or anorexia after long exposure to this kind of content. The most striking aspect of it all is that the platforms persist in plastering these videos everywhere not because they are fact-checker friendly or respectful of any culture, but because they perform well.

The result is a slight but constant influence on the nature of ambition. Girls are told that they are free to "be anything" — and consequently but they are bombarded with images of "anything" with the conditions that these should be: entrepreneurial are glamorous, educated are the charming, opinionated are the softly spoken. The algorithmic self— the version of oneself that wins the most digital platforms—turns into a product of handling: tasty, glossy, not to say profitable. Visibility has become not only the coin of the realm but also the golden handcuffs.

Nevertheless, a set of phenomena has gained strength through artificial means, i.e. they have not found the actual environment, nevertheless, they show resistance. In India, a series of countermovements are emerging that are beginning to challenge those algorithmic defaults. These forces, rather than saying no to technology, are trying to rewrite its logic. Communities such as Kool Kanya are creating for women career guidance and financial literacy that is culturally suited to Indian women, thus challenging the superficiality aimed at getting more clicks. Local feminist groups like Feminism in India and The Pink List India are taking advantage of their own algorithmic strategies to make sure that their content trend is of a progressive nature, using memes, reels, and keyword optimisations for this goal to be achieved on platforms created for a different purpose.

It is not only the role of educators and technologists to stand up and be counted. One instance of this is the partnerships that the Mozilla Foundation has created with many Indian developers, who later developed tools employed as pilots, by users, for example, are they able to "tune" their feed towards educational or inclusive content. Furthermore, researches at IIIT Hyderabad have taken up the subject of recommendation systems and are working on strategies that will lead to more transparent systems of the same, which will allow users to know why a few videos are promoted over others and with the information gotten, their feedback will be necessary.

Women at the community level are making collaborative efforts to embark on a mission of creating micro-networks that give priority to sharing of purposeful content. Telegram, WhatsApp, and even Pinterest have curated channels with feminist podcasts' lists, such as women-led coding tutorial materials, readings of regional language poetry, and critical media literacy. These are the quiet spaces of individual agency that work as a medium of rebelling but persistently gaining an advantage. The choice of what to see is indeed a political act.

Then there are content creators that are challenging the algorithm on purpose. They not only are they aware of the game but also they dig for something more within their content. For example, a fashion influencer is giving body-positivity messages at break points of their styling tips. A dance reel really makes a point out of casteism when the choreography is accompanied by a voice over referring to the issue. A YouTube channel is taking the opportunity to teach economic advice to domestic workers who are at the same time cooking. These people know that change often has to be disguised as if it were the same old thing that people usually accept.

Leadership is another sector that is starting to notice the disparities in the technology space. Although the 2021 IT Rules of India have some limitations, they were the stepping stone in the creation of the grievance redressal system in content moderation. Several civil society groups are still out there advocating for audits of algorithms, challenging the platforms to comply with their responsibilities and have a gender-sensitive AI design. However, such actions are still their infancy, and at times, even insignificant. The transformational shift will take place when algorithms are not just made to engage more people but also to be fair; this is what it comes to when tech design thinks of respect, diversity, and democracy.

In this case, the 'aspiration for' discussion is not the argument of ambition per se, but the question of the setting of ambition. It is more about the structures that encourage, reward, and carry forth the idea of ambition. Not only do algorithms objectify certain people and silence those that they do not want to be heard, but also they uplift a specific form of intelligence. In such instances, they are instruments of ideology, and they are far from being neutral tools. To aspire again to the ability of being heard is to gain back the power of determining the extent to which the invisible can be taken as being visible.

For young women in India, their struggle is on a very serious level. It is not a matter of mere self-esteem or the time of leisure while facing the screens. Rather, it is about what is no or yes, what are the available choices, what futures do they see, which narratives can they urge to be unveiled. The digital world is not a place without patriarchy, but a less visible one which still operates within that rule. However, apart from all that, it remains a space for change if we are able to identify the digital code and decode its prejudices and then rewrite a different script altogether.

In its essence counter-programming is all about the potential to redefine what the digital world can offer, and not to withdraw from it. The quest is to abdicate the position of the algorithm's pawn and actually become the creator of it. The major message behind this is that dreaming is not already a given track but a matter of a particular opinion, a different kind of political regime, and off-chances..

Chapter 10

India Inc. in the Digital Mirror

What is in the economic data is what culture wants. As a nation undertakes projects, it unmasks the things that it appreciates. For example, in the case of India, the country is experiencing a digital revolution and, at the same time, an economic downswing. Here the start-up ecosystem, the gig economy, and the infrastructure of emerging tech are not just high-octane growth engines, but also cryptograms that reveal who we are and what our aspirations are. What they do is encoded, by the simplicity of their form, the questions we believe are important for solving, who can be made the builder, and what kind of labor can be left in the shadows. This chapter thus attempts to view the ethical features of the Indian industry through the glasses of the digital economy--the things it not only constructs, but also deems as right.

India's growth into a global tech hub has been a dominant topic of an array of articles. Statistics about it have been made known repeatedly: India houses over 100 unicorns, the third-largest start-up ecosystem in the world, the highest digital payment volumes in the world, and a second-largest digital user population only after China. Nevertheless, beyond the glitzy narratives of the industry are the stories that matter much more and depict the reality more vividly and comprehensively. The story it tells is the dichotomy within the Indian entrepreneurial sector, one that follows Silicon Valley's principles, that are, blitz-scale growth, and user acquisition, and another that is grounded in addressing deeply Indian problems such as vernacular literacy, rural banking, sanitation, women's health, and agricultural logistics.

Imagine a situation where companies such as Agrowave, a digitalized farm-to-mandi logistics platform, or Kutumb, a multilingual social community platform that interconnects the caste, creed, or regional boundaries, have become the voices of innovation. These companies agree that it is the social problems that will take the top priority on the digital economy's agenda by providing examples where entrepreneurship growth is directly related to the welfare of society rather than customer acquisition and value. On the other hand, bio-toilets are an example of sanitation startups targeting rural schools, while menstrual education in the third sector from health-tech platforms is another case. These businesses employ a different criterion of success. Not all of them will become unicorns, however, their influence may be far greater and a more sustainable contribution to India's digital tomorrow. These activities are doing without the idea that innovation can only be disruptive. Instead, they are affirming that innovation can be continuity, continuity in the provision of care, inclusion, and accessibility.

The digital economy is no different—a world of social innovation-rooted standing on the shoulders of the workers who are invisible; workers who are not introduced even in company presentations. The 'ghost workers' of India: those who simply noticed on the content like the graphic designers who are working on the said jobs and those who worked the land by only using their algorithms, click farm operators who cheat on the real engagement, and unemployed translators who translate the global but do not even have a safety net of any kind or a professional reputation in their field. They are not given the stage at the launch of a product, but they are the life of the machine.

India's middle class is facing a paradox: although they are increasingly becoming people of instant commerce, smooth interfaces, and AI-generated personalization, they do not realize that their lifestyles are the result of the very hard and demanding human labor they hope not to see. The example of content moderation is illustrative here—even though the youngsters are employed through third-party agencies, and they have employment, they are still victimized, for their labour is ignored, and they are put in the first place only in the jobs market. It is an ethical blind spot in the glittering narrative of Indian tech progress

Further, there are delivery workers—a picture of the gig economy—who, despite being hearty souls, have to suffer from terrible conditions because the workplace environment is just a cover for it—they have worsening work conditions but still managing and making the ends meet. While the routes, the salary determining factors, and even happiness scores in delivery people are controlled by algorithms, the matters about dignity, safety, and fairness are seated in the fridge of convenience and scale. Indian legislative bodies have not been able to protect the livelihood of the workers and the platform companies are still finding ways to bypass their obligations. It is quite clear that the future of working is already here. However, it is not fair and humane.

The Indian story, however, is not only a deficit story. It is also a test ground for creativity, innovation, and the ability to jump forward. This is confirmed by the Indian engagements with blockchain, decentralised finance, and digital identity infrastructure as the early applications of the country which clearly demonstrate the above-mentioned. Many Western scholars are still sceptical about the viability of Web3, while in practice, India with Aadhaar and its layered stack—JAM (Jan Dhan, Aadhaar, Mobile)—is on the right path to create an inclusive kind of digitisation, which can be followed by the Western world. E-RUPI vouchers' wide-ranging availability, the fast pace of the Unified Payments Interface (UPI), and the occurrence of DigiLocker are not just technological achievements but are also the political system which could transform access most radically.

Decentralized tech prosperity is offered by risk awareness. Only by the reduction of corruption through blockchain-based land records, but who confirms the truth of the records in a system which has a history riddled with dispossession? Is digital identity the right solution? Will it be the target of surveillance and exclusion?

Web3 language is not the only expression India employs; it is also the place to deal with Web3's moral issues when codes override discretion, and public institutions give way to platforms. Equally as urgent is the matter of trust. Because Indian customers are familiar with digital tools, the public's trust depends on other qualities that businesses possess such as good customer service, user-friendly interfaces, and a good algorithmic image. This change can lead to new winners and losers. While some older companies are still in mid transitioning and try to figure out what to do next, startups find it easy to win the trust of the customer with UX design and partnerships with influencers.

However good the systems that have been built to create trust may be as they rely on ratings, reviews, and virality as their foundations, there is also a dark side that compromises those exact systems. It is then that the so-called watchdogs of the digital space (companies whose purpose is to dispense rewards for transparency and customer satisfaction) show a strong presence. This is a moment when they will be more involved in ensuring the real trustworthiness.

But who is on the losing side in these electronic businesses and the networked society? Indeed, those who come out as negative entities in the game are just as likely to switch roles with the wrongdoers. Thus, finding the truth among massive numbers of verified and trusted users is a hard and uncertain experience. On top of that, real decisions are not made by the users, but by the systems behind digital economies, whose unethical practices do the users even recognize?

The hunger of India for the consumption of digital ideologies is extremely phenomenal. The rapport by which the rural sector of the nation is going for the smartphones, the resourceful manner in which the kirana stores are putting the QR codes, the adaptability of the old people to bhajans available on video calls and the WhatsApp banking, are clear signs. These are very much accepted as an integral part of digital India and not just stories from urban areas.

It is for this reason that the chapter does not give India Inc its usual portrayal as that in the quarterly reports or in the number of new IPOs. Instead, it focuses on the broader cultural transitions that are the basis of those reports and stock-market records. The chapter defines enterprise as a matter of personal and collective social issues and not just a figure in business governance. The level of labor is no longer just the financial budget, rather the correspondence process. And it likes to deal with technology not as a gift from above, but as a battle with the powerful, distributed territory—every one of the devices becomes the place where openness and mutual participation can be achieved with maximum efficiency, control, and scale on the one side, love, and care on the other side on the other side.

India Inc., with the help of digital media, on one hand, has a clear view of the bigger picture but also is not afraid of reality. It portrays creativity and fresh thinking, sure—but also unmoved minds. It reveals unfinished goals, as well as passed-over issues. It extols the attainment and at the same time hides those who are taking the credit. The first challenge that is in the future is not whether India is capable of generating more unicorns, but if it is able to raise new values, which will cause the transmission of value smoothly and economically, ethically, and inclusively.

If a nation is most often considered to be the "next big thing," we should be more concerned about shaping it in an appropriate way. To give more context, the authors, in this chapter, not only answer but provide the means to ask better questions.

The Great Indian Jugad Tech: Exporting Frugal Innovation in the Digital Age

Jugad, at the first impression, may invoke the image of grassroots innovation -a jugaadu mechanic fixing up a broken pipe with available parts, or a local shopkeeper improvising a billing system-. But beyond that de facto, lies one of the most inspiring achievements in 21st-century digital governance: revamping a frugal innovation powerhouse in India. The same spirit that once repaired bicycles is now creating digital public infrastructures with global potential being pursued, researched, and, in some cases, being jealous by the developed world.

The digital experiments in India are no longer playing catch-up but taking the lead outright. UPI's uninterrupted payment system, the biometric identity system of Aadhaar, and ONDC's open e-commerce protocols, along with being the scale of the initiatives, are instances of the same design philosophy that is accessible, modular, and cost-effective. They are not the shiny Silicon Valley clones, nor are they the bloated state-run dinosaurs. They represent the uniquely Indian character in the way the country has chosen to solve their problems, and the ambition they have has become even more evident: Instead of its private ownership, to make digital infrastructure a public good.

Think of the Unified Payments Interface that has, by now, doubled its monthly transaction volume to 10 billion. This remarkable performance gives UPI the status of being a Payment Infrastructure only.' As a trust protocol, a consent engine and a disintermediator, UPI plays a lead role in revolutionizing payment systems and financial inclusion in our country. With credit card systems that have moved away from a hands-on approach and made money by deducting a percentage of every transaction, the UPI system has been built on a completely different philosophy where no MDR (Merchant Discount Rate) is levied by the bank, fin-techs, and finally, the customer is spared. On top of that, this is indeed a practical transfer from most European and US payment models that charge users quite high fees. There are countless examples of scenarios such as a chaiwala in Jaipur or a any executive in Bangalore, who with the help of UPI can carry out a very comfortable financial transaction using a QR code. UPI knows no boundary of elitism and poverty, it moves in a manner that it is unheard of in any other financial arrangement where the digital poor are to be found just 'in the next block'.

Aadhaar, too, is frequently misportrayed as a biometric profiling apparatus and a 24/7 surveillance tool in media debate, where the real purpose gets often obscured. It was always meant to be an umbrella for different identities, not just a digital version of the physical body. The main idea behind it is that of an identity layer that citizens can opt to be included in the ecosystem of welfare systems, SIM card issuance, tax compliance, and digital banking. When associated with eKYC and DigiLocker, Aadhaar is no longer a surveillance tool but a way for the unbanked and undocumented to prove their existence and access digital services. An iris scanner could not be where the Aadhaar brilliance is located; it is rooted in the design of an infrastructural, on top of which the government can, in a very efficient manner, at reduced quantities of leakages, provide its people with their fair shares of welfare benefits. A mother who due to the Aadhaar system gets a direct LPG subsidy in her Jan Dhan account in Bihar, bypassing both middlemen and corruption, is a lady of a kind that trust has become programmable in stack.

Nevertheless, the innovative experiment that is currently in progress is perhaps ONDC—the Open Network for Digital Commerce. Designed as a counterforce to platform monopolies, ONDC does not attempt to create a platform that would be as popular as Amazon or Flipkart; instead, it aims to break down such platforms. Being based on a range of public protocols, ONDC permits any buyer app to locate any seller without being obliged to use one that is closed. Theoretically, this favours e-commerce to the hilt, that is, even for a kirana shop, handicraft vendor, or a last-mile delivery agent. In practice, free-wheeling value creation is explored for digital capitalism. The question is not yet answered whether ONDC would be as scalable as UPI—but the game-changing goal of ONDC is clear: commerce as a joint venture.

The success of India's JugadTech model is more than just frugality and it's built on the fundamental principles of architecture. India Stack is not a set of distinct technologies; rather, these are the foundations the entire ecosystem is built upon. These four pillars, namely identity (Aadhaar), payments (UPI), data consent (DEPA), and digital documents (DigiLocker) are all scalable, modular, and API-driven. All things considered, each is a public digital good. India's approach is quite distinct from the Chinese platform-first models or the surveillance capitalism in the West. It is a form of digital federalism where private and public sectors have common access to a railway of the digital age. And the result is inspirational.

The development of India's Digital India program has started to be observed by the international community. Brazil is incorporating some parts of the India Stack into its projects. The Philippines may soon have an Aadhaar-like identification system. UPI-like payments have generated a great deal of interest in Rwanda and Morocco. Besides, the World Bank's projects for high-speed internet service, which usually do not refer to India's DPR (Digital Public Infrastructure) model directly, are actually extracted from this model and can be used as a model given that India's method of digital public good delivery has become the standard for developing economies. The software being exported is more than just software but also development of a governance model. This model provides transparency and scalability for the state, citizen, and market transactions.

But this success tale is also beset with controversies. Critics are right to bring up points on consent, surveillance, exclusion, and data protection. The very same Aadhaar system that makes direct benefit transfer feasible can block out the elderly who biometrics are not working. The zero-MDR policy that fuels the spread of UPI may as well have sustainability concerns for private payment players in the longer term. Nonetheless, ONDC's anti-monopoly aspirations are ominous as they aim to create a balance between actual size and stability in a highly competitive e-commerce environment. The case of Jugad is a valid one, and yet it is not a conclusion of development if we are delivering the same without institutions and instead with Jugad.

Moreover, there is this problem which is known as techno-solutionism, and it is believed that complex social issues can just be developed as a solution. A digital identity does not, by itself, guarantee people's dignity. Also, the fact that transactions are completed in real-time does not mean that structural inequality has been eradicated. APIs are not a solution without holding someone accountable. The government must ensure that digital technology does not become a thing that takes over human governance. That digital technology should form a part of the code of governance that is a benefit to, not the withdrawal of, the public. The conclusion is quite simple: the same thriftiness that is the backbone of JugadTech's scalability can also be the weakness that results in it turning stiff if it does not retain the elements of rights, redressal, and public oversight.

Undoubtedly, India's accomplishments are absolutely tremendous. It speaks of a digital infrastructure that is non-exploitative and that is empowering. This is the view of infrastructure not as a product but as a protocol. The essence of the idea is that it is not about building unicorns but instead, it revolves around a utility. Further, it is also the idea of digitalization which can play the role of a public service that caters to democratic needs, which is not in spite of the scale, but because of it. It is the same with the ingenuity that in the past was used for assembly of motors and the conversion of milk vans that today, essentially, is now changing the internet for the better and is making it the property of the many and not just a few.

In the digital age of today, as the gap between people who have access to technology and those who do not increases, JugadTech offers a solution to this problem. Silicon Valley, which is ad-driven and controlled by monopolies, and Beijing, a surveillance state, both do not have the answer to this problem. However, JugadTech is an organization where the true spirit of technology has been realized that is not about the price of the company but also about the consumers who might receive the new technology as a result. This vision is not unrealistic and, in fact, is so realistic that in India, it is synonymous with need.

Startups with Soul

When the topic of Indian innovation comes up, investors most often concentrate their attention on unicorns; the themes then slide to the valuation process, and the fast growth of businesses with the acquisition of tremendous amounts of users by them. However, this specific discussion, besides being profitable, hides a totally different story, which is even more profound and probably more influential in a moral sense since it is about the creators of digital tools who instead of following the law of the jungle in Silicon Valley, are aiming at solving such stubborn and specific to India problems with a clear conscience and practical demeanor. In upshot, these are the startups that are not building lean for the final takeout but are doing so it's a matter of dignity, where success is determined not only by the amount of money raised, but in fact, the number of toilets built, the number of farmers served, or the number of vernacular learners empowered as well. Their presence may not be very strong in the tech sector, but without them it is not unthinkable that no progress and no future would be possible in the same discovery and applications of new products and services that germinate in the digital economy.

This world of entrepreneurship is no longer on the margins but rather forms the core. A quiet revolution is happening as innovation cohabits with the local ethos and language, and aligns with ethical values to define the digital face of the Indian nation. An example of it is the toilet hygiene crisis whereby lack of safe sanitation facilities is the problem of the majority of Indians daily. As Swachh Bharat has provided the infrastructural needs, behaviour change and maintenance have not matched. The new genre of social entrepreneurs are the ones who are now the game-changers in the industry. The GARV Toilets are one example - the combination of the IoT sensors, solar-powered maintenance technology, and the employment models using solar power to make it a sustainable business and to create the local employment it has become an incredibly important venture since it happens at the intersection of digital and real meaning. The said solution is not at all fancy, neither can it be value-laden for a VC and must be far from people's everyday work, but an additional level of solidarity has been brought into play through it; it has become the voice of the people in their unique mutant culture and the outercities whose infrastructure has been ignored by the government.

Vernacular literacy is a characteristic that India shares with the vast majority of its citizens—this is one of the silent barriers that ensures that a large number of the population will be excluded from digital engagement. Over the years, government education policies and digital access programs have been oriented towards English, often at the expense of other languages, which were treated as usability drawbacks. However, innovative ventures like Kutuki and Pratilipi have changed this mindset. Kutuki, a minority language early learning platform, which caters to the communities speaking Tamil, Kannada, and Marathi languages, where it is not mere translation of English to the local languages, it is another form of teaching through tales, music, pictures, etc. that resonate with their local population by (those who) personally (are) part of it. So, basically it is not a product of Western platforms, but a new concept developed from indigenous ideas and inspirations which came from children of semi-urban India. Pratilipi, a vernacular storytelling platform, like-wise, has opened up the space and allowed writers in Hindi, Malayalam, and Bengali to publish and earn, which is different from the traditional way of publishing and also a gesture of nonviolent language extinction. These two platforms do not only let the non-English speaking people in; they are the primary issue.

Although, truth be told, the influence of the enterprise that is driven by a mission, such as uncovering in the rural farmland and farmers in India, may even be the most (significant) one. For a long time, the agricultural tech has been mostly concerned with the dissemination of messages from above to the farmers, which included local weather forecasts, market prices, and field status reports, via SMS. Nevertheless these efforts failed to provide workable solutions as technologists did not consider the fact that farmers could neither read nor write, have low or no connectivity, and did not trust traditional institutions. Nonetheless, a new breed of startups led by rural-born founders is changing the status quo. For example, DeHaat, a full-stack platform, promises complete service to the farmers, meaning from seed beside the purchase, helping with the crop, and even to the guarantee of the market further. All of this is done by local micro-entrepreneurs who serve as farmers directly as they ask questions and consult about their agriculture at the same time. This human-tech model recognizes a reality that most e-commerce businesses have not—namely, access is not just digital, rather it is relational. Now DeHaat, by using this hybrid system, has reached out to over a million farmers in many states, but by not circumventing but by reinventing the role of the physical intermediaries.

Of prime importance is that those startups do not exist by themselves. The advent of those startups itself is a mirror that has been put in a broad context of the change of attitude towards entrepreneurship in India. The preference that was traditionally given to IIT dropouts who then became crypto bros is slowly and steadily being shifted to engineers who go back to their home districts, social workers who learn coding and women who leverage WhatsApp as a bootstrap before an app is built. This change of the aspirational logic is not just a figure of speech, it has changed the whole tone of the funding conversation. Although most of these startups started with donor or government support, many of them now attract impact investment which is the reason behind the premise of the sustainable development goals. Villgro and Acumen Fund are the two main organizations that are the forerunners of this social funding movement. This process is not easy, it is slow, and it contains many compromises, but one thing is for sure, it reveals a more accurate picture of what might be considered a sustainable transformation.

First and foremost, we must agree that the impact-driven startups are still open to criticism. For some, the issues of retention and monetization are standing in the way, especially if they rely mostly on users who are economically weaker. Some others are facing difficulties with the unclear regulatory environment, especially in fields like education or health where technology goes at a faster pace than policy. At times, the mere ethical aura of the impact covers up the incompetency of the organizations or the weak leadership. However, these failures might occur not only in this area, but they are prevalent in the entire industry of startup companies. The difference is not only the purpose but also the way it is achieved. A lot of these entrepreneurs' focus lies in the development of the business, not in the competition, so they lead as co-creators allowing stakeholders, communities, even critics to be a part of the innovation process. Their set of KPIs, usually, also carries those aspects that are not counted by the traditional VCs. Traditional KPIs would eliminate such things: trust, cultural relevance, dignity.

One illustrative tension in the area that remains controversial is the conflict between the impact of the solution and the number of people to whom it can apply. Do deeply contextual innovations like a menstrual health startup initiated in tribal Jharkhand, for example, resonate in Tamil Nadu or Rajasthan without losing their potential for the replication of the idea? The answer can not be given in one sentence. On the one hand, there are some startups that follow the example of SNEHA or Saathi Pads and have opted for modularity rather than uniformity, that is, they have chosen technology or materials as their core that can now be managed in a decentralized manner. On the other hand, those like Arthan or i-Saksham have created a platform where grassroots entrepreneurs can meet and discuss various issues on their own, and that has become a way for the network to move forward and spread while the solution is still local. This move also undercuts the conventional wisdom among startups that standardization is synonymous with efficiency.

What if the future of success depends on establishing systems that thrive with variety rather than crushing it? However, the one who doesn't recognize the variety as a key success factor will eventually vanish, or maybe could be even successful too, but will certainly find it more challenging to thrive.

For the past few years the role of women in tech in companies has been increasing what's more essential here is their active participation in the whole process, from ownership and supply to the provision of financial support. For example, the development of a sector such as the small-scale energy by Ajaita Shah, through her project, Frontier Markets, and then by her by employing rural women creates a new position of women at the very front of the distribution line--Solar Sahelis means they are merchants of solar lamps, clean cookstoves and also digital services in the country side. Carefully designed for these women, product, and platform adapt to their constraints and strengths. In brief, the launch of the organization functions as expected for those it was meant for while meeting a real need and clearing adverse consequences of no complete deployment of such enterprises. The last result thus shows the outlook of gender intelligent business with some good results for their intentional inclusion in technology. That is why women should be spared the old concept of the inclusion of new skills in them instead of giving technology another form that conforms to women's activities and CFs.

What is more, these young ventures are not set against Silicon Valley giants, but rather, they position themselves as an alternative. They might not always have access to the most innovative algorithms, but they are the ones who often come up with better, more thought-provoking questions: Who is left out of this system? What sort of assumptions does our UI have about literacy, gender, or trust? Is it possible for profit and ethics to be in harmony—not only in theory but in financial statements, too? These questions lead the discourse around entrepreneurship to the point of being more about design justice than merely pursuing innovation for the sake of it.

Similarly, they are also getting more recognition. Now, the government is using its own incubators like Startup India and Atal Innovation Mission to scout for social ventures. Furthermore, incubators in rural universities and Tier-II cities are getting bigger. In addition to this, not unicorns but such more silent actors drive much of the debate on the future of a digital India— about issues such as climate resilience, health equity, or tech localisation. As such, their power is not really in going viral but in revealing the real.

Getting into the skin of these startups tells us that we are witnessing an Indian future different from the copy-paste West-obsessive and valuation-chart-worshipping India, a future that is more about dealing with empathy, the modesty of designers and the contextuality of scaling. And what is ironic in this context, is that this is probably the most transferable or adoptable concept. While the developing world is in search of a non-extractive path to build the digital economy, India's "startups with soul" propose an idea that is more of a compliment than a strategy: frugal innovation coupled with care has a chance in the competition against the well-capitalized and, most of the time, victorious counterparts.

Amid the rubble and debris where remains of ancient homes crept its pathway through the streets and half submerged by the inflow of the flood, while the once glorious community that thrived is now a place of longing where memories are only the reality of kind. Such dreadful changes that nobody of the country, not even of the grave, will be able to record where they live the life of miserable unknown people.

Doomed to live surrounded by their past through wall murals and shutter artwork, people were unable to shake off the feeling of nostalgia even if they were brave enough to see the walls of their houses being taken away by the water. However, as it turned out, the paintings were not the only thing around that was there during the disaster. As they recall, more than ten families who lost their homes continue to wait for a transient influx of hotel guests to move out which was about to be their makeshift shelter.

All this indicates that society still has yet to prepare for sudden climate changes and that nature gives us signs of upcoming inconvenience. The villagers sang and yelled in despair, but there was no way of salvation as the floods brought terror, particularly to women and children, leaving everyone scattered and vulnerable.

General practitioner Dr. Meyer admitted that her clinic was just around the corner, but the deluged streets hindered her to reach it. She held on to her bag with all her strength while debris swirled around her, blocking her way. Later on, the nurse informed her that she only fell, and she was unharmed.

This invisibility does not only go as far as moderation. India's large multilingual speaker base has converted it into the hotspot for training large language models. Thousands of contractual workers not only transcribe, but also tag, translate, and "correct" digital content in many languages spoken in India so that AI systems that range chatbots to voice assistants can work as if they had a human touch. Belonging to being devoid of a central source, the chore is low-paying and carried out by people who are often using platforms that are not regulated in any way. The outsourcers are normally paid per task, some of them will only receive a few rupees per task, and as a rule, they are the ones to provide the digital infrastructure (devices, data, electricity). As a result, the AI achievements in India are at the expense of the low paid workers in the language and linguistic departments.

A great example is the gig economy workers who are too deeply dependent on their digital devices. Swiggy, Zomato, and Blinkit distribution agents perform their jobs with the help of apps, which give them the possibility of crossing cities that are managed by intense algorithms. In practice, the drivers' mobile applications specify the kind of work they may or may not receive, their route and delivery speed, ratings they are supposed to have, and their customer visibility. These workers are people who are marked as the highest leaders at one time but as soon as the need falters no attempt is made to acquire them. They are only onboard but not on salary schedules. An oversight of their delivery or one report—whether this report is true or false—will rob them of their income in a flash. No HR, no up or out system, no commodity security measure. The algorithm has the job of deciding who the offender is, providing the criminal justice system, and carrying out the capital punishment.

Meanwhile, digital translators continue to work under these suffocating terms as they facilitate app interfaces, websites, or customer service templates into Tamil, Bengali, or Marathi. It's funny to note that although it is them who "vernacularise" digital India and extend the technological inclusivity, they're essentially still excluded by the economical terms of their work. A small minority of translators earn subscriptions, sign papers agreeing to work for a long time, or are given the right to participate in the negotiation and make their presence visible. Their thinking is just a part of the brand's gloss that usually does not require any mention. It's a fact that the primary builders of digital India are the ones whose names will never be counted with the great minds.

Ghost work is not only gender-biased but also has a female face. A large percentage of women, particularly from the cities of tier-2 and tier-3, are brought to micro-tasking platforms for one simple reason, they are being recruited because the work is remote and "flexible". However, many of these women have their movements and deadlines set for any arbitrary task snatching and quickly getting to the domestic chore at the same time. The empowerment is promised only to meet the irregular payment, closed evaluation, and emotional burden of the oppressive, low-level work. It's a shame that they are invisible on the list of tech employees and official indicators of digital inclusion. The platform economy has been consuming their time without recognizing their input.

The policy landscape is not in line with this radical change. As India's labor laws are not completely conversant with the digital era, these labor codes are outdated and hence unable to address dispersed, digital, or task-based labor. The term "gig worker" is still not legally defined and if it is used, it is a much narrow term that does not cover workers in differently established criteria other than those in the delivery or ride-hailing sector. The institutions have not been able to design any form of support especially for mental health for the content moderators. Nor has any effective systems been brought into light that can be used in the wage transparency for micro-taskers or bringing their grievances for the same to the workers. On the other hand, the state is still in the dilemma of fostering digital India or rather regulating its intrinsic contradictions. In the vacuum, a new form of workers of the invisible class manifests.

In terms of platform companies, they are, in fact, promoting their companies under the constant euphemisms that they have developed. Gig workers are now known as "partners". Moderators refer to themselves as "safety specialists". Translators are labeled "community contributors". The jury is still out on whether the vile language used was gender-based or not, but it is not just the choice of words, it is, in fact, an art of precise selection from the employers' side in order to slip away from any employer obligations. The platforms, while getting the maximum benefit, also try to get rid of the liabilities as much as they can. For example, if a delivery person gets hit by a car, the company will blame the accident on the person's contractor. In a case of a trauma to a content moderator, the vendor takes the responsibility for their emotional health issue. In short, the platforms are so successful in dividing the responsibilities that they can almost narrowly escape being held accountable for their actions.

However, opposition is gradually becoming visible. For instance, last year, food delivery drivers from Bengaluru carried out coordinated protests in response to the reduction of their wages and the increase in fuel prices. AI translation workers, who have formed collectives on WhatsApp, have started to be the voice of their communities by exchanging rates, discussing exploitation, and even agreeing to boycott contracts that are poorly paid. Feminist technologists and digital labour scholars have raised the issue of the cognitive and emotional load of invisible tech work in their academic research. These voices may not have much impact, but their power and influence continue to grow.

But this crisis also points to a very deep question, philosophically speaking: who are these knowledge workers in digital India? If a person is training a language model in Odia, or is reading and checking fake news in Malayalam, are they not, in fact, preparing the ground for the AI of the future? Is there no need, then, for their work to be seen as skilled, essential and of the future? Instead, what happens is their labor is treated as though it were nothing, unseen, and paid as if it were an additional thing. This is more than an economic disparity, it is epistemic injustice, i.e. the power to decide whose knowledge is relevant in the new digital economic order.

The global community has already experienced the challenges around this kind of labor. For example, in the United States "ghost workers" in Silicon Valley have become the topic of Senate hearings and the subject of lawsuits and journalistic exposes. In Europe, digital platforms are under the watchful eyes of the labour authorities so that the gig workers can receive de facto employee status in some countries. India, with its vastness and variety of languages, is obviously facing a different situation; nonetheless, it may also become the leader of ethical digital labour worldwide. This, however, calls for political willingness, institutional change, and a new way of assigning value.

There is no digital utopia without human scaffolding. Chrome is not alone for the user exp but a person is working manually for the data control, toxicity moderation, or the delivery person is panicking to drop parcels in 45°C. These labors are no sidelines but India's digital story creators, period. The failure to notice them means more than being unfair; it is something that cannot survive in the future. The future of a society that is based on invisibilized labor might be in reality weaker than everyone thinks it is. The issue is not about the existence of ghost work; it is more about the question of whether or not we are ready to see it, count it, and value it.

Trust, Tokens, and Tech

Trust is the invisible infrastructure of every economy. It is the oil that flows in the channels of commerce and binds institutions. It is the one by which people can interact with the system they do not fully see. In the old days, trust was often transferred through human intermediaries like banks, governments, notaries, clerics. Right now, in the digital era, it is mostly that code, platforms, and protocols that have responsibility. Nevertheless, within the context of what software developers call Web3, trust that can be decentralised, verifiable, programmable, and perhaps even sovereign is emerging as a new concept. Given India's recent tradition of adopting new technologies, its growing population, and its distinctive digital public infrastructure strategy, the country is likely to be not only a recipient but a creator of such tools.

The question central to the next phase of tech sounds both age-old and pressing: Who is the owner of someone's identity, and who has the right to grant legitimacy? In the Web2 period, the platforms had a tight grip on the user data and monetised it in return for the users' access. That is what particularly distinguishes Web3 from Web2; it assures folks the ability to own their data, identify themselves independently, and perform peer-to-peer without being watched by external regulators. Blockchain gives the technology of Web3 its backbone, in which individuals authorise transactions, create a network identity, and have a code of conduct for contracts and community through a shared ledger, which is not only for cryptocurrency but also for identity, credentials, and related community issues.

The discussion around Aadhaar in a way has been an early indicator of this change. At the beginning, Aadhaar emerged as a biometric identification system, which was initiated for the welfare of the people and the financial inclusion, and consequently, it set up a digital infrastructure through which big crowd service could be provided. Up to now, over 1.3 billion people of India have registered themselves. The Aadhaar project has resulted in significant purchasing efficiencies (entering data in real-time, handouts of direct benefits, and mobile-based authentications) but it also exposed many concerns that have still not been dealt with such as spying, approval, and exclusion.

The implementation of Aadhaar system opened up the negotiations of the centralized identification systems. With India ready to embrace its next phase of digital transformation, it not just remains the only country in search of a trust reformation through regulatory means but also has the solution at the programming level.

Now, the time for introducing DIDs, SSI, and verifiable credentials has come. The idea is that these solutions can be used by users to manage their own identity data, decide on their identity revelation, and reduce their reliance on centralized organizations. Such would be the case that one of the rural Maharashtrian graduates would be able to virtually present a digital certificate that can be verified to their probable employer if the digital certificate has been signed-off by the university.

Moreover, the migrant worker gets an opportunity to prove his/her employment history no matter where in the states they have been to without the need to double the documentation for every new place of work. This play makes trust mobile.

The public digital infrastructure of India, which is also a by-word for the "India Stack", is an exemplary case of the test drive of such new techniques. It was built as microservice architecture and open APIs making it different from the widely used corporate platforms. It has not only empowered UPI (for fast money transfers), DigiLocker (for safe data storage), and Account Aggregators (for strictly consensual data exchanges) but also has allowed for the implementation of such big social changes that these thins were also the governing architectures for India's digital future—public, interoperable, and inclusive and thereby user-controlled.

Some of the initial tests show that it can. School records and DigiLocker have already started to be used with a blockchain credentialing system. The verifiable documents can be used as a certificate of degree to be shared with employers or organizations without any counterfeit. The use of blockchain in land records management has been suggested by the Supreme Court as a step forward to the reduction of fraud and litigation in property ownership. The project was implemented in Andhra Pradesh and Telangana, where a transparent and secure system was introduced, ensuring the reliability of the records.

On the contrary, DeFi applications have not gained a significant number of users yet, but are mostly being adopted by cities in the country, where technology is dominating. DeFi projects provide opportunities for staking, lending, and asset exchange without relying on the middlemen in the conventional banking system. This ambiguity of the sector frightens most users, but they are still curious about the service. It is not that India will become a haven for crypto-trading in the conventional Western sense; rather, the blockchain technology might have relevance for the community in terms of proof of welfare eligibility, community voting protocols, transparent supply chain, and decentralized health records.

A notable development that most of us overlook is "tokenized governance"—a concept that includes the community in decision-making with the help of programmable, transparent, and auditable systems. The present political landscape might make it look odd, but there is the possibility of local governance initiatives (like participatory budgeting in Kerala or digital grievance redressal in Karnataka) being upgraded through token-based systems which would stimulate a sense of trust and incorporate the community's power and voice. Blockchain can be the source of trust.

Nevertheless, the belief that the technological development is necessarily a good thing has to be balanced with the real state of affairs. The fact that something is not centralized doesn't make it a democracy. Nor does every token help people. A large part of the initial crypto surge was overshadowed by the fact that it was all about the mania of speculators, 'pump-and-dump' schemes, and environmental issues. On the regulatory front, India has decided to be conservative, so they tax digital assets quite heavily and at the same time have postponed the adoption of legal frameworks for innovation. The concern is that too much regulation will stifle innovation; the threat is that too little regulation will give fraudsters access to the public. In the middle of these two options is a chance to govern features instead of the over-hype. Simplify the problem—just look at the applications, forget about the prices.

India, in its special capacity, is in a position to develop its public infrastructure both in terms of scalability and legitimacy. The World Wide Web

3.0 ideology is mainly about conservatism and keeping off from the government; still, India's approach can be unique representing a new kind of pro-public Web3. This approach is a way of using decentralized resources to improve the effectiveness of the government and empower citizens, while, at the same time, rendering every process transparent, not dubious. The approach is also confirming that not all issues necessarily require the usage of blockchain; some are more of a policy, others a cultural nature while some need the humble choice of simpler tools.

However, the basic concept is still there. It is possible to think of an Indian farmer in Bihar who could claim the harvested insurance through a smart contract with no bribery, no delays, and no errors involved. Also, it's an example of a gig worker in Coimbatore who earns micro-loans based on tokenized evidence of earlier earnings. Or else it is the case of a tribal student from Jharkhand who holds a digital backpack of credentials that can be verified—retrievable, transferable, and universally applicable across the country. These are not just utopian works of imagination. They are real-life problems that need solutions and are waiting for the collaboration of technologists, policymakers, and civil society to come up with the resolutions.

An innovative point in India's journey will most probably not emerge from the habit of copying Western patterns as was previously the case. UPI is a typically Indian way of digital payments, which gave birth to a new environment where transactions are for free, not by copying the idea that credit cards have been using. Similarly, India could develop trust-tech not on Web0 grounds, trying to differentiate themselves ideologically but, by focusing on citizens' trust. Godwin, this project could be labeled differently. Nobody will call it an ideology, instead, it will be infrastructure, a coherent strategy, etc. The aim of trust in future will not only include cryptography but, above all, whether a person is credible or not.

The verification of information will be by how systems handle exceptional situations. A decentralized identity system, for example, can it still recognize a woman who changes her name after getting married, or a migrant who does not have his phone with him anymore? Another question to be considered is will smart contracts translated into Hindi, Telugu, or Santali still be valid as legal documents when they are used in that form? Or simplifying the question, is it possible for decentralized applications to be developed to such an extent that they can be used on low-capacity phones and accessed through non-uninterrupted networks? These are the questions that will show if trust-tech is a tool for all or if it is just for decoration. Here, India's challenge is not limited to achieving the next era of technology, but also to make it culturally relevant.

In the event of success, the new innovation will not only surpass the West in the area of innovation but will involve a self-leap in the way it interacts with the state-citizen-shadow regulation complex. The facilitation technique of security at a mammoth level will surely be the one ringing the bell for the move and not taking the high stake by introducing the next big thing that may or may not.

Chapter 11

The Philosophical Future

It is a puzzling fact about contemporary society, never before have humans been so globally connected and yet they are actually so internally fragmented. India, a nation whose culture is based on reflection, is paradoxically a leader in a world that is connected to an extent that it is almost beyond belief. The clash is not coincidental and is of great importance. It is of irenic nature. The spirit of the debate, in this case, is the duality of things - the Atman, the genteel inner self cherished by the Indic people, versus the global network of mental organs that are incessantly bent on stealing our selfhood, measuring our value, and driving our urges to profit.

India's digital [buldy1] future is not only about technology but also about its connection with our oldest and highly resilient ethical guidelines. If the previous sections have been devoted to examining infrastructure, innovation, and inequality, this one follows a line that can be described as more delicate - the way we read, think, and navigate the digital world. The article not only explores what India is constructing but who we are turning into. Therefore, its purpose is to motivate the readers to think about digital life from a philosophical, cultural point of view in the country where spirituality has always been a dominant factor in the material world.

At first, we are called to face the dichotomy between actual presence and the manifestation of our professional or personal identities. In traditional Indian philosophy, dharana, and dhyana (concentration and meditation) are not merely spiritual practices; instead, they are the means through which knowledge is created and the world is experienced. This contrasts strongly to today's digital platforms that are built for the purpose of dividing the user's attention, giving bonus points for mere superficial engagement, and supporting addictive behaviors. The average Indian smartphone user reaches for the device 2,617 times in a day. Every like, retweet, and notification acts as a vehicle to the journey from the present awareness to the performing level where the digital self has become a projected one, i.e., an entity that is overly concerned with the metrics of visibility. Likes become tokens; being viral, a measure of worth.

What if we speak about metaphysical and not just mere behavioral things here? Can it be that the attention economy does not only lead to time erosion but also mind transformation? That is the main question this chapter provides. It wants to be informed if Atman – a concept in Indian philosophy as a soul or spirit – transcendental and immortal— the eternal, observing self—is being occluded by a digital ecology that insists reactivity to be dominant and reflection to be in a passive position. Can a culture that once has the ability to make its sages practice deep inner peace silence now use the same way to show teenagers how to go offline with the right words? Or the production process of our tools has bypassed that of our moral vocabulary?

The other question is the result of the concept of "karma", not as a superstition, but as a theory of moral causality. That is, in the case of Indian ethics, morality is not reduced to a set of rules or principles; it is rather seen as the source of individuals, community, and future. Every action creates a consequence that is not only external but also internal by nature. Digital environment leads to a situation when it is challenging to determine this. For instance, if the trolling is carried out anonymously, the abuse is amplified by an algorithm, and disinformation is distributed through share buttons, then one can ask the question of the distribution of karmic responsibility. Can the moral law remain a living reality in a digital world that is not transparent?

The growing frequency of online cruelty, and particularly the gendered and caste-based accuse, is too flagrant to be taken as trifling acts such as merely trolling. In fact, this can be characterized as the externalization of latent social contaminants, which show that rage is being more and more engendered for the benefit of those who are engaged in these platforms. Nevertheless, the idea of digital karma can be considered valid as well. Thus, platforms do not only spread hate but they can also represent compassion, just like the same net that disseminates hate also carries with it love. The difference lies in our actions that follow our words. Here digital karma, becomes repulses and not so much a cosmic account, but an ethical feedback—do our actions in the online world develop the human person, or do they reduce him or her?

This leads to the third and culminating question: How can we describe Indian digital dharma? Not dharma in a religious sense but a kind of ethical structure - a set of duties to humanity in a shared area. In the Mahabharata, dharma is a term that is not situational, it is context-oriented, and it is dialogic. The responsibilities of a warrior and a monk are different; the role of a ruler is certainly not that of a teacher. Thus, digital dharma is not one that revolves around homogeneous regulations but one of sensitive duty. When one has awareness, what does it mean to act, to limit when, to moderate in balanced manner?

India is indeed the best in this matter if it is portrayed as an indicator and a promoter of this new concept and not as a revival of the past. While privacy and rights dominate the conversation in the Western world, Indian philosophers' traditions present moral patterns out of relationality. The self is not alone, it is one of the interdependence web nodes. Trust falls not only on people but also on the system. This perception might still remodel our computer designing and policy-making processes, as well as teach the computer users about ethical and existential topics concerning their learning process. This may guide the way to a system grounded on mutual respect, balance, and reciprocity rather than to the libertarian, individualist ideology ruling the Silicon Valley.

At present, such breakthroughs are emerging to the surface. Apps for mindfulness founded on Indian traditions are getting relocated to their cultural context, no longer as productivity tools, but spiritual aids again. People in online communities make the first experiments in a change to slower and intentional ways of conversation. Several startups are doing their best to build platforms that epitomize consent, transparency, and well-being instead of making money as principal influence. But these are merely the highlights. The task is to stretch these islands into continents and insert ethical reflection into the everyday flow of the designer's work, discussion's dialogue, and digital policy.

This chapter provides the reader with not just a definite response, but a series of questions, provocations, and forms of critical thinking. It's like the reader being a part of a symposium where people are ready to take, or better say provoke, a reaction. And, it is exactly these symposiums where readers may collectively solve some of the most urgent dilemmas of the digital age by way of ancient vivid ideas- karma, dharma, and the Atman. This is not to indicate a romanticizing of the past, nor a refusal of technology. It's about finding one's true path, i.e. placing one's resources at the service of one's best self. Can our tools not only display but also guide our solid truths? Can our platforms give life to our ethical standards? May digital India develop not only in extension but also in understanding?

Asking the questions above is not to choose a backward step from the current era of development; it is to redefine it. A possible revolution of philosophy is not to be regarded as a thing of wealth. In fact, in a world that is everywhere speaking to us, a world where everyone is found to be connected everywhere, it is the little, disciplined brain in the corner that will still be, may be, the most significant.

Can a Nation Have a soul in a Digital Age?

An attempt to define India against the backdrop of modernity has not been a simple and unambiguous task. To put it in other words, India is both an IT superpower and a land of live scriptures, where ancient traditions and hi-tech lifestyles mingle with great ease. This is a rather sarcastic position from some other viewpoints. However, given that India is undergoing an extreme makeover experience in the virtual world—something that literally impacts more than a billion of its citizens, the role of philosophy becomes as important as that of technology. It's not about whether or not-India is doing the digital thing, it's about which India is the coding process giving birth to. Can a civilization of this century become so digital-age interactive that it risks being without that seal of the aeonian, the soul left in it? inapp

You might think that digital infrastructure is only convenience or efficiency by which you can only get the job done a better way—bank, shop, learn, or connect. However, when these infrastructures begin to negotiate identity, dream, morals and even memory, they serve not only the needs of life but as an expression of norms. Aadhar is not just the biometric database; it is the answer to the question of what the identity is like in the 21st century. UPI is not a completely new product in the fintech world; it is the new and real trust that comes from the government and is what the citizens follow then. It becomes a state-based definition of trust, and that is no longer direct peer-to-peer relationships. The transformation from oral and communal traditions to the algorithmic filtering of experiences reveals a colossal shift in culture—from having a shared way of knowing things to attaining personalized consumption loops. This is not an insignificant change. This is the metaphysical reconfiguration process that appears in the facade of modernization.

For many ages through Indian philosophies, the soul "Atman" has been untainted by the matters of visibility, productivity, and social media. However, current digital platforms have grown to need these qualities in demand. One's visibility in society has become a matter of one's existence in it. There must be a spectacle by which one is recognized and of course, a person's performance is given recognition. This action dismisses former rules that favored service to vanity, quietness to voice. The outward appearance of a traditionally spiritual life that was more inward gazed than widely expressed through yoga and meditation changes beyond recognition. The nature of one's spiritual encounters thus moves from personal inquisition to community performance. Digital tools are not only a way to distill culture but also to create it.

This is definitely not to romanticize the past or to say that the tech has turned our world into a grim dystopia. India's strength has always been its incorporation ability — that's how it embraced aesthetics from Persia, colonial law, and the principles of post-liberal economics and weaved them into a common culture. The virtual space can be its next great phase of synthesis if the country pulls it off successfully. This union, nevertheless, has to be more deliberate and less involuntary. A confusion of ideas can turn the instruments of the digital era into solvents of civilization rather than those of unity. It's enough to change a matter of a digitally powerful society to one that is digitally overpowered.

One way of examining this friction is through the cognitive consequences of the life led by algorithms. One should first of all take into consideration the fact that recommendation engines – be it Youtube, Instagram or Amazon – are not mere suppliers of the essential; they are also the ones who help invent the desire. Eventually, these platforms understand through our actions what our preferences are, and then, they start curating our information for us. This is, however, just one side of the coin as such systems also trim down the information to its bare minimum, which is quite different from the Indian ideology which prefers the gray areas such as spirituality in the body and spirituality in the soul to binary ways of knowing. These outlets tilt the balance in favor of which is definitely not to make reason stand, but to determine whether a fact is true or not. And this condition is incompatible with traditions that expose individuals to hints, introspection and ethics ambiguity, " says the author, asking aloud.

The digital, too, carves out the time. The routine life in India, especially its religious festivals, was enlightenment the lunar-solar calendar. On the other hand, the clock in the digital age is a whole different story. Notifications start the clock at that very second, asking for immediate action. The zero-hours time frame leads to much play, content expires in just one day, etc. Therefore, the digital time is strikingly different from the one in the Hindu cultural heritage. Indeed, such a difference is important because profound philosophical thinking is often time-consuming, repetitive, and silent. These attributes happen to be the least in agreement with these current screens and their fast-moving styles.

Yet in the middle of these conflicts, the opposing side can still be seen. India is a source of digital tools adopters with a batch of people such as entrepreneurs, coders, thinkers and the emerging monk class who ask themselves whether the digital tools could be harnessed for non-AI goals or not. Can the blockchain technology be employed to foster trust in decentralized community finance instead of cryptocurrency speculation? Are the AI-generated language models capable of drawing knowledge retrieval tools from Indic texts to come up with knowledge systems that reflect Indian rather than Anglo-positivist epistemology? Can the software be made to enlighten the internal state—this time not through gamified meditation but with the help of stillness, ethical clarity, and self-inquiry building tools?

The question that brings more originality is not whether India will make digital systems, but whether it will put the systems with civilizational intelligence. After all, codes also carry their own sets of values. The style of an app, the design of a payment rail, the policy of a platform—each of them takes for granted what is worthy, what is standard, and what is permissible. If India's digital conversion simply re-enacts the West's one, it will not only import technologies but also ontologies—a state of mind of individualism, commodification, and performative identity. However, if India fills its digital future with ideas from its own philosophy, it will provide a new model to the world: one where the interconnectedness of things does not necessitate uniformity, and where size does not mean a loss of soul.

This is anything but a call for 'Indian alternatives' to Silicon Valley platforms. The thrust of it is more about the question of whether in the technological world, India's ancient spiritual wisdom traditions—including but not limited to Vedanta, Bhakti, Sufi and Sikhism—can enter into meaningful dialogue with people's practices. Can they be used to shape platform designs, data governance strategies, user education, and even the future of the public sphere? The attention economy goes beyond just bending people's concentration to capture it; the reprogramming of what is among things likely to catch anyone's attention is the fundamental aspect of it. Any positive reaction to that is through philosophy.

Imagine the ethics of data, for example. Most of the discussion on the subject in the world centers on privacy, security, and consent. It is indeed a matter of much importance. In Indian culture, the focus is rather on moral behavior. The right question is not just whether or not something is allowed, but also if it is the right thing or not. Also, the emphasis is not on the individual's desires but on what sustains the community. This dharmic principle is not just a matter of the law, but also the moral aspect. A digital ethic based on dharma would not only be reasonable to insist on opt-in checkboxes, but also inquire as to whether the systems support swadharma (individual integrity), lokasangraha (collective well-being), and samatva (equity). in the process, we first ourselves about surveillance, data brokerage, AI ethics, and digital infrastructure.

Now, let's move the topic to the matter of identity. Aadhar may very well authenticate fingerprints, however, it is powerless to erase the demography, social class, kinship, dialect, and ritual territoriality encountered in India. While it is quite a real danger that Indian subjectivity has been reduced to that of a KYC-compliant entity of an all that has the potential to change this is the same tool of technology, depending on how it is run, narrated, and defended. The essence of a nation does not rest in temples and texts only. It is embedded in the technology that people use to communicate with-in their social systems, i.e., with the state and among themselves, with time and truth.

Okay, let's take, for example, if a country can have a digital soul. It depends on how the nation uses the word soul and the kind of digital we allow our imagination to be. When we say "soul," we mean the highest moral aspirations and the deepest feeling of a society; that is, the spirit of the nation. Such a thing is to be found in society naturally. It must be nurtured, programmed, and defended. The Indian digital soul will still be there when faster applications or cheaper phones are gone. If our infrastructure is devised with insight, technology with a sense of moderation, and our thinking with ethical imagination, then our digital soul as a nation is in the making.

The evolution of India's digital realm is beyond being a matter of engineering, it's a civilizational issue as well. The core of this question is whether we are to digitalize only the outer shell, or will we have the courage to go ahead and digitalize the inner self with all due respect to biometric but at the same time philosophical context. Is the new internet-driven India going to be more filled with sagacity, with liberty, and with integrity, or will it just be more interconnected?

Here's the question. Nothing but the traffic jam is left.

The Attention Economy vs. Atman

Our current epoch is marked by an intriguing contradiction: while the unlimited cascade of notifications, reels, and retweets on one side, and our minds being pulled into numerous directions – the infinite, and essentially regressive character of that process – and on the other side there is this old civilization model that leads us to the idea of freedom in silence. The core of the matter is not about the addictiveness of the modern technology. The question lies in the idea that perhaps modern digital systems are developed with such axioms that are fundamentally inconsistent with the Indian philosophical traditions that have been nurtured for thousands of years. What happens if Silicon Valley's money-making exploitation of human attention meets Atman, one of the noblest concepts of the Indic philosophy, a pure, self-contained, and unreflecting soul? Some remember what has gone before, only putting rose-tinted glasses on, others are only living in the present, but there are a few people, who don't sit and ponder on what happened, but draw the bridge and plan for years to come. Atman is traditional and stereotypical, Silicon Valley is progressive but disrespectful of the environment. The answer is neither negative nor positive. However, it remains a serious issue.

It is no longer just a motto. it has become a guiding principle that human attention is the most sought-after scarce resource in this era. Every interface of a phone is structured to monetize every second that the user spends there: from the delivery of infinite flows of information, the automatic play of content, intermittent dopamine rewards, to nudges, alerts, and pings. The platforms are getting profit by capturing and selling the attention present in the cognitive space. Tristan Harris, a technology analyst, highlighted that these systems do not only present choices to their users, they also make the decisions for them. But this is simply seen as manipulative, which means that the more profound change that is taking place has been missed. The fact is that the present digital experience, in terms of the application's architecture, is treating the user not as a self-ruling entity to whom the choice confers a statistically predictable future but as a potential subject of a strategic game of interest in the domain of attention, where the user is easily commodifiable as data and the soul of the very user is a matter that can be overlooked.

On the other hand, the perspectives in the Indian tradition focus on the mind's inwardness as the most important rather than as a method to be productive. The description in the Yoga Sutras of the mind is chitta, a place where thoughts constantly transform. Chitta vritti nirodhah is a goal that implies the calming down of the mental waves created by the fluctuations of the mind. Hence, concentration is not the gateway to making profits; it is a means of spiritual enlightenment. According to the Upanishadic pattern, it is not that consciousness is colorless. It is the middle of existence. That which you think about, you become. Yad bhāvam tad bhavati. We can find the complete opposite of the fast click-driven logics of social media platforms which always like the people to be in agitation, shock, novelty, and vanity. It is true that the digital marketplace is because it is a place where you are not when you are not calm, you are a little off-balance—twitched, cheered, provoked.

At the same time, one should not hold the belief that technology naturally ruins spiritual life. However, the current system of rewards indeed does. With one of the world's biggest and fastest digitalization campaigns, India has finally removed the barrier and connected people to hundreds of millions. The change has not only affected the digital space but has also reshaped the mentality thus the behavior of the masses. To ignore the philosophical impact of this shift is a very short-sighted approach. The attention structure incentivized by a culture is identical to its ethical norm. When each digital action is a tribute to distraction, then stillness starts to be subversive.

One remarkable and illustrative demonstration can be observed from the rise of the "mindfulness" apps, most of which borrow the ideas from Buddhist and Yogic traditions and then use them as the best available attention-hacking UX strategies to the user community. A user will be the beneficiary of a range of digital coping mechanisms that the app provides a constant reminder of such as the streaks, badges, and the overall game-like ease in using those serenity methods. Thus, inner peace is broken down into algorzhythmically digestible pieces. Along the same line, we are left with a much more fundamental question to ask ourselves: Is it really possible to instill peace in such a way on a platform of which the profits clock in through your commitment? Is the possibility to change from within real in a context whose primary agenda is to push it on?

One might perhaps argue that the Atman—the realizing self—is basically impossible to be manipulated by external forces. However, cultural conditioning has the paramount role in determining our experiences. Consequently, when the mind is enslaved, the power of being aware is crushed. Today's scenario is not a clash between East and West, rather two paradigms of attention: one that tries to make it a slave and the other that honors its independence.

Yet the social costs of distraction which is not a free choice are escalating even from a pragmatic viewpoint. The average screen time per day for Indian teenagers has risen way above 7 hours, and at the same time, mental health indicators have been depreciating. The matter of the fact is not the exposure itself but the generation and feeling of being enclosed in a vicious cycle of wanting more and comparing with others. For one, beauty filters on Instagram are not just additional decorations to the photos; they can also change the perception of oneself. TikTok's viral algorithms which prefer multi-emotion over single thought are also tricks used by platforms to come up with the most probable scenarios, thereby affecting our judgment of our being, success, and significance.

Moreover, there's an epistemic burden. C. Thi Nguyen, a political scientist, has made a point that attention systems which are gamified are reducing various extensive initiatives like truth or righteousness to mere figures: likes, shares, and followers. What gets registered is what is getting registered. Indian philosophical tradition, in contrast, embraces concepts of pratyaya (false constructs) and pratyaksha (direct knowing). Here, such distinctions among concepts are vital when it comes to civil discussion. The more we rely on trending content to define our reality, the harder it will be for us to detect the subtle, the lasting, or the unsuitable.

However, a paradox is still there. Despite devices taking away your focus, they are also still capable of refocusing it too. Digital media is not limited to the scope of online news or entertainment platforms. Chosen meditation podcasts, digital copies of ancient texts, and thought-provoking documentaries are perfect examples of digital materials. The problem is not if screens themselves are good or bad; the main issue is whether or not the systems that are built on those screens encourage awareness or contribute to its destruction. It is absolutely possible that online media environments could be reshaped to make reflection an organic part of the user's decision-making process rather than an external compulsion. The obstacle is not the media tool; it is the manner of generating value that companies follow.

A group of Indian thinkers and technologists are now adopting alternative ways of thinking and working. The idea of "digital dharma" is being pursued by designers who are keen on developing digital tools that are in line with India's ethical codes of conduct. The intention of these developers is not just to be gunas neutral, but to create such technologies that play a part in enhancing the well-being and the realization of human potential in its full sense. Sattva and Chitti, for example, are such like apps that are used for meditation with the Vedic religion at their core and on the other hand, they are also the early products based on Indians' languages and social values. The purpose of the above-mentioned activities is not to put the tradition for the tech-savvy generation, but rather to make the findings of tradition relevant to the design of the human attention system. The idea here is to make these insights the architecture of our attention systems.

How about the designing of an interface that embodied tranquillity? Such an interface would probably avoid the use of endless scrolls. It would suggest some comfortable thresholds and methods to halt and might as much as speech. Also, it would be the decision of the designer making it to maintain the difference and not be attracted to the popularity of his works. A transformation of this kind of magnitude will not only call for a shift in language but also a shift in awareness, time, and goal.

That leads us to the field of education where the majority of the Indian edtech platforms are involved in the delivery of skills and performance in exams while a very minimal number of them are talking about the moral faculty of attention. This latter is a golden opportunity that has been lost. Rather than imitating the tactics of Silicon Valley, India should offer a creative non-violent resistance to the status of being deliberately absent that can reach not only technology users but also all the citizens - a version extending to the whole of the society.

The education of the aspect of attention demand not to be labeled as a wellness trend only but as a civic infrastructure too. We often talk about and insist on the absolute necessity of digital rights, such as privacy, access, and security, but the discussion of digital virtues is not so frequent. Forbearance. Transparency. Kindness. These are not hardware components but ethical principles. The Hindu, Buddhist, and Jain lines of thought all point to viveka- discernment- to be a key instrument in one's own freedom. Applied in digital games, it means saying no just to the automatic, asking back the subliminal message and realizing the intention of persuasion. The platform is not the action. It is capable of clearly and visibly guiding the way or of obscuring it.

A nation like India, with its philosophical tradition that accommodates a very deep introspection and, at the same time, encourages a very stimulating public debate, is in a very good place to change the rules of the attention governance. But for this, the country has to be ambitious; not for the sake of being the top app store seller, but by setting the ethical rules of the interface itself. This objective could be pushed away as it might be thought as beyond reach in the face of apps manipulated by billion-dollar ad engines and internet users having very short attention spans. Nevertheless, civilizations are not just empty users of technologies; indeed, they can be the creators of these technologies. That is why they can disapprove and reshape the technology they are using. To achieve this, the lesson is that they have to recall.

The Atman is not driven by trending nor is it the subject of constant requests nor does it need any changes in order to be appealing to others. It observes. And in that very observation, a new possibility for a digital order emerges, which is characterized by the fact that human attention is not treated as an SKU but as sacred.

Karma in the Cloud: Digital Deeds and the Ethics of Anonymity

In earlier days, the web was an imagined oasis of free access to ideas—unlimited, unlimited and decentralized. But as digital life has turned out to be indistinguishable from actual life, the philosophical implications of our online activities have begun to demand emphatic rethinking. Every 'like', every retweet, every foul-mouthed comment or digital seal of support is now in the bigger picture of the influence matrix. What we do online is not something of a passing cloud. It leaves the observer marks. It influences reputations, mental health, discourse, and policy. But are these actions karmic? In other words, can they have ethical consequences in the deeper, civilisational sense which karma was defined in Indian thought—not only cause and effect but a metaphysical accountability that binds intention, context, and outcome? Moreover, and even more rudely now, what is to be the face of ethics in the age of digital anonymity?

The idea of a digital public square characterized by the laws of karma is not an attempt to take over a religious vocabulary for stylistic purposes. It is a question of whether an old civilisational system of morality—one that claims that actions are intertwined with the intentions and the chain of effects from action—can we understand, and perhaps adjust, our online behaviour. Unlike the legal or the penal system, which has laws to estimate acts, karma, according to classical Indian philosophy, assesses the moral liability of an act as per the conscience which is behind it. A lie told to save a life is not the same as a lie told to deceive. A public charity act done for show does not have the same intentions as the same act done with the heart's willingness but quietly. Karma, through its flexibility, its refusal to disentangle behavior from the background and the motive, makes its way to a deep, non-binary ethics—this makes it a unique candidate for a more us world where the public and private selves are ineluctably mixed, and where platforms of digital nature encourage people to perform very well, but not to introspect.

The paradox of the digital life is the fact that it creates an extraordinary abundance of actions - clicks, shares, swipes - but at the same time makes people less accountable for the things they do online. Platforms are designed specifically for boosting their users' engagement and number of participants but not for making the community more wise and accountable. A post becomes viral not because of its truth; provocation is the principal key to success. An algorithm, instead of promoting nuancedness, is structured so that outrage is the only choice that gets a response. Yet each of the actions of digital circulation bears instead the burden of negative influence. The consequences have been introduced which are as follows: a label-less video going viral around the globe of millions can end with lynching. Deepfake productions that deceive people can cause the loss of someone's career. Moreover, an individual could go through moral and psychological torture if he/she is a target of trolling, the motive of which is the government, females, as well as those in the minority.

These are not just by-products of a neutrally designed technology; they are mainly the products of large-scale decisions. Karma as a tool for scrutinizing a situation comes in handy at this point and its significance and necessity both are beyond doubt.

For example, imagine a user who unknowingly spreads a rumor because he didn't care to see if it was true, and he did it either to boost his ego, to get approval of his views, or he was just simply gratified to see that he got more followers. From the karmic perspective, this is one problem-free event. The cause - the person's enthrallment, the matches of the of the self with the world, or the market's imprinting - is significant. Common traits that mark the end of any discussion on this point are the ways in which misinformation can rapidly take unpleasant turns, and consequently empathy that used to be among the community members vanishes. The most important to mention is that this user does not notice in any way the mess he/she has brought about. The whole system, that is, the algorithm takes away the possible outcomes of a person's actions and places them outside the individual, hence creating what we term digital disembodiment. The real challenge here is to explain the situation to yourself using karma among the clouds, and because of that, the cause and result chains have been completely blurred and, in fact, there is no longer a system where if a person behaves poorly they definitely receive some less reward, a form of giving and taking, even if they do not help anyone.

Anonymity's veil not only allows the disconnection to exist but it makes it much worse. On forums and also in comment sections, individuals are so bold that they can do anything and go as far as to use abuse, defamation, threats, doxxing practices. These are the standard behaviour of Indian citizens in the virtual world, especially due to the deep political division in the nation and the oppression of women having conducted online. However, anonymity is not always associated with immorality because it is the very same that allows people to be even if those who are really at risk allow it to be. When practiced as a weapon, anonymity becomes a great obstacle. After all, without karma, which means no consequence, there can be no reflection and hence no moral development.

On the other hand, this is not a situation that is to be seen as a moral crisis or a phobia arising from being technologically backward. The main difficulty is not in the internet, it is, rather, the unexamined architecture of the platforms, incentives, and behaviours that have thrived in the digital age. If we want karma to exist in the digital world, we must create structures that not only encourage ethical conduct but also integrate it. This is where the line between design philosophy and dharma must be drawn in the sand: platforms should not be full of forgotten values. Recommendation engines are not there only to help people stream as long as they want or click the links; their main focus should be on facts, respect, and building relations. The moderation that comes with the digital age should be proactive, multilingual, and a model of transparency. The ideal situation, however, is that the literacy level in India should not only be limited to empowering people with simple and functional skills but it should also emerge as a subsystem of fostering ethical intelligence so that people can make it clear to themselves that they are still within the moral universe even if they are in the online world.

Some of the pilot studies in progress already suggest that this is the case. The "Pause Before You Post" feature, which is being tried out on a few social media networks, encourages users to reflect on the effect of their words. A number of Indian NGOs have taken the initiative and designed campaigns to show people the ripple effects of online hate (i.e., how a share can grow into a tragedy). However, these projects are just a drop in the ocean, and the ocean may be rising. We should not settle for mere reform, but move towards a cultural shift; namely, the appearance of what is referred to as digital karma consciousness. This would involve educating users who are not only aware of the fact that they are not safe under the cloak of anonymity but who also realize that each action—be it visible or invisible, real or pseudonymous—will leave a mark on the screen and society's moral balance.

Furthermore, we have to tackle a more fundamental philosophical question— whether karma, as it has always been understood, can be transported to the digital age at all. Can it be functional in a world where machine learning and metadata prevail and thus the causality effect is usually less direct and the human intention is not seen in the way that it affects algorithms but rather inferred from them? A possible way forward may be to reinterpret karma not as a mechanism that brings cosmic retributions but simply as a principle of interconnectedness. In this sense, digital karma implies that we have to realize that our deeds, no matter how insignificant or virtual they might seem, are still part of a great chain of cause and effect that shapes our collective awareness. Thus, ethics could become the process of being here rather than a set of rules to follow as a commitment to be attentive, rather than casual, in every relationship.

Above all, certain streams of classical Indian thought even anticipated the paradox of the inner world and the outside world. The Bhagavad Gita may wrongly be taken as a text of determinism, but the central idea of karma yoga—taking the path of just action not for sake of reward but guided by a clear vision of duty and intent—is highly appreciated. The situation where one's self-worth and one's achievements are evaluated by others has made man very vulnerable and even the most modest principle — karma yoga — becomes both revolutionary and antigeneric according to the standard of society. Virtuous acts performed dharma style in the ocean of the World Wide Web imply, indeed, working for a cause without the noise of continuous festive activities, talking and bypassing without humiliating, and arguing without having to insult others.

The prioritization of karmic frameworks in the world of technology is definitely likely to get the criticisms of many, who believe that such an action might lead to technology that is over-spiritualized and moralized. The thing that should be let unsaid is the real picture of it. The risk is that the code of conduct is not enough, but the code without the ethics is the hazard. If we fail to question the nature of our digital systems that influence our moral instincts, a day will come when there is no compassion at all, the frictionless spread of lies will be present, and the individuality will be determined by the metrics not the meaning. Karma in the cloud may not have religious connotations but it is social necessity.

Effectively, the question is not whether karma is for real in the digital space but whether we are prepared to invest the moral attention needed to notice it. Every society has to come up with its set of rules on digital ethics lest it suffers from anarchy. For India, a civilization that has always considered thought, speech, and action as interconnected, it would be an act of great neglect to be solely inspired by the logic of Silicon Valley. The very nation that once had the Nyaya Sutras and the Dhammapada can certainly find philosophical resources to imagine new ways to be responsible even in the absence of visibility, even when online.

It's been proven that we can't isolate the code from karma. Additionally, it's not that karma ceases, just that karma can still be present in different domains--apart from us, slowly but invisibly, and only a few of us begin to sense this unfolding.

Establishing Digital Dharma

It is no longer enough to check if technology is good or bad. Today, the more mature and crucial question to ask is: how to coexist with it? In this crucial historical junction, the challenge is before India, a civilization with a legacy of thought deeply entrenched in the teachings of balance, duty, and collective good. It is their monumental task of dictating the course of the question of how humans conduct themselves with digital technologies for the billions of Indians who are embracing digital infra at the same time. The test is neither of nostalgia nor nativism but a moral architectural project that is scheduled to stand as an orientating force in digital conduct: Digital Dharma.

Dharma is often misconstrued as "religion" or "law"; it is actually better described as the right conduct in context—a fluid ethic that changes by time, role, and circumstance. It is not a rigid commandment but a responsibility that is relative to the situation. In the digital world, law does not just mean policing the cyberspace but is a good way to balance the libertarian spirit brought by Silicon Valley that advocating the freedom of speech over the responsibility to listen and pursuing growth over taking care of the community. This way of thinking does not contradict the concept of the rights of an individual and the duties associated with the rights; these rights are not opposites, but rather, they complement each other: if you have the right to make your voice heard, you, in turn, have to take the fainral obligations to silence the voices of others. Having internet access, on the one hand, necessitates that one should keep it clean. Digital Dharma is not a system of surveillance nor of censorship rather it is about the shared responsibility, mutual benefit, and moral clarity in the digital age.

If we want to establish such an overall structure, we have to begin by acknowledging that the present digital architecture is mostly exploitative in its nature. The platforms are designed for the sole purpose of engaging the users, where no one cares about improving the lives of those users. Time is just a means of making money. Instead of interacting with people in an ethical manner, data is collected in the most unethical ways. Furthermore, the users, particularly those from the global South, are almost never involved in processes to set the value frameworks of these systems. This creates an ethical misalignment. The logic of utility, ter will shape the way we act, which is devoid of the principle of humanity. In order to challenge this, India has to be assertive in shaping norms, not just as a tech consumer but as a purveyor of the moral virtues of technology.

A case in point is the Indian government's initiative to digitise infrastructure through the like of Aadhaar, UPI, and ONDC, which have demonstrated how digital goods by state approval can serve as vehicles of inclusion, not just profit. Policy can be a potent and influential instrument used in influencing people's minds as well. Culture, education, and imagination need to be in lockstep with one another. A Digital Dharma could hinge on three core principles: Sahishnuta (mutual tolerance), Samvaad (ethical dialogue), and Sangha (community orientation). These are not just mere high-flown ideals; rather, they are the very principles that can be translated into real action—through platform design, civic education, and user behavior.

Think of Sahishnuta. With the present digital surroundings that are full of trolling, cancellation, and polarisation, tolerance is not silently watching it happen. It is an endeavor to follow. The readiness to stay with opposing opinions non-defeated and in the absence of dehumanization of the other is a basic necessity in a digital commons. Indian cultures have always had a direct contact with pluralism—not because they have to, but simply because this is their special strength. This spirituality can be the basis not only for the community moderation policies but also for the algorithms that do not only reward the virality but also the civility. Suppose there is a platform that not only demotes hate speech but also encourages dialogic disagreement. Sahishnuta would need a switch from quantity to quality—something that India, in a very special way, could be a pioneer at.

Next, there is Samvaad—dialogue in an ethical way. In the Mahabharata, some of the most complex morally charged issues are hashed out at great length and with all complexity: hence, there are no absolute villains, and there are no supermen. Such debate traditions can give birth to online forums where the battle of opinions is not a zero-sum game, but the transformation of each other through their interactions. Teaching courses in civic literacy can not only inform young Indians about the media literacy but also imbue them with the moral literacy within the cyberspace. Rather than asking users to do nothing but avoid falsehoods, might we not bring in the idea of users thinking about how their conduct online contributes to the public speaking. Each share, like, or repost is a verbal statement—either it leads to a clear situation or adds vagueness to the public square. Samvaad seeks the decision before the demonstration.

And lastly, Sangha—communal well-being orientation—dictates that digital systems must take account not only of individual preferences but also of the impacts on the whole society. Recreations of algorithms should be sensitive to the loss of social welfare. The policies of a platform should be such that they not only examine the effects on marginalized communities but also understand systemic effects. Indian tech creators could be in the lead in incorporating Sangha { in } their designs: platforms that can lead users to the feelings of empathy, gadgets that are not only for the few but also for those who are linguistic [communities], people in rural areas, and the disabled who are [so] often [excluded from] design thinking. Digital Dharma stands against the user that functions all alone and opts for the citizen who { is } actively participating in society.

This framework should also closely include power. A dharmic digital ethic is not naive about equality in the situations where the existing injustice structures originate. The abuse of gender, discrimination based on caste, and religious polarization are not only issues of bad behavior; they are potential manifestations of the hierarchies moving from the offline world to the online one. A useful framework must make explicit the ways that the aforementioned means are used to harm people in digital spaces, i.e. through the operation of biased algorithms, unequal moderation, or inaction on the part of the platform. Digital Dharma cannot pretend to be agnostic to color, caste, or content and this stance is essential for the ideology behind it, the essence of which is to be clearly just.

Unfortunately, sometimes it can even be said that profit-driven platforms and user disinterest prove that ethical frameworks are very much like ideals. But Indian history has many indications that moral constructs have led to changes in society. The Non-Cooperation Movement was not simply a political strategy; it was a call for a moral stand. The Green Revolution, despite all the criticisms, was a result of the deeply felt moral obligation to feed the people of the nation. The current digital revolution insists on a similar moral attention. To give birth to Digital India without digital dharma would be similar to constructing a soulless infrastructure.

There are indeed practical ways forward. Regulatory frameworks like the Digital Personal Data Protection Act could be a key starting point to include the safeguards essential system, but legislation cannot play the role alone without social culture. Digital ethics courses in schools and colleges that draw from India's philosophical traditions can be a great way for the ancient to the modern to directly link up. Tech incubators can offer incentives to startups applying ethical design and promoting societal gamesmanship. Civil society organizations must continue to demand transparency, fairness, and accountability in digital governance. The miracle of Indian technology is not happening only down in Bengaluru, it is taking place through the talks of people in Kanchipuram, the traditional values of Varanasi, and the stories of Shillong.

Certainly, India has one idea for the world, the idea that technology should be employed for human flourishing and not vice versa. And that flourishing is not only GDP growth or user retention; it is social, reflective, and responsible. The virtual world does not have to be a hindrance to the spiritual; it can even be its broadening. As long as digital systems are made and used with dharma as the primary consideration, they can not only help to achieve political independence but also inner freedom, i.e. Swaraj.

It is really a big job: to even come close to fulfilling the demand for the systems that would be ethical as well as efficient, flexible on the one hand, and stable on the other, open without being abusive. The scope is as wide indeed. India can play the leading role not only in terms of the digital decade (users and innovation) but also in terms of values and vision. In the world dominated by digital tools that influence our perception, thinking, and relations, the question no more is whether India will digitise but with what Dharma it will.

What we see here is not a set of pangs for bygone times, but a willful and mindful shifting of gears—towards a digital civilization where the age-old insights of interdependence, self-restraint, and mutual respect are rediscovered and given a fresh impulse. "Digital Dharma" is neither a hotchpotch of words nor a mere figure of speech. It is both a proposition and with a bit of luck, it might even be a global contribution.

Conclusion

A Billion Futures, One Signal

India has never been singular. It was always diverse in languages, which were prayed in hundreds of places to gods and with billion votes through rationalities. India keeps resisting simplification—geographically, culturally, politically. Nevertheless, what the previous parts of the text have conveyed is that virtual revolution that happens to be in the country has started producing coherence to some extent—not resembling one another but connecting. What evolves is not really a united whole, but an amalgam of Indian characteristics that winds its way through the days—omate, disputed but increasingly coordinated. The core issue is no longer if the digital is going to shape India's future; it among other things also determines if India is capable of managing the digital impact on its own grounds.

Let me stress that this last chapter is not a summary, nor is it a conclusion. It is a look forward: a conscious effort to align the threads of past probes—on gender, governance, identity, innovation, ethics — into a big picture. It clarifies that India's digital transition is way beyond the common apps, the known networks, or the familiar policies. The change is of a broad scope involving how people perceive themselves in a position of responsibility, how people look at being a citizen, and how they define their life purpose in the information age. A billion futures carry with it a sense of not just the size but the variety, the problem is not to make ones the sole ruler but to find distinctiveness through this multitude of voices that are also shared dreams.

What characterizes this signal is not a single voice spreading the message. It is a cross-cutting of various sectors both public and private, the spiritual and technical, the hyperlocal and planetary. To illustrate, let's talk about the Digital Public Infrastructure (DPI) of India. It is a structure that boosts financial participation of the peasant in Jharkhand as well as serves as a facilitator of blockchain projects in Mumbai. And you could also mention the societal advancement which had women operate phones for purposes more than just escaping, i.e., for economic independence, microlearning, and personal empowerment. Or just think about the strange case of a generation that is equally good at memes and meditation, digital data and dharma, Silicon Valley standards and Nalanda ethics. Such situations are neither paradoxes nor conflicts; they are sure signs that we are in the process of constructing a coherent society through digital means. It is not the dominant voice but the harmony of ideas that leads to the signal.

However, coherence without a path in a moral compass can lead to terrible outcomes. Although the platforms that bring people together and allow communication can also be used for manipulation. The very strong visibility that supports helps can also hurt. The speed of machine learning has the ability to increase not only the production of new ideas but also the income gap. This is why apart from the technological success, more profound philosophical, social and moral issues should go hand in hand. Can trust be made into a code? Can basic human feeling be done by machines or at a larger scale? Can a digital society be not only efficient, but also fair? These are real- not just theoretical- questions. They indicate that these design problems are just around the corner. From the beginning not only do India's infrastructures have the power but perhaps also the obligation to respond to these questions with imagination.

India has a rich history of resources that can be utilized for this imaginative work. Thinking that focused more on the exercise of the mind than on the body, the devotion to the relation among people rather than the separation and the obsession with the process instead of the result have much to say about how digital systems are to be developed, discussed and launched. As long as these values are not taken up just for show but are actually lived out, the good old traditions can be put to use. For example, a concept like Dharma should go beyond a tech slogan and become the concrete manifestation of its impact on platform governance, AI ethics, data stewardship, and the way digital spaces are being built and maintained. The civilizational resources of India not being antiques, are objects that facilitate various activities, even today, if we accept to adjust them without idealizing them.

The future path of India is going to be a rough walk. The very large number of the population is the reason for the complexity of the situation; the division of politics causes the noise, the distinction in the infrastructure brings the inequality. But in the confusions and disturbances that exist, there can be an ignition of the spark of creativity. As it was demonstrated earlier in the book, indeed, India is an example of a country where tech citizens are built and are shaping and renewing the whole image of the society themselves where the entrepreneurs are working on improving the living conditions in the villages, some emergency workers no more to be cloaked in invisibility as they create their niche among the workers in the digital economy, and the rest of the women encourage each other for support and visibility through selfies taken with bravery though they face hostility. All these instances are not just flukes; they are also a form of structural indication that India is busy not only taking technology as a consumer but also making it a part of the local and global arena.

The global stakes are high. While most of the world is thinking of digital fatigue, surveillance capitalism, algorithmic nihilism, the Indian case offers digital vitality with a social twist. Of not only, but it is understood that it is since it is a chaotic, multi-ethnic, and spontaneous phenomenon. Indian bracket of 'Jugaad' culture, which is usually considered as the bypassing psyche, is actually the very foundation where innovations will happen quietly, smoothly, and in a friendly way. It's not so much about software as it is about feelings.

However, to actualize this prospect, India will have to grapple with the most difficult challenges in terms of not only infrastructure and access but also imagination and intention and will have to deal with concepts of fairness in various forms of leverage of digital technology. Will digitalization be tolerated that eliminates diversity or respects diversity? Will platforms perpetuate inequalities or facilitate social mobility? Will officials consider the digital commons as human rights, or will they give them over as privileges? These are not trivial questions. They are the ones that help a girl from a small city in Tier 3 to form her dreams and that lead to the hiring— or not hiring— of a coder from a slum in Bengaluru. They also ascertain if India's digital progress is only a matter of the technology, or if it is indeed governed by democratic principles.

Undoubtedly, technology will keep transforming, policy frameworks will keep changing, new platforms, and start-ups will keep coming. Nevertheless, values such as care, equity, participation, and respect should remain the guiding principles of all our endeavours. In making this point, we are not calling for digital moralism, but mostly for the moralisation of ourselves—you, the users, the developers, the controllers, the educators, and the citizens. The digital world is not a machine—it is, for the most part, a reflection of who we decide to be, not just of what we build.

A billion futures could never be controlled. They are, however, open to shaping through cultivation. Furthermore, if India will be able to discover the right signal—grounded in respect, aimed for fairness, suitable for diversity—then it would be able to bring the world something not commonly found: a sense of purpose. This is not when it is used as a brand, not as a show. But it is used as the way society and technology both can coexist wisely.

What Kind of India Are You Helping to Code?

The question here is not about the role of technology in India but of Indians shaping technology. Replacing one word for another, a subtle change, that becomes necessary, nevertheless, catapults the whole discussion to a different segment, thereby, it forcefully makes way for a new pattern in our way of looking at digital citizenship, responsibility, and power. Throughout the discussions on the digital transformation of India, it has always been the story of access: more users, more devices, and an abundance of services through a simple click. But access without agency is irrelevant. Connecting digitally doesn't fully express oneself, and getting to a technological level that creates apps that are non-moral is not acceptable. The closing of the book should not be about the impact of technology on India, but it should rather invite a reflection on the choices made by India about technology.

In India, the digital revolution, though expansive, is not a neutral current, it keeps being scripted—line by line, decision by decision—by both public institutions, private firms, and millions of users and their daily choices. The problem-solving technology world today can take various forms—the nudge into savings for women via a fintech platform, a vernacular news app that encourages divisive content for more clicks, or a government dashboard where the citizens left out are those not able to read English. These are not the system's issues, but they express the system's intention: the design utilized reflects the values preferred by the creators, and many times the mirror betrays the practicality of the new ideas of the social platform, the kidneys of the ethical code, and the words' shallow and speedy availability.

The importance and relevance of this context are vital in a nation like India, where the digital world is not just a mere add-on to the society but has now become the core infrastructure. Datafication of everything from welfare to work, from identity to intimacy and the platform economy of the data-led state are now the drivers of people's ordinary lives. But what happens to the moral side when those systems have no shared values? Who is included and who is excluded? Who does better because of the model of optimisation, and who is disadvantaged due to the unpredictability of the system?

Those are no longer abstract questions. They are questions that need immediate, practical, and political answers. To illustrate the gravity of the present, look at the Indian digital infrastructures that have gone beyond being local to find international acceptance with digital ID Aadhaar, digital payments with UPI, and digital commerce with ONDC. In fact, these systems show an ability to be improvised technologically—frugal, scalable, interoperable.

At the same time, their design gives an impression that governance can be made simple through the use of large databases, inclusion can be tracked by compliance with the biometric and that efficiency can be a substitute for the power of reasoning. What starts off as an act of innovation, can quickly become a creed. These platforms are not just for conducting transactions, they also determine what can be and is transacted, and, as a logical consequence, also what is considered valuable.

The impression of all this does not stop at engineering and entrepreneurs, but it reaches the entire citizen who becomes part of the construction of the digital India where the digital trail, they provide data by the platforms they patronize, and behavioral habits, they consider being normal. The swipe, the share, the upvote are not just random acts of individuals. These are the signals that they pass to the system. The system then runs the algorithms which in turn become the norms. In this feedback economy, silence is a cue of consent to the system's operations. Every interaction counts as a participation, and eventually, an accumulation of these patterns of participation gives a print of society in the digital domain.

Now, even the most basic point is to consider is that whether or not a digital India that is capable of high technology is possible with the moral standing of the nation? Is ethical retrogression, the byproduct of technical acceleration, also true?

The response solely lies in ensuring whether India can develop digital authorship or not—where it is not only about digital skills but also about digital authorship—the quality of actually creating something new either in writing, research, or art. Creation of such qualities in citizens will ensure not just digital education but also the dimension of ownership and sense of responsibility. This is not a call for coding at the community level but a call for civic coding i.e. the concept of using our knowledge and skills to the technology we design and the platforms we use to uphold ideas such as justice, dignity, pluralism, and wisdom that are becoming the new standard of people everyday life.

The reason we should be optimistic about the future is that India follows certain philosophical codes that act as strong constraints to the ruling digital age principles. Indian ethics reinforce dharma, which is a teaching based on right action, the right person, and the right time, those being the virtues of balance, truthfulness, responsibility, character, and others. The Western tech culture excels in branding and personal performance but in India, there is the flooding of the spiritual inner by the Indian spiritual systems.

This is not an old story from the past; it is much more a vivid demonstration of the fact that numerous value systems not only exist but are also in line with the theme of innovation. Moreover, they may even prove to be the very essence of innovation that is to be both, sustainable and humane, thus it becomes a more and more persuading reason for innovators to adopt them.

Anyway, we can point out that there are quite a few instances of implementation of a fundamentally different approach in practice. There we can mention, for example, groups like DEF or the feminist digital communities Breakthrough and Point of View. These communities do not attract investments as much as big unicorn corporations, but, nevertheless, they have changed the very approach to digital activities in India. Their activities like making safety tools for women, creating data commons for rural communities, or educating citizens so that they can participate in the audit of tech policies represent a different ethos of innovation focused not only on scale, but rather on equity, not only on code, but also on care.

Moreover, regulatory systems can not just be used as control instruments but can be employed to imagine new scenarios as well. The argument about the Digital Personal Data Protection Act in India, as embarrassing as it is now, suggests the people's wish to see those who are responsible, not just those who are flexible. There is a demand for more appropriate regulations that are written by all parties, understood within their own specific contexts, and consistently transparently enforced. Thus, the process refers to evolving from fighting against to advancing with our own ideas and resembles the questions related to this subject: Can the Indian people be provided with the chance to take the initiative in deciding about their own digital future? And what else is needed to be in place, in order to maintain the future in that way?

Then, it also means that it calls to change the facts of Indian society on a global scale.. So a large part of the information that Indian people are in contact with comes from the algorithms that have been trained on Western data, programed with Western biases, and controlled by the firms that come from the Western culture. From the decision to apply beauty filters, through the use of language models, creation of influencers scores and even to making the rules about creating the content that is to be published, it's true to say that the Indian digital experiences are of colonial nature but only if we leave them postcolonial in their flavor. The concept of real digital sovereignty will require more than one step towards the localization of servers or banning applications. It will rather mean epistemic sovereignty, which is the capacity to determine the nature of knowledge, value, and well-being in the era of digital technology.

Indeed, the question being put forth by this chapter is not hypothetical. What kind of India are you (by any means) programming? Are you like the rest of the people who keep the biases of the real world or do you bring change to them? Do you create digital tools (technologies) that allow broad access or simply add to the number of consumers? Do you engage in the digital culture that supports the reward of the spreading of controversial ideas and their being viral or instead do you prefer to have a culture where nuance and dignity are fostered? These are not questions just for policymakers; they are also for users, educators, engineers, designers, parents, and poets.

Digital India has no finished design yet - that YOU may see the great opportunity in it. The code is still in the process, the architecture is still flexible, and the protocols are still negotiable. But that door of opportunity is closing. When platforms become monopolies and machine learning turns into machine memory, the defaults we pick now can be the canons of the future. The task, in this case, is to be the main actors of our participation – not just take digital convenience for granted, but be wary of digital conscience.

We close the book but this does not represent the end. It's a new beginning. It's more of an image not a map. Not a reflective statement, but an encouragement - to think and to react, and most importantly, to create with purpose The future is not a destination but a creation hence in the case of India, it is a thing built by the decisions, choices, and signals of a billion hands and a billion people – each an input of the world's largest digital democracy. The question we should be asking is: What instructions are we passing to it?

About the Author

Ananya Mehta is a renowned digital anthropologist and cultural commentator with over two decades of experience exploring the intersections of technology, society, and identity in South Asia. Holding advanced degrees in Sociology and Media Studies, her work delves deep into how digital transformations influence cultural narratives and individual lives. Ananya has contributed to leading journals and think tanks, offering insights into India's evolving digital landscape. Her unique perspective combines academic rigour with accessible storytelling, making complex technological shifts relatable to a broad audience. "Digital India: How Technology is Reshaping a Billion Lives" is her latest endeavour, encapsulating years of research and on-the-ground observations.

www.ingramcontent.com/pod-product-compliance
Lightning Source LLC
Chambersburg PA
CBHW031323230926
51848CB00001B/65
9789348738974